Land Records

of

YORK COUNTY
Pennsylvania

Libers E and F
1771–1775

Mary Marshall Brewer

HERITAGE BOOKS
2018

HERITAGE BOOKS

AN IMPRINT OF HERITAGE BOOKS, INC.

Books, CDs, and more—Worldwide

For our listing of thousands of titles see our website
at
www.HeritageBooks.com

Published 2018 by
HERITAGE BOOKS, INC.
Publishing Division
5810 Ruatan Street
Berwyn Heights, Md. 20740

International Standard Book Number
Paperbound: 978-0-7884-5862-0

CONTENTS

INTRODUCTION

Land records can often be the answer to a genealogical puzzle. The land in Colonial America was cheap and available and the land records begin with the arrival of the first Europeans. And in the earliest records a significant amount of genealogical date is found. In many of the forgoing deeds the line of ownership reveals the relationship of parents, grandparents, spouses and others. This is especially helpful when the ancestor died intestate or without a will.

The land records of York County begin with the founding of the county in 1749. This book represents abstracts from Deed Book E (1771-1774) and Deed Book F (1773-1775). Deed Book A (1746-1763) and Deed Book B (1763-1764) were published as one volume in 2004. Deed Books C (1764-1768) and D (1768-1771) were published in 2002 as a single volume. Deed Books G (1775-1785) and H (1785-1793) were published as a single volume in 2004.

York County was created out of Lancaster County. At its inception it included all of present-day York and Adams Counties. Adams County was established in 1800.

Most of the early settlers of York County were Germans. The Scotch-Irish settlers began arriving shortly after the Germans, settling the southeastern region of the county.

Copies of the deed books are available at the courthouse in York and the York County Archives. Microfilm copies are available at the Historical Society of York County, the Historical Society of Pennsylvania, and the Family History Library. Land warrant registers for all Pennsylvania counties are available on microfilm at the Pennsylvania State Archives. The warrant registers for Lancaster County, 1732-1750 (photocopies) are available at the Historical Society of York County.

F. Edward Wright
Lewes, Delaware
2004

ABBREVIATIONS

a. - acres
ackn - acknowledged
adj - adjoining
adminr - administrator or administratrix
afsd - aforesaid
atty - attorney
br - branch
co - county
cr - creek
dau(s) - daughter(s)
decd - deceased
dep - deputy
e - east
esqr - esquire
gent - gentlemen
Junr - junior
mi - miles
n - north
pt/o - part of
purch - purchased
rd - road
s - south
sd – said
Senr - senior
tr - tract
w - west
w/o - wife of
wit - witness

YORK CO, PENNSYLVANIA
DEED RECORD
E Book
1771-1774

14 Dec 1771. Deed. MICHAEL HAHN of York Town, York Co locksmith and
Elizabeth his wife for £100 sold to ADAM HEINICKE of York Township, York
Co yeoman a 175 a. tr of land ... whereas the Proprietaries by their patent dated
at Phila 29 Oct last past did grant unto PHILIP BENTZ Junr a 175 a. tr of land
called *Huntsman's Hall* on Little Codorus in York Township adj CONRAD
RICHY, JOHN HERNISH & ADAM HEINICKE's other land. Whereas the
said PHILIP BENTZ and AGNESS his wife on 13 Dec instant did release the
afsd tr of land unto the said MICHAEL HAHN ... . Wit: LODWIG HETICK
(HETIG), CARREL BAWNÛTZ (BROWITZ). Ackn 14 Dec 1771 before
JOHN ADLUM justice. (E:pg 1)

30 Jul 1771. Deed of Mortgage. LODWICK DERWICKLER (TARWATER)
of Manheim Township, York Co yeoman ackn myself to be indebted unto
GEORGE ROSS atty at law for £46 to be paid to him in 12 mos, and for
securing the payment of the same, and for 5 shillings, I have sold to the said
GEORGE ROSS a 120 a. tr of land whereon I now live bounded by GEORGE
ROSS & Company & PHILIP WERKINGS ... provided that if the said
LODWICK DERWICKLER shall pay to the said GEORGE ROSS £46 &
interest after deducting 40 shillings for every a. that the said LODWICK
DERWICKLER has cleared which he was employed to cleare at MARY ANN
FURNACE for the said GEORGE ROSS then this deed to be void ... . Wit:
JOS THORNBRUGH, CHRISTIAN MILHEIM. Proved 4 Jan 1772 by
JOSEPH THORNBRUGH before RICHD MCCALISTER justice. (E:pg 3)

3 Jan 1771. Deed of Mortgage. JACOB SHRAM of York Town, York Co
weaver for £19.4.10 sold to HENRY PINSLER of Dover Township, York Co
yeoman the dwelling house and ½ pt/o a lot of ground, No. 238, bounded by
Water Street & the remaining ½ pt/o the lot, in breadth 14' and in depth 125' ...
provided that if the said JACOB SHRAM shall well and truly pay unto the said
HENRY PINSLER £19.4.10 with interest within 1 year then this bill of sale to
be void ... . Wit: PHILIP PISSER, JNO MORRIS. Ackn 3 May 1771 before
JOS UPDEGRAFF justice. 25 Apr 1774 HENRY PINSLER discharged
mortgage. Wit: SAML JOHNSTON recorder. (E:pg 3)

28 Mar 1771. Deed. CONRAD FRY of Windsor Township, York Co yeoman
for 5 shillings sold to JACOB SEGNER (STAGNER), ADAM HAINDEL
(HAINDLE), JACOB RUBY & STEPHEN SLIFER of same place trustees of
the Lutheran and Presbyterian Congregation in trust for the use and benefit of

the Dutch Lutheran and Presbyterian Congregation a 1 ½ a. tr of land pt/o a 100 a. tr of land ... in pursuance of a warrant dated at Phila 22 Jan 1767 there was granted unto the afsd CONRAD FRY 100 a. of land in the afsd township adj ADAM GUIRE, GEORGE STEVENSON, BARRETT FRY, JOHN FISHER & JACOB RUBY ... . Wit: PHILIP PYFER, JNO MORRIS. Ackn 28 Mar 1771 before JOHN ADLUM justice. (E:pg 4)

3 May 1771. Deed. NICHOLAS FIRESTONE of Paradise Township, York Co farmer for £150 sold to JOSEPH FIRESTONE of same place farmer a 159 a. tr of land adj JACOB BALSLE, COTLEEP PRIECHNER & LAWRENCE MCMULLEN ... whereas the Proprietaries did grant unto FREDERICK JOLLADGE 50 a. of land adj Pigeons Hills in Paradise Township by two warrants, one dated 28 Oct 1751, the other dated 4 Apr 1754, and the said FREDERICK JOLLADGE on 11 Aug 1755 sold unto FREDERICK EICHELBERGER two improvements in Paradise Township, 100 a. with two warrants taken for the said land by JOHN BRADY, and the said FREDERICK EICHELBERGER on 15 Nov 1760 did assign over all his right of the afsd deed unto NICHOLAS FIRESTONE father of the afsd parties, and the said NICHOLAS FIRESTONE died intestate possessed of the lands, 300 a., leaving his relict and issue the said NICHOLAS FIRESTONE his eldest son and eight children. On the petition of the said NICHOLAS FIRESTONE eldest son the real estate of the intestate was valued and the said NICHOLAS FIRESTONE as eldest son made satisfaction to the other children for their shares ... . Wit: CONRAD DOLL, THOS ARMOR. Ackn 18 Nov 1771 before HENRY SLAGLE justice. (E:pg 6)

18 Dec 1771. Deed. SAMUEL JOHNSTON and MICHAEL SWOOPE of the Town of York, York Co esqrs for £30 sold to PETER PRINGLE of Manchester Township, York Co yeoman a 75 a. tr of land ... whereas in pursuance of a warrant dated 29 Mar 1768 there was surveyed and laid out for the said SAMUEL JOHNSTON and MICHAEL SWOOPE esqrs a 75 a. 121 perches tr of land in Codorus Township near Codorus Cr adj MICHAEL SPRINGLE, FREDERICK EICHELBERGER & the Baltimore Road ... . Wit: JOHN CLARK Junr, THOS SMITH. Ackn 18 Dec 1771 before JOHN ADLUM justice. (E:pg 8)

24 Sep 1770. Deed. JOHN HARRIS of Paxton Township, Lancaster Co, PA yeoman & MARY his wife for £850 sold to PHILIP SHRYNER of Mainham Township, co afsd, yeoman a 325 ½ a. tr of land in Newbury Township adj MARGARET FINLEY, WILLIAM CHESNEY & River Susquahanna and also a 43 ½ a. island called *Harris' Island* ... whereas the Proprietaries by their patent dated 16 Mar 1737 did grant unto JOHN HARRIS decd a 820 a. tr of land then in Lancaster Co on the w side of the River Susquahanna now in Newburry

Township, York Co, and whereas by another patent dated 20 Oct 1743 the Proprietaries did grant unto the afsd JOHN HARRIS decd a 200 a. tr of land adj the afsd tr including an island in the River Susquahanna, and the said JOHN HARRIS decd by his will dated 22 Nov 1746, dying seized of the afsd trs of land and island, did after devising to his sons JOHN HARRIS & WILLIAM HARRIS 420 a. pt/o the said tr of 1020 a. to be divided to them in the upper pt/o next to DAVID PRIEST, directs as follows " I leave to EASTER my wife in lieu of her dower 600 a. of land including an island being the residue of my 1020 a. tr provided she continues my widow during her natural life and at her death or marriage, the 600 a. to be divided amongst my children allowing my son JOHN two shares" ... and the said EASTER HARRIS after the death of the said JOHN HARRIS married and is since dead so that the said 600 a. came to JOHN HARRIS, WILLIAM HARRIS, SAMUEL HARRIS & DAVID HARRIS sons of the said JOHN HARRIS decd and EASTER w/o Doctor WILLIAM PLUNKITT a dau of the said JOHN HARRIS decd, and to EASTER FINLEY now EASTER PATTERSON & MARGARET FINLEY heirs of ELIZABETH FINLEY another dau of the said JOHN HARRIS decd, and JOHN HARRIS one of the parties to this indenture hath purch the share of WILLIAM HARRIS & MARGARET his wife 19 Sep 1761, and the said JOHN HARRIS has also purch the share of SAMUEL HARRIS & ELIZABETH his wife 19 Sep 1761, and the said JOHN HARRIS has purch of WILLIAM PATTERSON & EASTER his wife their share 11 Sep 1770, and by virtue of a petition JOHN HARRIS' share and the shares purch as above have been surveyed off the afsd tr of land to the said JOHN HARRIS ... . Wit: [?], WILLIAM MCCLURE, [?]. Ackn 11 Nov 1771 before WILLIAM RANKIN justice. (E:pg 9)

30 Dec 1771. Deed. MARTIN REILY (REYLE) of York Town, York Co taylor and ELISABETH his wife for £60 sold to JACOB KERN of same place taylor ½ pt/o Lot No. 39 in the Town of York, in breadth 32'6" and in length 230' ... whereas the Proprietaries by their patent dated at Phila 27 Dec 1753 did grant unto JOHN GUITINGER a lot of ground in the Town of York, in breadth 65' and in length 230', bounded by High Street, Lot No. 40 & Lot No. 38 (Patent Book A vol. 18 pg 172), and the said JOHN GUITINGER on 31 Mar 1758 conveyed unto the said MARTIN REILY the e ½ pt/o the said lot of ground (Book A pg 274) ... . Wit: JOSEPH GARRETSON, WM KERSEY. Ackn 12 Dec 1771 before JOSEPH UPDEGRAFF esqr justice. (E:pg 12)

20 Dec 1771. Deed. MARTIN EICHELBERGER esqr surviving executor of the will of DIETRICK UHLER late of Manchester Township, York Co yeoman decd for £1108.10 sold to MICHAEL HARE of York Co yeoman a 217 ½ a. tr of land ... whereas MARTIN JOSE (by the name of MARITIN JOSEPH) obtained a grant under the hand of the Proprietaries dated 30 Oct 1736 for 300 a. of land on the w side of Susquehanna River in the Mannor of Springetsbury

(then in Lancaster Co) but now in York Co, and the said MARTIN JOSE on 26 Aug 1742 did sell unto the said DIETRICK UHLER (by the name of TEETER WOOLERICK) ½ of his right to the grant of 300 a., and the said DIETRICK UHLER afterwards died having first made his will and appointed the said MARTIN EICHELBERGER esqr and GEORGE MEYER executors and impowered them to sell his real and personal estate (not by the will otherwise disposed of), and the said MARTIN JOSE died intestate owner and seized of the ½ pt/o 300 a. of land leaving issue to survive him (to wit) NICHOLAS JOSE, HANNAH w/o JACOB UTTINGER, MARGARET w/o ISAAC LERUE, MAGDALENA w/o JACOB NEASE & JOHN JOSE, and the said NICHOLAS JOSE being of full age also died intestate unmarried and without issue and his part became vested in his brother the said JOHN JOSE, and the said JACOB NEASE and MAGDALENA his wife on 18 Aug 1760 conveyed unto the said JACOB UTTINGER all their share of the 300 a. (Book C pg 212), and the said JOHN JOSE and MARY his wife on 30 Sep 1762 conveyed their share in the 300 a. unto the said JACOB UTTINGER together with the share of the said NICHOLAS JOSE decd (Book C pg 214), and the said ISAAC LARUE and MAGDALENA his wife both died intestate leaving MARY MAGDALENA LERUE to survive them, and the said MARY MAGDALENA LERUE on 28 Aug 1766 conveyed all her share of the 300 a. unto the said JACOB UTTINGER (Book C pg 199), whereas the said JACOB UTTINGER and HANNA his wife on 13 Dec 1766 conveyed unto the said MARTIN EICHELBERGER esqr and GEORGE MEYER executors of the will of the said DIETRICK UHLER decd 75 a. of land pt/o the ½ pt/o the original grant (Book C pg 206), and in pursuance of the several conveyances afsd there was surveyed and laid out a 371 a. 81 perches tr of land in Manchester Township pt/o the land held under the original grant adj MATHIAS SMISER Senr, NICHOLAS HARMAN, PETER SCHRIVER Junr, SIMON WIDTMEYER, PHILIP HAINTS Junr, JACOB UTTINGER & JOHN HOKE, and MARTIN EICHELBERGER esqr and GEORGE MEYER executors in pursuance of the directions of the said will did on 28 Apr 1770 expose to publick sale a 217 ½ a. tr of land pt/o the last above described tr adj MATHIAS SMISER Senr, ADAM UHLER, PETER SCHRIVER Junr & SIMON WIDTMEYER and sold to the said MICHAEL HARE for £1108.10 he being the highest bidder, and the said GEORGE MEYER since also died … . Wit: CHAS LUKENS, JNO CLARK Junr. Ackn 20 Dec 1771 before JOHN ADLUM esqr justice. (E:pg 15)

4 May 1771. Deed. JACOB DAUTEL of York Town, York Co tanner and ANNA MARIA his wife for £300 sold to ANDREW BOLLY of Paradise Township, York Co yeoman two trs of land in the whole 300 a. … whereas in pursuance of a warrant dated at Phila 10 Sep 1753 there was surveyed and laid out unto ULRICH PEELER a 150 a. tr of land in Paradise Township adj TETTER SALTSGAVER, JOHN BAKER, BARNET SINCE & WILLIAM

OLLER, and the said ULRICK PEELER on 7 May 1752 did convey the tr of land unto CHRISTIAN CROLL (father of PHILIP CROLL) for the joint use of the said CHRISTIAN CROLL and GEORGE STEVENSON ... in pursuance of another warrant dated at Phila 19 May 1752 there was surveyed and laid out unto the said GEORGE STEVENSON a 150 a. tr of land in Paradise Township adj RUDOLPH SPENGLER & TETTER SALTSGAVER, for the joint use of the said GEORGE STEVENSON and the said CHRISTIAN CROLL, and the said CHRISTIAN CROLL made his will dated 31 Jul 1758 and did devise to his said son PHILIP the afsd land, and the said GEORGE STEVENSON and MARY his wife, PHILIP CROLL and MARIA EVA his wife on 2 Jan 1767 did convey the two trs of land unto the afsd JACOB DAUTEL and MICHAEL DAUTEL, and the said MICHAEL DAUTEL and MARGRETA his wife on 29 May 1769 did convey ½ pt/o the two trs of land unto the said JACOB DAUTEL ... . Wit: JOHN MEEM, GEO LEWIS LESLER. Ackn 4 May 1771 before JOS UPDEGRAFF justice. (E:pg 19)

6 Aug 1771. Deed of Mortgage. FREDRICK HUBER of the Town of York, York Co locksmith for better securing the payment of £89.13.9 and also 5 shillings sold to JACOB BLAZER of Manchester Township, York Co yeoman four lots of ground on the w side of George Street in the Town of York, Nos. 114, 115, 116, & 117, bounded by Princess Street, as appears on the General Plan and expressed in four certificates under the hand of GEORGE STEVENSON ... whereas the said FREDRICK HUBER standeth bound unto the said JACOB BLAZER for £161.7.6 conditioned for the payment of £89.13.9 on 1 Feb 1772 ... provided that if the said FREDRICK HUBER shall well and truly pay unto the said JACOB BLAZER £89.13.9 then this obligation to be void ... . Wit: PHILIP PYFER, JNO MORRIS. Ackn 14 Aug 1771 before JOSEPH UPDEGRAFF esqr justice. (E:pg 21)

27 Jan 1767. Deed. DETER MYER (MAYER) of Manchester Township, York Co farmer for £300 sold to MICHAEL SMYSER of same place tavernkeeper a 84 ½ a. tr of land (pt/o a 400 a. tr of land) in Manchester Township adj ANDREW HOKE (HOOK) & the said DETER MYER ... whereas the Proprietary on 30 Oct 1736 did grant unto DENNIS MYER 400 a. of land on the w side of SASQUEHANNA RIVER on the br of Cadoras Cr to include his improvement, and the said DENNIS MYER on 18 Jun 1762 conveyed the afsd tr of land unto the said DETER MYER (Book B pg 16) ... . Wit: GEO EICHELBERGER, JACOB [?]. Ackn 29 Nov 1771 before MARTIN EYCHELBERGER justice. (E:pg 23)

25 Jan 1772. Deed of Mortgage. DANIEL RISHER (REICHER) of Paradise Township, York Co yeoman for better securing the payment of £200 and also 5 shillings sold to MICHAEL HERR of Manchester Township, York Co yeoman

an improvement and a 272 a. tr of land in Paradise Township adj JOHN APPELMAN, PETER MOHR, WILLIAM WINANT & CHRISTIAN SEINBACHER ... whereas the said DANIEL RISHER standeth bound unto the said MICHAEL HERR for £400 conditioned for the payment of £200 on 25 Mar 1774 ... provided that if the said DANIEL RISHER shall well and truly pay unto the said MICHAEL HERR £200 then this obligation to be void ... . Wit: HENRY MILLER, JOHN CLARK Junr. Ackn 25 Jan 1772 before MICHAEL SWOOPE esqr justice. 26 Mar 1774 MICHAEL HERR discharged mortgage. Wit: SAML JOHNSTON recorder. (E:pg 25)

14 Jan 1772. Deed. CHRISTIAN WYANBRENNER of Manheim Township, York Co yeoman and CHRISTINA his wife for £174 sold to MORDICAI WILLIAMS of Dover Township, York Co taylor a 162 a. tr of land ... in pursuance of a warrant dated 5 Mar 1756 there was surveyed and laid out for the said CHRISTIAN WYANBRENNER a 162 a. tr of land in Dover Township adj PHILIP HENRY MOORE, land late of VALENTINE ERTLE, MELCHER BENEDICK, JACOB CARPENTER & CONRAD HEAK ... . Wit: FRANTZ [?], JOS BOUDE. Ackn 14 Jan 1772 before RICHD MCCALISTER justice. (E:pg 26)

25 Nov 1771. Deed of Mortgage. JOSEPH ADLUM of York Town, York Co skinner for better securing the payment of £50 and also 5 shillings sold to SAMUEL JOHNSTON of same place esqr a lot of ground whereon the said JOSEPH ADLUM now dwells on the e side of George Street in the Town of York, in breadth 57 ½' and in length 250', bounded by Lot No. 207 ... whereas the said JOSEPH ADLUM standeth bound unto the said SAMUEL JOHNSTON for £100 conditioned for the payment of £50 on 24 Nov next ensuing ... provided that if the said JOSEPH ADLUM shall well and truly pay unto the said SAMUEL JOHNSTON £50 then this obligation to be void ... . Wit: HENRY MILLER, JOHN CLARK Junr. Ackn 5 Nov 1771 before JOHN ADLUM esqr justice. (E:pg 28)

12 Oct 1771. Bond. SAMUEL EDIE & ROBERT MCPHERSON esqrs of Cumberland Township and DAVID MCCOUGHY esqr of Menallen Township, York Co are firmly bound unto our Sovereign Lord GEORGE the Third for £2000 ... upon condition that whereas the afsd SAMUEL EDIE esqr on 1 Oct instant was elected sheriff of York Co as by an indenture remaining in Phila dated 2 Oct instant between JOSEPH ADLUM coroner of York Co of the first part and FREDERICK WOLF, JOHN MENTIETH, WILLIAM GEMMILL, HUGH DUNWOODY, WILLIAM LAW & THOMAS STOCKTON assistant judges and WILLIAM SCOTT, JOHN MICKEL Junr, JAMES BLACK, SAMUEL LEWIS, ANDREW HART Junr & JOHN THOMPSON inspectors, freeholders of York Co of the other part ... now if the said SAMUEL EDIE shall

well and truly serve and execute all the Kings Writs and Processes to him directed without delay and according to law ... then this obligation to be void ... . Wit: HENRY MILLER, JOHN CLARK Junr. (E:pg 29)

31 Oct 1771. Deed of Mortgage. ANDREAS NEBINGER of the Town of York, York Co innkeeper and MARY his wife for better securing the payment of £500 and also 5 shillings sold to HENRY KEPPELE Junr of the City of Phila, PA merchant Lot No. 71 on the n side of High Street in the Town of York, in breadth 65' and in length 230', bounded by BALTZER SPANGLER & GEORGE [STAKE?], and an 8 a. 34 6/10 perches lot in York Township adj MARTIN DANNER, JOHN HAY & MATHIAS SITLER (being the same piece of land which MATHIAS SITLER and CATHARINE his wife on 11 Dec 1766 granted unto the said ANDREAS NEBINGER) ... whereas the said ANDREAS NEBINGER by his bond stands firmly bound unto the said HENRY KEPPELE for £1000 conditioned for the payment of £500 on 31 Oct 1773 ... provided that if the said ANDREAS NEBINGER shall well and truly pay unto the said HENRY KEPPELE £500 then this obligation to be void ... . Wit: PHILIP ZIEGLER, JOHN HUBLEY. Ackn 1 Nov 1771 before JNO POPE justice. 20 Dec 1777 HENRY KEPPELE Junr discharged mortgage. Wit: ARCHD MCCLEAN recorder. (E:pg 30)

20 Nov 1771. Deed of Mortgage. WILLIAM MACKEY of Fawn Township, York Co yeoman for better securing the payment of £31.12 1 penny and also 5 shillings sold to CUNINGHAM SAMPLE of same place a 300 a. tr of land in Fawn Township adj ALEXANDER MCCANLESS, JAMES WHITE & JOHN CRUMMY, which was surveyed to JOHN EDMISTON in pursuance of a warrant dated 4 Apr 1754, and the said JOHN EDMISTON on 11 Feb 1760 granted unto ROBERT LUCKEY, and the said ROBERT LUCKEY on 26 Aug 1765 granted unto the said WILLIAM MACKEY ... whereas the said WILLIAM MACKEY stands firmly bound unto the said CUNINGHAM SAMPLE for £63.4.2 conditioned for the payment of £31.12 1 penny on 1 Jan next ensuing ... provided that if the said WILLIAM MACKEY shall well and truly pay unto the said CUNINGHAM SAMPLE £31.12 1 penny then this obligation to be void ... . Wit: WILLIAM SMITH, ANN SMITH. Ackn 20 Nov 1771 before WILLIAM SMITH justice. 2 Dec 1785 CUNNINGHAM SAMPLE esqr discharged mortgage. Wit: JACOB BARNITZ recorder. (E:pg 32)

25 Jan 1772. Deed of Mortgage. DANIEL REICHER of Paradise Township, York Co farmer for better securing the payment of £800 and also 5 shillings sold to MARTIN EICHELBERGER of Manchester Township, York Co esqr surviving executor of the will of DIETRICK UHLER decd a 217 ½ a. tr of land in Manchester Township adj MATHIAS SMISER Senr, ADAM UHLER,

PETER SCHRIVER Junr & SIMON WIDTMEYER, the same tr of land granted
to MICHAEL HARE by the said MARTIN EICHELBERGER as surviving
executor, and by the said MICHAEL HARE on 24th this instant conveyed to the
said DANIEL REICHER ... whereas the said DANIEL REICHER by eight
obligations standeth bound unto the said MARTIN EICHELBERGER for £1600
conditioned for the payment of £800 in payments before 25 Mar 1779 ...
provided that if the said DANIEL REICHER shall well and truly pay unto the
said MARTIN EICHELBERGER £800 then this indenture to be void ... . Wit:
HENRY MILLER, JOHN CLARK Junr. Ackn 25 Jan 1772 before MICHAEL
SWOOPE justice. 14 Mar 1775 MICHAEL EICHELBERGER discharged
mortgage. Wit: SAML JOHNSTON recorder. (E:pg 33)

28 Dec 1771. Deed of Mortgage. JOHN AMENT of Windsor Township, York
Co miller for better securing the payment of £210.4.7 and also 5 shillings sold to
ANTHONY AMENT of same place yeoman a messuage, grice mill and oil mill
and 230 a. of land in Windsor and Chanceford Townships adj JOHN KIRK,
JAMES HINES & land late of GEORGE [HACHTEL?] ... whereas the said
JOHN AMENT standeth bound unto the said ANTHONY AMENT for £420.9.2
conditioned for the payment of £210.4.7 on 28 Mar next ensuing ... provided
that if the said JOHN AMENT shall well and truly pay unto the said
ANTHONY AMENT £210.4.7 then this indenture to be void ... . Wit: GEO
EICHELBERGER, CHAS LUKENS. Ackn 28 Dec 1771 before MICHAEL
SWOOPE esqr justice. (E:pg 36)

26 Mar 1772. Deed of Mortgage. JACOB PLAUSER of Manchester Township,
York Co yeoman for better securing the payment of £323 and also 5 shillings
sold to TOBIAS BOYER of Shrewsberry Township, York Co yeoman a 106 a.
92 perches tr of land in Manchester Township adj Big Cadorus Cr, PHILIP
KING & MARTIN CRONEMILLER, being the land which by patent dated at
Phila 9 Jul 1767 was granted unto ISRAEL MORRIS of the City of Phila, and
the said ISRAEL MORRIS with PHEBE his wife on 24 Jul 1767 transferred the
land unto the afsd JACOB PLAUSER ... whereas the said JACOB PLAUSER
standeth bound unto the said TOBIAS BOYER for £646 conditioned for the
payment of £323 on 1 May 1773 ... provided that if the said JACOB PLAUSER
shall well and truly pay unto the said TOBIAS BOYER £323 then this indenture
to be void ... . Wit: PHILIP PYFER, JNO MORRIS. Ackn 26 Mar 1772
before JOSEPH UPDEGRAEF (UPDEGRAFF) esqr justice. (E:pg 37)

28 Mar 1772. Deed of Mortgage. EPHRAIM PENITON of York Town, York
Co cordwainer for better securing the payment of £93 and also 5 shillings sold to
DANIEL RAGAN of Dover Township, York Co mason a ½ lot of ground on the
w side of Water Street in York Town bounded by the Widow UPDEGRAFF &
Codorus Cr, being ½ of the lot of ground which HERMAN UPDEGRAFF esqr

late of York Town decd did by his will devise unto his wife ANN URSULA his house and lot in York Town adj JOHN MEEM, during her natural life ... whereas the afsd EPHRAIM PENITON by seven obligations stands bound unto the afsd DANIEL RAGAN FOR £186 ... provided that if the said EPHRAIM PENITON shall well and truly pay unto the said DANIEL RAGAN £93 then this indenture to be void ... . Wit: JOSEPH GARRETSON, WM LEAS. Ackn 28 Mar 1772 before JOSEPH UPDEGRAFF justice. 3 Jun 1789 DANIEL RAGEN discharged mortgage. Wit: J. BARNITZ recorder. (E:pg 39)

13 Mar 1772. Deed of Mortgage. JACOB LORENTZ of Germany Township, York Co yeoman for better securing the payment of £33 and also 5 shillings sold to ISAAC DRUGGET of Hanover Town, York Co tobacconist two lots of ground in the Town of Petersburg bounded by ISAAC DRUGGET & JACOB PARR together with a compleat set of nail smiths tools ... whereas the said JACOB LORENTZ stands firmly bound unto the said ISAAC DRUGGET for £66 conditioned for the payment of £33 on or before 15 Mar instant ... provided that if the said JACOB LORENTZ shall well and truly pay unto the said ISAAC DRUGGET £33 then this indenture to be void ... . Wit: JOS BOUDE, [?]. Ackn 13 Mar 1772 before RD MCCALISTER justice. (E:pg 40)

7 Nov 1771. Deed. JOHN FREY of Reading Township, York Co carpenter for £300 sold to CATHERINA FREY and ANNA FREY of same place spinsters a messuage and 200 a. tr of land in Reading Township adj FRANCES HODGE, PHILIP SHRIBER, THOMAS CRISHWEL, JOSEPH BROWN & WILLIAM MOCLEHANEY ... whereas in pursuance of a warrant as it appears by a receipt from THOMAS COOKSON decd that JACOB YOUNGBLOOD has lodged in his hands £5.7.6 to procure him a warrant for 100 a. of land in Reading Township dated 20 Apr 1747, and the said JACOB YOUNGBLOOD on 7 Mar 1749 did convey the tr of land unto the afsd JOHN FREY, and in pursuance of another warrant dated 26 Jun 1749 for 100 a. of land to be surveyed unto me adj the afsd tr of land in Reading Township then in Lancaster Co but now York Co ... . Wit: MICHAEL BOWER Junr, [?]. Ackn 7 Nov 1771 before JOHN SMITH justice. (E:pg 42)

27 Jun 1767. Deed. JAMES CLARK of Newbury Township, York Co yeoman and MARGARET his wife for £570 sold to BALTZER KNATZER of same place yeoman a 200 a. tr of land ... whereas ALLEN ROBINET hath obtained a warrant dated 19 Feb 1746 to take up 200 a. of land in Newbury Township (Lancaster Co then) but now York Co adj RICHARD ASHTON & RICHARD PETERS on Yellow Breeches Cr, the same being surveyed by THOMAS COOKSON esqr, and the said ALLEN ROBINET by a power of atty did appoint his trusty friend WILLIAM COPELAN of York Co yeoman his atty, and the said WILLIAM COPELAN did sell unto HENRY WAGGONER of Bethel

Township, Lancaster Co blacksmith the afsd tr of land, and the said HENRY WAGGONER did sell unto the said JAMES CLARK the tr of land on 22 Feb 1760 ... . Wit: JAMES WELCH Junr, ELIZ WELCH. Ackn 27 Jun 1767 before JAMES WELCH justice. (E:pg 43)

26 Apr 1771. Deed. ZACHARIAH NORTON of Strasburg Township, York Co yeoman for £170 sold to GEORGE ISENHARDT of Frederick Co, MD yeoman a 150 a. parcel of land in Strasburg Township adj WILLIAM GREER, JACOB CROW & ISRAM HENDRICKS, it being the land which HENRY HENDRICKS transferred to ZACHARIAH NORTON on 25 Apr 1767 ... . Wit: [?], JNO MORRIS. Ackn 27 Apr 1771 before JOHN ADLUM justice. (E:pg 44)

3 Sep 1768. Deed. ELIJAH ETTING for £3 sold to MICHAEL GROSS a tr of land in the Manner of Springetsbury adj CONRAD REFF & JOHN HARNIST, surveyed to me in pursuance of a warrant dated 28 Oct 1765 ... . Wit: JAMES BENEZET, JAS SMITH. Ackn 3 Sep 1768 before MICHAEL SWOOPE justice. (E:pg 46)

24 Mar 1769. Deed. MICHAEL GROSS of the Borrough of Lancaster, Lancaster Co merchant for £67 sold to JOHN GROVE of Newberry Township, York Co yeoman a warrant with all lands surveyed ... whereas the Proprietaries granted to ELIJAH ETTING a warrant for 200 a. of land to be surveyed and laid out to him in the Manner of Springetsbury adj CONRAD REIGLER & JOHN HARNISH, and the said ELIJAH ETTING on 3 Sep 1768 did sell unto the said MICHAEL GROSS his right in the warrant ... . Wit: GEO EICHELBERGER, JAS SMITH. Ackn 24 Mar 1769 before MICHAEL SWOOPE justice. (E:pg 47)

18 May 1770. Deed. JOHN GROVE of Newberry Township, York Co yeoman for £29 sold to MICHAEL HAHN of York Town, York Co locksmith a warrant with all lands surveyed ... whereas the Proprietaries granted unto ELIJAH ETTING a warrant for 200 a. of land to be surveyed and laid out to him in the Mannor of Springetsburry adj CONROD RICH & JOHN HARNES, and the said ELIJAH ETTING on 3 Sep 1768 did sell unto MICHAEL GROSS of the Borrough of Lancaster merchant, and the said MICHAEL GROSS on 24 Mar 1769 did convey unto the afsd JOHN GROVE the afsd warrant with the lands surveyed ... . Wit: RUDOLF SPENGLER, GEORGE MOUL. Ackn 18 May 1770 before JOHN ADLUM esqr justice. (E:pg 48)

16 Oct 1771. Bill of Sale. GEORGE MANICKEL of Manheim Township, York Co yeoman for £20 sold to JACOB SHEARMAN of York Co effects, goods and chattels [long list followed] ... . Wit: JOS BOUDE, GEO SEIVERT.

Proved 12 Nov 1774 by JOSEPH BOUDE & GEORGE SEIVERT before
RICHD MCCALISTER justice. (E:pg 50)

25 Apr 1767. Deed. HENRY HENDRICKS of Shrewsbury Township, York Co
yeoman for £40 sold to ZACHARIAH NORTON of York Town, York Co
cordwainer a 100 a. tr of land in Shrewsbury Township adj WILLIAM GREER,
JACOB CROW & ISRAM HENDRICKS ... . Wit: WILLIAM
UPDEGRAEFF, JACOB BILLMEYER Junr. Ackn 25 Apr 1767 before JOHN
ADLUM esqr justice. (E:pg 51)

7 Feb 1767. Deed. Know ye that our beloved father ALEXANDER
MCCANLESS Senr now decd of Faun Township, York Co farmer for £100 sold
to THOMAS COOPER & JOHN BOYD of York Co a tr of land in Faun
Township on River Susquehana which our father gave a bill of sale & bond of
performance binding him to make a deed to the afsd THOMAS COOPER &
JOHN BOYD for the afsd messuage and 111 a. tr of land adj land patented
under MD called *Coopers Addition*, land patented under MD called *Elishas Lot*,
land patented as afsd to JOHN COOPER called *Desarts of Arabia*, we JAMES
MCCANLESS & ALLEXANDER MCCANLESS sons & heirs of
ALLEXANDER MCCANLESS Senr decd do make known to all persons to
defend the 111 a. by a patent granted from the Proprietors Office of PA to our
father, from us to the afsd THOMAS COOPER & JOHN BOYD, and SARAH
MCCLANLES (their mother) the widow of the said ALLEXANDER
MCCANLES decd doth freely give up all my right of dower unto the said
THOMAS COOPER & JOHN BOYD ... . Wit: GORGE PATEN, WILLIAM
ROBINSON. Ackn 7 Feb 1767 before CUNINGHAM SEMPLE justice. (E:pg
52)

6 May 1772. Deed of Mortgage. JOHN OTT of Codorus Township, York Co
weaver for better securing the payment of £74 and also 5 shillings sold to
JACOB LEEDY of same place yeoman a 170 a. tr of land in Codorus Township
adj JOHN VERNOM, surveyed and laid off in pursuance of a warrant for 50 a.
dated 31 May 1762 ... whereas the said JOHN OTT by three obligations stands
bound unto the afsd JACOB LEEDY for £148 conditioned for the payment of
£74 in payments before 1 May 1775 ... provided that if the said JOHN OTT
shall well and truly pay unto the said JACOB LEEDY £74 then this indenture to
be void ... . Wit: JOHN UPDEGRAFF, WM LEAS. Ackn 6 May 1772 before
JOHN ADLUM justice. 21 Aug 1778 JACOB LEEDY discharged mortgage.
Wit: ARCHD MCCLEAN recorder. (E:pg 53)

13 Apr 1772. Deed of Mortgage. CHRISTIAN RIEF of York Township, York
Co yeoman for better securing the payment of £50 and also 5 shillings sold to
JOHN RIEF of Newberry Township, York Co yeoman a 100 a. tr of land in

York Township adj GEORGE GUSSLAR, JOSEPH SHONK & ABRAHAM WELSHANCE ... whereas the said CHRISTIAN RIEF standeth bound unto the said JOHN RIEF for £100 conditioned for the payment of £50 on 13 Oct 1772 ... provided that if the said CHRISTIAN RIEF shall well and truly pay unto the said JOHN RIEF £50 then this indenture to be void ... . Wit: STEPHEN RIETINGER, JNO MORRIS. Ackn 13 Apr 1772 before JOSEPH UPDEGRAFF esqr justice. 26 Nov 1773 JOHN RIEF discharged mortgage. Wit: SAML JOHNSTON recorder. (E:pg 55)

6 Aug 1771. Deed. DIETERICK FAHNSTICK Senr of Cocalleco Township, Lancaster Co yeoman and MARGARETHA his wife for £100 sold to DANIEL FAHNSTICK of Manchester Township, York Co yeoman son of said DIETERICK FAHNSTICK a 100 a. tr of land in Manchester Township adj Bermudian Cr, land granted to BENJAMAN FAHNSTICK & the mill land, it being pt/o a 400 a. tr of land granted to EDWARD SMOUT decd by patent dated 12 Apr 1751 in Phila (Patent Book A vol. 15 pg 60), and the said EDWARD SMOUT departed this life having first made his will dated 20 Jun 1751 and did direct that his executors, to wit, ELIZABETH SMOUT, MARCUS YOUNG & JOHN HOBSON should sell the afsd tr of land, and on 27 Nov 1755 they did sell the tr of land to JAMES MOORE, and the said JAMES MOORE and ANN his wife on 28 Nov 1759 granted the same to the said DIETRICK FAHNSTICK ... . Wit: GEO GARBER, PETER MILLER. Ackn 8 Aug 1771 before JOS UPDEGRAFF justice. (E:pg 56)

6 Aug 1771. Deed. DIETERICK FAHNSTICK Senr of Cocalleco Township, Lancaster Co yeoman and MARGARETHA his wife for £100 sold to BENJAMAN FAHNSTICK of same place son of said DIETERICK FAHNSTICK yeoman two trs of land in Manchester Township, a 94 a. tr adj TORRIS FAHNSTICK, the mill & DANIEL FAHNSTICK and a 6 a. tr of land adj Bermudian Cr, the mill & the mill race both trs being pt/o a 400 a. tr of land granted to EDWARD SMOUT decd by patent dated 12 Apr 1751 in Phila (Patent Book A vol. 15 pg 60), and the said EDWARD SMOUT departed this life having first made his will dated 20 Jun 1751 and did direct that his executors, to wit, ELIZABETH SMOUT, MARCUS YOUNG & JOHN HOBSON should sell the afsd tr of land, and on 27 Nov 1755 they did sell the tr of land to JAMES MOORE, and the said JAMES MOORE and ANN his wife on 28 Nov 1759 granted the same to the said DIETRICK FAHNSTICK ... . Wit: GEO GARBER, PETER MILLER. Ackn 8 Aug 1771 before JOSEPH UPDEGRAFF justice. (E:pg 58)

Deed of Mortgage. PETER MORE of Manchester Township, York Co yeoman for £100 sold to GEORGE ERNSTMEYER of same place two bay horses, one gray mare, two black cows, three heffers, eight head of sheep and four hogs ...

provided that if the said PETER MORE shall well and truly pay unto the said
GEORGE ERNSTMEYER £100 before 14 Apr next ensuing then this bill of
sale shall be utterly void ... . Wit: MATSIN [OTBOR?], HENRY MILLER.
Ackn 27 Apr 1772 before MARTIN EYCHELBERGER justice. 25 Feb 1778
BALZER RUDISILLY one of the executors of the will of GEORGE
ERNSTMEYER decd discharged the mortgage. Wit: ARCHD MCCLEAN
recorder. (E:pg 61)

7 Apr 1772. Quit Claim. FREDERICK SHULTZ one of the sons of PETER
SHULTS late of Heidelberg Township, York Co decd, MARTIN WEYGEL
(who intermarried with CATHARINA one of the daus of said decd, who is also
dead) and DIETER RUBERT and MARGARET his wife (also a dau of the said
decd) for £85.14.3 (to each) quit claim unto PETER SHULTS (eldest son and
heir at law of said decd) a 209 a. tr of land ... whereas JOHN DIGGES of
Conewago gent on 15 Nov 1749 did sell unto the said PETER SHULTS a 209 a.
tr of land pt/o a larger tr called *Digges' Choice* in Heidelberg Township (Book E
I No. 12 fol. 26&27 in MD) ... . Wit: BROWG KINTZ, JACOB BILLMEYER
Junr. Ackn 7 Apr 1772 before JOHN ADLUM justice. (E:pg 61)

11 Oct 1767. Deed. JACOB ZIEGLER of Manchester Township, York Co
farmer for £8.10 sold to JACOB ZIEGLER Junr tanner a 17 ¾ a. tr of land pt/o a
285 a. tr of land adj JOHN EMIGH, tr laid out for a Church, part granted to
GEORGE ZEIGLER & CHRISTIAN OISTER ... whereas in pursuance of an
instrument of writing signed by the Proprietaries dated 30 Oct 1736 there was
surveyed and laid out unto the afsd JACOB ZEIGLER on 8 Apr 1746 a 285 a. tr
of land (then in pt/o Lancaster Co) now Manchester Township, York Co adj
CHRISTIAN OISTER, JOHN EMIG & JACOB GREYBIL ... . Wit: GEO
STEVENSON, THOS ARMOR. Ackn 30 Dec 1771 before MARTIN
EYCHELBERGER justice. (E:pg 63)

9 Dec 1771. Articles of Agreement. Between JACOB ZIEGLER of Manchester
Township, York Co tanner and FREDERICK KUHN of Berwick Township,
York Co innkeeper ... the said JACOB ZIEGLER for £130 paid by the said
FREDERICK KUHN hath sold unto the said FREDERICK KUHN a 17 ¾ a. tr
of land in Manchester Township adj JACOB ZIEGLER, JOHN EMIGH
(EMICH), land laid off for a Church & CHRISTIAN OISTER ... it is mutually
agreed by the parties that the said JACOB ZIEGLER and SUSANNA his wife
shall before 1 Feb next ensuing execute a deed for the conveying the said land
unto FREDERICK KUHN ... and the said JACOB ZIEGLER is allowed to live
and dwell on the said premises till 1 Apr next ensuing ... they bind themselves
in £260 ... . Wit: EPHM PENITON, JACOB BILLMEYER Junr. (E:pg 65)

24 Mar 1772. Deed. FREDERICK KUHN of Berwick Township, York Co innkeeper and CATHARINE his wife for £130 sold to PETER WOLF of Manchester Township, York Co innkeeper a 17 ¾ a. tr of land ... in pursuance of an instrument of writing signed by the Proprietaries dated at Phila 30 Oct 1736 there was surveyed and laid out unto JACOB ZIEGLER on 8 Apr 1746 a 285 a. tr of land pt/o Lancaster Co now in Manchester Township, York Co adj CHRISTIAN OISTER, JOHN EMIG & JACOB GRAYBLE, and the said JACOB SIEGLER on 11 Oct 1767 did sell unto his son JACOB SIEGLER 17 ¾ a. pt/o the afsd tr of land adj JOHN EMIGH,, land laid off for a Church & part granted to GEORGE ZIEGLER ... . Wit: DAVID MCCONAUGHY, HANS MORRISON. Ackn 24 Mar 1772 before ROBT MCPHERSON justice. (E:pg 66)

20 Apr 1765. Deed. WILLIAM STALLWORTH of Fawn Township, York Co for £54 sold to WALTER ROBISON of same place a 25 a. tr of land in Faun Township adj JAMES CRUMEY, which was granted unto me by warrant dated 6 Aug 1753 ... . Wit: ALEXANDER MCCANLESS, THOS ARMOR. Proved 16 May 1770 by THOMAS ARMOR (ALEXANDER MCCANLESS is since decd) before JOHN ADLUM esqr justice. (E:pg 69)

1 May 1765. Deed. SAMPSON ARCHER of Berwick Township, York Co tavernkeeper for £20 sold to GEORGE STEVENSON of York Township, York Co esqr a 100 a. tr of land between WILLIAM ORR and JOHN FINLEY in the Barrens in Shrewsbury Township, which was granted unto me by warrant dated at Phila 11 Jun 1762 ... . Wit: THOS ARMOR, JOHN BOYD. Proved 18 Dec 1771 by THOMAS ARMOR & JOHN BOYD before JOHN ADLUM esqr justice. (E:pg 70)

21 May 1772. Deed of Mortgage. MARTIN KAP of Lancaster Co, PA yeoman for better securing the payment of £600 and also 5 shillings sold to GEORGE NESS of Manchester Township, York Co yeoman a 159 a. tr of land in Manchester Township adj GEORGE ERNEST MYER, JACOB RUDISIL, JOHN WOLF, GODFREY KING & ANDREW SMITH ... whereas the said MARTIN KAP by eight obligations stands bound unto the said GEORGE NESS for £1200 condition for payment of £600 in payments before 1 May 1780 ... provided that if the said MARTIN KAP shall well and truly pay unto the said GEORGE NESS £600 then this indenture to be void ... . Wit: JOHN HECKENDORN, WM LEAS. Ackn 21 May 1772 before JOS UPDEGRAFF justice. 13 May 1782 GEORGE NESS discharged mortgage. Wit: ARCHD MCCLEAN recorder. (E:pg 70)

1 Mar 1760. Deed. JOSEPH MCKINNEY of Manchester Township, York Co yeoman for £35 sold to GEORGE STEVENSON of Kent Co esqr a 261 a. tr of

land in Barwick Township adj land patented to JOHN DIGGS under MD, JACOB KEGGY, land patented to ROBERT OWEN under MD, WILLIAM WAPLER & HENRY KERR, being the same which was surveyed to me 7 Mar last by virtue of a warrant dated at Phila [*blank*] ... . Wit: WM MAILAY, JOHN BOYD. Ackn 25 Mar 1762 before THOS ARMOR esqr justice. (E:pg 72)

25 Apr 1771. Deed. GEORGE STEVENSON of Carlisle, Cumberland Co, PA gent for £108 sold to THOMAS ARMOR of York, York Co surveyor a 261 a. tr of land ... whereas the Proprietaries by their warrant dated at Phila [*blank*] there was surveyed and laid out unto JOSEPH MCKINNEY a 261 a. tr of land in Barwick Township [*same as above*], and the said JOSEPH MCKINNEY on 31 Mar 1760 did sell unto the afsd GEORGE STEVENSON the afsd tr of land ... . Wit: ROBT STEVENSON, JAMES DILL. Ackn 26 Apr 1771 before WILLIAM DELAP esqr justice. (E:pg 74)

17 Feb 1772. Deed of Mortgage. DAVID NEALS (NEALLS) (NEEALS) (NEELS) of Manorighan Township, York Co for better securing the payment of £24.4.10 and also 5 shillings sold to MARY NEALS of same place a messuage & tr of land held under pt/o a warrant granted unto ROBT NEALS decd dated at Phila 28 Oct 1757 adj JAMES CROUTHERS, now GEORGE EALLEY by a conditional line, JOHN KEER & the mountain ... whereas the said DAVID NEALS on 13 Sep 1771 stands bound unto the afsd MARY NEALS for £48.8.10 conditioned for the payment of £24.4.10 ... provided that if the said DAVID NEALS shall well and truly pay unto the said MARY NEALS £24.4.10 on 30 Sep 1773 then this indenture to be void ... . Wit: CHARLES BOYERS, LEWIS LEWIS. Ackn --- 1772 before MATTHEW DILL justice of the peace. (E:pg 75)

27 Apr 1772. Deed. GEORGE HANEY for 5 shillings sold to PHILIP HOFFMAN of Manchester Township, York Co (and £50 at or before the sealing and delivery hereof) the right in an application No. 3263 by me entered in the Proprietaries Land Office and received on 30 Mar 1767 for taking up 100 a. of land in Manchester Township adj CHRISTIAN BIXLER Junr, CHRISTIAN HEID & Big Codorus Cr ... . Wit: [?], JACOB BILLMEYER Junr. Ackn 27 Apr 1772 before JOHN ADLUM justice. (E:pg 77)

19 Dec 1771. Deed of Mortgage. LEONARD WOLF of Manheim Township, York Co yeoman only son and heir at law of FREDERICK WOLF late of York Co yeoman decd for better securing the payment of £25.6.3 and also 5 shillings sold to JACOB SHEARMAN of Manheim Township, York Co yeoman a 125 a. tr of land in Manheim Township bounded by GEORGE FOX, GEORGE GAILEY, FRANCIS HOSTETTER & NICHOLAS HOSTETTER, it being the

same improvement and piece of land whereon the said FREDERICK WOLF lately dwelt, also two horses, one grey and the other a sorrel ... whereas the said LEONARD WOLF by his bond stands bound unto the said JACOB SHEARMAN for £50.12.6 conditioned for the payment of £25.6.3 on or before 19 Dec next ensuing ... provided that if the said LEONARD WOLF shall well and truly pay unto the said FREDERICK WOLF £25.6.3 then this indenture to be void ... . Wit: JOS BOUDE, JO CHRISTIAN BERK. Ackn 29 Dec 1771 before RICHD MCCALISTER justice. (E:pg 78)

27 Apr 1772. Deed of Mortgage. PETER MORE of Manchester Township, York Co yeoman for better securing the payment of £100 and also 5 shillings sold to GEORGE ERNSTMEYER of same place yeoman a 100 a. tr of land whereon the said PETER MORE now dwells in Manchester Township adj JACOB SHIPE, PETER SCHNEIDER, JACOB BONE & the *Oar Bang* late the property of WILLIAM BENNETT ... whereas the said PETER MORE standeth bound unto the said GEORGE ERNSTMEYER for £200 conditioned for the payment of £100 on or before 14 Apr 1773 ... provided that if the said PETER MORE shall well and truly pay unto the said GEORGE ERNSTMEYER £100 then this indenture to be void ... . Wit: JACOB ROTHROCK, HENRY MILLER. Ackn 27 Apr 1772 before MARTIN EICHELBERGER esqr justice. 25 Feb 1778 BALTZER RUDISILLY one of the executors of the will of GEORGE ERNEST MEYER decd discharged mortgage. Wit: ARCHD MCCLEAN recorder. (E:pg 79)

11 Jan 1770. Deed. CHRISTMAN LAW (LAU) of Manchester Township, York Co miller for £200 sold to MICHAEL LAW, one of the sons of the said CHRISTMAN LAW, of same place ½ pt/o of a 347 ½ a. tr of land ... whereas in pursuance of a warrant dated 10 Apr 1750 there was surveyed and laid out unto the said CHRISTMAN LAW (by the name of CHRISTIAN LOW) a 347 ½ a. tr of land in Manchester Township adj PHILIP LAU, Little Codorus Cr, FREDERICK REMER, GEORGE CONROD, land late of NICHOLAS SHUSTER now of the said CHRISTMAN (alias CHRISTIAN) LAW, PETER LAW, FELIX MILLER & Little Codorus Cr ... . Wit: [?], JACOB BILLMEYER Junr. Ackn 11 Jan 1770 before MARTIN EICHELBERGER esqr justice. (E:pg 81)

28 Mar 1769. Deed. VALENTINE HESS of Paradise Township, York Co and RACHEAL his wife for £75.10 sold to MICHEAL PRISSEL of the same place whealright a 65 a. tr of land pt/o a larger tr granted unto us by a warrant dated at Phila 10 Mar instant in Paradise Township adj VALENTINE PRISSEL (BRISSEL), NICHOLAS DELLOW & other land of the afsd VALENTINE HESS ... . Wit: [?], NICHS BETTINGER. Ackn 28 Mar 1769 before HENRY SLAGLE justice. (E:pg 83)

27 Apr 1772. Deed of Mortgage. PHILIP HOFFMAN of Manchester Township, York Co yeoman for better securing the payment of £38.5.2 and also 5 shillings sold to CASPAR KNAB of same place yeoman a 100 a. tr of land in Manchester Township adj CHRISTIAN BIXLER Junr, CHRISTIAN HEID & Big Codorus Cr, it being the same which GEORGE HANEY obtained an application No. 3263 dated 30 Mar 1767 who on the same day did convey the same to the said PHILIP HOFFMAN ... whereas the said PHILIP HOFFMAN standeth bound unto the said CASPAR KNAB for £76.10.4 conditioned for the payment of £38.5.2 on 27 Oct 1773 ... provided that if the said PHILIP HOFFMAN shall well and truly pay unto the said CASPAR KNAB £38.5.2 then this indenture to be void ... . Wit: [?], JACOB BILLMEYER Junr. Ackn 27 Apr 1772 before JOHN ADLUM esqr justice. 26 Jul 1777 CASPER KNAB discharged mortgage. Wit: ARCHIBALD MCCLEAN recorder. (E:pg 84)

19 May 1772. Deed of Mortgage. MARTIN HAUKE of Ruffo Township, Lancaster Co, PA yeoman for securing the payment of £180 and also 5 shillings sold to WILLIAM EDDY of Hopewell Township, York Co a 175 a. tr of land in Hopewell Township adj JAMES MCCULLOUGH & HENRY CRAIG ... whereas the said MARTIN HAUKE by ten obligations standeth bound unto the said WILLIAM EDDY for £360 conditioned for the payment of £180 in payments before 15 Apr 1782 ... provided that if the said MARTIN HAUKE shall well and truly pay unto the said WILLIAM EDDY £180 then this indenture to be void ... . Wit: JOHN SHULTZ, WM KERSSEE. Ackn 19 May 1772 before JOHN ADLUM esqr justice. 1 May 1784 WILLIAM EDIE discharged mortgage. Wit: ARCHD MCCLEAN recorder. (E:pg 86)

17 Oct 1766. Deed. JOSEPH POLK Senr of Barwick Township, York Co yeoman sold to JOSEPH POLK Junr of same place yeoman (for 1/3 pt/o all the produce of the tr of land to be yearly rendered to the said JOSEPH POLK Senr during his life and at his decease the said JOSEPH POLK Junr to pay £10 to the legatees of the said JOSEPH POLK Senr) a 100 a. tr of land... whereas the Proprietaries by their warrant dated at Phila 10 Nov 1748 did grant unto JOHN HEUSTON a 100 a. tr of land in Barwick Township (then pt/o Lancaster Co) adj one BROWN on Little Cannewaga, the same since conveyed to the said JOSEPH POLK Senr ... . Wit: JOHN MENTIETH, JOSEPH POTTER. JOSEPH POLK Junr doth bind himself in the penal sum of £100 for the performance and discharge of the within consideration. 27 Apr 1767 JOSEPH POLK Senr & BARBRA his wife ackn before HENRY SLAGLE justice. (E:pg 87)

2 Jan 1771. Deed. BALTZER SPANGLER Junr and MICHAEL SWOOPE esqr executors of the will of BALTZER SPANGLER late of York Township, York Co yeoman decd for £200 (being the residue of £250) sold to FRANCIS

PICKLE of same place yeoman a 130 a. tr of land pt/o a 487 a. tr of land adj land of RUDOLPH SPANGLER (now of JAMES SMITH) & land late of GEORGE HOKE (now of JAMES SMITH) ... whereas the Proprietaries by patent dated at Phila 24 Feb 1763 granted to the said BALTZER SPANGLER a 487 a. tr of land in York Township adj York Town lands, land late of MARTIN FRY, CONRAD HOLTZBAUM, GEORGE HOKE & RUDOLPH SPANGLER (Patent Book AA vol. 4 pg 257) ... whereas the said BALTZER SPANGLER (in his lifetime) on 4 Mar year last mentioned by Articles of Agreement between him and the said FRANCIS PICKLE for £250 the said BALTZER SPANGLER agreed to make a deed for a 130 a. tr of land in York Township adj RUDOLPH SPANGLER, JAMES SMITH (formerly of GEORGE HOAK) and the said BALTZER SPANGLER's other lands, and before any deed was executed the said BALTZER SPANGLER died having first made his will and by a codicil the said BALTZER SPANGLER directed his executors to execute deeds to several children for several houses, lots and lands and also to execute a conveyance to such other persons the testator sold lands to... . Wit: GEO EICHELBERGER, JAS SMITH. Ackn 2 Jan 1771 before JOHN ADLUM esqr justice. (E:pg 89)

27 Mar 1772. Deed. FRANCIS PICKLE of York Township, York Co yeoman and ELIZABETH his wife for £680 sold to JAMES SMITH of York Town, York Co atty at law a 130 a. tr of land [same as above] ... . Wit: GEO EICHELBERGER, DAVID GREER. Ackn 27 Mar 1771 before JOHN ADLUM esqr justice. (E:pg 92)

18 Sep 1771. Deed. JAMES WRIGHT of Hempfield Township, Lancaster Co, PA esqr and RHODA his wife, JOHN WRIGHT of Hallam Township, York Co gent and SUSANNA WRIGHT of Hallam Township, York Co spinster for £50 sold to JAMES EWING of Hallam Township, York Co gent a 26 a. tr of land adj WILLIAM WILLIS, pt/o a 278 a. tr of land ... whereas the Proprietaries by their patent dated at Phila 7 Apr 1752 did grant unto JOHN WRIGHT late of Hallam Township, York Co decd, the said JAMES WRIGHT and WILLIAM WILLIS a 480 a. tr of land in Manchester Township adj Codorus Cr, town land, NICHOLAS BUTT (BUT), FRANCIS WORLEY, JOHN SMITH, one OPIS land & CHARLES JONES (Book A vol. 16 pg 146), and after obtaining the patent it was mutually agreed between the said JOHN WRIGHT in his life time, the said JAMES WRIGHT and WILLIAM WILLIS that the said JOHN WRIGHT the elder and JAMES WRIGHT should received for their 2/3 part 278 a. of the 480 a. tr of land and WILLIAM WILLIS received the remainder. The said JOHN WRIGHT the elder is since dead but before the time of his death made his will dated 3 Dec 1753 and did devise his real and personal estate to be divided into six shares "to my wife one share, to my two sons ROBERT and JOHN three shares, and the plantation whereon I now live to my two daus each a share" and impowered his executors, his wife ELEANOR WRIGHT and the said

JAMES WRIGHT, to make sale of any other of his lands if they should think proper, his plantation where he then lived only excepted ... whereas the said WILLIAM WILLIS and BETTY his wife on 5 Feb 1767 did release all their right of the 278 a. of land unto the said JAMES and ELEANOR WRIGHT (Book C pg 240) ... and the said ROBERT WRIGHT, after the death of the said JOHN WRIGHT the elder, died unmarried, intestate and without issue, and the said ELEANOR WRIGHT since also died intestate leaving the said JOHN WRIGHT, PATIENCE now w/o the said JAMES EWING and the said SUSANNA WRIGHT, her issue by the said JOHN WRIGHT decd ... . Wit: THOS MINSHALL, SAMUEL WRIGHT. Ackn 18 Sep 1771 before THOS MINSHALL justice. (E:pg 95)

2 Dec 1771. Quit Claim. JOSEPH HERSEY of Paradise Township, York Co yeoman and MAGDALENA his wife, JACOB HERSEY of Warwick Township, Lancaster Co yeoman and BARBARA his wife, JOHN HERSEY also of Warwick Township yeoman and CATHARINA his wife, PETER HERSEY of Paradise Township, York Co yeoman and ANN his wife, JACOB SCHNEIDER of Rapho Township, Lancaster Co yeoman and MARY his wife, JACOB HEISTANDT of Hempfield Township, Lancaster Co yeoman and ELISABETH his wife and JOHN SCHENCK of Elisabeth Township, Lancaster Co and BARBARA his wife (the said JOSEPH HERSEY, JACOB HERSEY, JOHN HERSEY, PETER HERSEY, MARY SCHNEIDER, ELISABETH HEISTANDT & BARBARA SCHENCK being the children of CHRISTIAN HERSEY late of Warwick Township, Lancaster Co yeoman decd) for 5 shillings quit claim unto ANDREW HERSEY of Paradise Township, York Co yeoman eldest son of the said CHRISTIAN HERSEY decd a 156 a. tr of land on both sides of Codorus Cr in Paradise & Codorus Townships adj GEORGE ROSS, ANTHONY MOULE & PETER HERSEY's part of the tr called *Hirsey's Mount*, and a 94 a. tr of land pt/o a second tr in Paradise Township adj the afsd tr, said PETER HERSEY's part of *Hirsey's Mount*, GEORGE SWOOPE & the heirs of THOMAS WILSON ... whereas the Proprietary of MD by patent dated 17 May 1734 granted unto the said CHRISTIAN HERSEY (the father) a 400 a. tr of land on the main br of Codorus Cr (the land deemed to be in Baltimore Co, MD) called *Hirsey's Mount* (but now is in Paradise and Codorus Townships, York Co) (Patent recorded in Liber E T No. 1 fol. 77 in MD) ... whereas the Proprietaries of PA by their patent dated 16 Aug 1756 did grant unto the said CHRISTIAN HERSEY (the father) a 331 a. tr of land in Paradise & Codorus Townships lying contiguous to the afsd tr (Patent Book A vol 19 pg 188 in Phila) ... the said CHRISTIAN HERSEY was seized in the afsd two adj trs of land with divers other lands in Lancaster Co and being so seized died intestate on 19 Apr last past leaving the afsd children to whom his estate descended, and the said parties have agreed to made division of the whole estate, and the two afsd trs to be divided between the said ANDREW HERSEY, the said JOSEPH

HERSEY and the said PETER HERSEY, being three parts divided and they have agreed to release unto each other their share ... . Wit: ROBT WHITE, ARCHD MCCLEAN, CHRISTIAN HERSEY, ABRAHAM CASSALL. JOSEPH HERSEY & MAGDALENA his wife and PETER HERSEY and ANN his wife ackn 18 Dec 1771 before RICHARD MCCALISTER esqr justice. CHRISTIAN HERSEY & ABRAHAM CASSALL by their solemn affirmation did declare on 6 Apr 1772 before JOS UPDEGRAFF esqr justice that they saw JACOB HERSEY & BARBARA his wife, JOHN HERSEY & CATHERINE his wife, JACOB SNIDER & MARY his wife, JACOB HESTANT & ELISABETH his wife & JOHN SHANK & BARBARA his wife sign, seal & deliver the foregoing deed unto ANDREW HERSEY and they also saw BARBARA HERSEY widow and relict of CHRISTIAN HERSEY decd sign, seal and deliver the release of her right of dower unto ANDREW HERSEY. (E:pg 100)

2 Dec 1771. Quit Claim. BARBARA HERSEY widow and relict of CHRISTIAN HERSEY late of Warwick Township, Lancaster Co, PA yeoman for 5 shillings quit claim unto ANDREW HERSEY of Paradise Township, York Co (eldest son of the said CHRISTIAN HERSEY by the said BARBARA) all my right of dower in two trs of land in the whole 250 a. [see above] ... . Wit: CHRISTIAN HERSEY, ABRAHAM CASSALL. Proved 6 Apr 1772 by CHRISTIAN HERSEY and ABRAHAM CASSALL before JOS UPDEGRAFF justice. (E:pg 105)

2 Dec 1771. Quit Claim. ANDREW HERSEY of Paradise Township, York Co yeoman and ELISABETH his wife, JACOB HERSEY of Warwick Township, Lancaster Co yeoman and BARBARA his wife, JOHN HERSEY also of Warwick Township yeoman and CATHARINA his wife, PETER HERSEY of Paradise Township yeoman and ANN his wife, JACOB SCHNEIDER of Rapho Township, Lancaster Co yeoman and MARY his wife, JACOB HEINSTADT of Hempfield Township, Lancaster Co yeoman and ELISABETH his wife and JOHN SCHENCK of Elisabeth Township, Lancaster Co and BARBARA his wife (the said ANDREW HERSEY, JACOB HERSEY, JOHN HERSEY, PETER HERSEY, MARY SCHNEIDER, ELISABETH HEISTANDT & BARBARA SCHENCK children of CHRISTIAN HERSEY late of Warwick Township, Lancaster Co yeoman decd) for 5 shillings quit claim unto JOSEPH HERSEY of Paradise Township, York Co yeoman one of the sons of said CHRISTIAN HERSEY decd a 105 a. tr of land pt/o a tr of land called *Hirsey's Mount* in Codorus Township adj Codorus Cr, PETER HERSEY's part & JOHN KOONTZ and also a 146 a. tr of land pt/o a tr of land in Paradise & Codorus Townships adj GEORGE SWOOPE, PETER HERSEY'S part, Codorus Cr, PETER LOW & CHRISTIAN LOW ... whereas the Proprieties of MD and PA [same as E100] ... . Wit: ROBT WHITE ARCHD MCCLEAN., CHRISTIAN KERSEY, ABRAHAM CASSALL. Ackn 18 Dec 1771 before RICHARD

MCCALISTER justice and 6 Apr 1772 before JOS UPDEGRAFF justice [*same as above*]. (E:pg 106)

2 Dec 1771. Quit Claim. BARBARA HERSEY widow and relict of CHRISTIAN HERSEY late of Warwick Township, Lancaster Co, PA yeoman for 5 shillings quit claim unto JOSEPH HERSEY of Paradise Township, York Co (son of the said CHRISTIAN HERSEY by the said BARBARA) all my right of dower in two trs of land in the whole 251 a. [*see above*] ... . Wit: CHRISTIAN HERSEY, ABRAHAM CASSALL. Proved 6 Apr 1772 by CHRISTIAN HERSEY and ABRAHAM CASSALL before JOS UPDEGRAFF justice. (E:pg 111)

2 Dec 1771. Quit Claim. ANDREW HERSEY of Paradise Township, York Co yeoman and ELISABETH his wife, JOSEPH HERSEY of Paradise Township, York Co yeoman and MAGDALENA his wife, JACOB HERSEY of Warwick Township, Lancaster Co yeoman and BARBARA his wife, JOHN HERSEY also of Warwick Township yeoman and CATHARINA his wife, JACOB SCHNEIDER of Rapho Township, Lancaster Co yeoman and MARY his wife, JACOB HEISTANDT of Hempfield Township, Lancaster Co yeoman and ELISABETH his wife and JOHN SCHENCK of Elisabeth Township, Lancaster Co and BARBARA his wife (the said ANDREW HERSEY, JOSEPH HERSEY, JACOB HERSEY, JOHN HERSEY, MARY SCHNEIDER, ELISABETH HEISTANDT & BARBARA SCHENCK children of CHRISTIAN HERSEY late of Warwick Township, Lancaster Co yeoman decd) for 5 shillings quit claim unto PETER HERSEY of Paradise Township, York Co yeoman youngest son of the said CHRISTIAN HERSEY decd a 134 a. tr of land pt/o the tr of land called *Hirsey's Mount* on both sides of Codorus Cr in Paradise and Codorus Townships adj ANDREW HERSEY's part & JOSEPH HERSEY's part and a 122 a. tr of land in Paradise and Codorus Townships adj afsd tr, ANDREW HERSEYS's part, heirs of THOMAS WILSON, THOMAS ARMOR, PETER LOW & GEORGE SWOOPE ... whereas the Proprieties of MD and PA [*same as E100*] ... . Wit: ROBT WHITE, ARCHD MCCLEAN, CHRISTIAN HERSEY, ABRAHAM CASSALL. Ackn 18 Dec 1771 before RICHARD MCCALISTER justice and 6 Apr 1772 before JOS UPDEGRAFF justice [*same as above*]. (E:pg 112)

2 Dec 1771. Quit Claim. BARBARA HERSEY widow and relict of CHRISTIAN HERSEY late of Warwick Township, Lancaster Co, PA yeoman for 5 shillings quit claim unto PETER HERSEY of Paradise Township, York Co (son of the said CHRISTIAN HERSEY by the said BARBARA) all my right of dower in two trs of land in the whole 251 a. [*see above*] ... . Wit: CHRISTIAN HERSEY, ABRAHAM CASSALL. Proved 6 Apr 1772 by CHRISTIAN

HERSEY and ABRAHAM CASSALL before JOS UPDEGRAFF justice. (E:pg 117)

30 Apr 1768. Deed. DAVID MCCONAUGHY esqr sheriff of York Co for £320 sold to GEORGE ROSS of Lancaster Co a messuage and ½ of Lot No. 108 in York Town on High Street bounded by JOHN EMIGH & PHILIP ENTLERS, in breadth 32'6" and in depth 230' ... whereas MICHAEL GROSS lately in the Court of Common Pleas recovered a debt of £600 and 62 shillings 11 pence damages against NICHOLAS HONING and ANN his wife (late ANN DAVIS), THOMAS MINSHALL and WILLIAM DAVIS executors of the will of THOMAS DAVIS decd ... the sheriff seized in execution a messuage and ½ of Lot No. 108 in York Town which were of THOMAS DAVIS late of York Co yeoman/husbandman decd at the time of his death and exposed the same to sale at public vendue on 25 Jan 1768 and sold to GEORGE ROSS of Lancaster Co atty at law for £320 he being the highest bidder ... . Wit: JAMES SAYRE, DAVID GRIER. Ackn 30 May 1768 before SAML JOHNSTON prothy. (E:pg 118)

30 Jun 1768. Deed. GEORGE ROSS of Lancaster Borough, Lancaster Co atty at law and ANN his wife for £400 sold to JOSEPH SMITH of York Town, York Co innholder ½ of Lot No. 108 in York Town [same as above] ... . Wit: WM THOMSON, J MOORE. Ackn 30 Jun 1768 before SAML JOHNSTON esqr justice. (E:pg 122)

13 Dec 1770. Quit Claim. JAMES SMITH of York, York Co esqr and ELINOR his wife for £5 quit claim unto JOSEPH SMITH of same placed innholder a messuage and ½ lot of ground [same as above] ... whereas the Proprietaries by their patent dated at Phila 27 Sep 1753 did grant unto GEORGE HOOK late of York a lott of ground on the s side of High Street in York Town (Patent Book A vol. 18 pg 169), and the said GEORGE HOOK and BARBARA his wife on 1 Mar 1753 [1762 written in] did convey ½ of the lott afsd unto the said JAMES SMITH (Book A pg 585), and the said JAMES SMITH being so seized of the messuage and ½ lott of ground sold the same to THOMAS DAVIS late of York Co yeoman now decd for £600 and entered into a bond for £1200 dated 9 Oct 1762 which the said JAMES SMITH was to execute and deliver unto the afsd THOMAS DAVIS a deed of conveyance for the messuage and ½ lott of ground, and the said THOMAS DAVIS being so possessed soon after the agreement departed this life having first made his will and appointed his wife ANN DAVIS now w/o NICHOLAS HORNEL, THOMAS MINSHALL & WILLIAM DAVIS executors before a deed of conveyance could be made ... soon after the decease of the said THOMAS DAVIS the sheriff seized in execution the afsd messuage and ½ lot of ground and sold the same at public vendue (for satisfaction of the said THOMAS DAVIS decd's debts) to

GEORGE ROSS esqr of Lancaster Co ... the said GEORGE ROSS and ANN his wife on 30 Jun 1768 conveyed the messuage and ½ lott of ground unto the afsd JOSEPH SMITH ... . Wit: GEO EICHELBERGER, DAVID GRIER. Ackn 13 Dec 1770 before JOHN ADLUM justice. (E:pg 123)

13 Dec 1770. Deed. JOSEPH SMITH of York Town, York Co innholder and BARBARA his wife for £425 sold to PHILIP ENTLER of same place innholder a messuage and ½ lot of ground [same as above] ... . Wit: JAS SMITH, DAVID GRIER. Ackn 13 Dec 1770 before JOHN ADLUM justice. (E:pg 126)

8 May 1772. Deed. JOHN STRICKLER of Hellam Township, York Co blacksmith for £300 sold to HENRY STRICKLER of same place yeoman a 136 ½ a. tr of land pt/o a 212 ½ a. tr of land adj JOHN DREICHLER, said JACOB STRICKLER's land (alias JOHN STRICKLER) & Widow KOONTZ ... whereas the Proprietaries by their patent dated at Phila 22 of Apr last past did grant unto the said JOHN STRICKLER a 212 ½ a. tr of land in Hallam Township called *Strickleburg* adj HENRY KANN, the heirs of MICHAEL KEENTZ, JOHN DREICHLER, JOHN STRICKLER (but in reality belonging to JACOB STRICKLER), DANIEL HARMAN & Stony Run (Patent Book AA vol. 13 pg 91) ... . Wit: [?], JACOB BILLMEYER Junr. Ackn 16 Jun 1772 before JOS UPDEGRAFF justice. (E:pg 130)

0 Jun 1772. Deed. HENRY STRICKLER of Hellam Township, York Co yeoman and MAGDALENA his wife for £100 sold to CONRAD STRICKLER of same place yeoman two trs of land pt/o a 136 ½ a. tr of land, the one a 5 ¾ a. tr adj JOHN DREICHLER, said HENRY's land, the heirs of MICHAEL KUNTZ & Widow KOONTZ, and the other a 4 ¼ a. tr adj said KUNTZ & HENRY STRICKLER ... whereas the Proprietaries by their patent dated at Phila 22 of Apr last past did grant unto the said JOHN STRICKLER a 212 ½ a. tr of land in Hallam Township called *Strickleburg* adj HENRY KANN, the heirs of MICHAEL KEENTZ, JOHN DREICHLER, JOHN STRICKLER (but in reality belonging to JACOB STRICKLER), DANIEL HARMAN & Stony Run (Patent Book AA vol. 13 pg 91) ... and the said JOHN STRICKLER did convey unto the said HENRY STRICKLER pt/o the afsd tr of land [see above] ... . Wit: [?], JACOB BILLMEYER Junr. Ackn 9 Jun 1772 before JOHN ADLUM justice. (E:pg 132)

24 Jun 1772. Deed. ANDREW BOWER of Warrington, York Co yeoman and ELIZABETH his wife for £28 sold to ABRAHAM BOWER of Huntington Township, York Co yeoman a 9 a. 150 perches tr of land pt/o a 181 ¼ a. tr of land in Warrington Township adj Bermudian Cr, other land of the said ABRAHAM BOWER & JOHN LERNER ... whereas the Proprietaries by their patent dated at Phila 8 Jun 1744 did grant unto MICHAEL BOWER a 423 a. tr

of land in Manchester Township, Lancaster Co, but now in Huntington and Warrington Townships, York Co adj SAMUEL COX, THOMAS DILL, ANDREAS BAYLE, WILLIAM RICHARDSON & THOMAS CANWORTHY (Patent Book A vol. 12 pg 137) ... and the said MICHAEL BOWER and CATHARINE his wife on 13 Nov 1764 did sell unto the said ANDREW BOWER a 181 ¾ a. tr of land pt/o the 423 a. tr of land adj part laid off for MICHAEL BOWER Junr, Bermudian Cr, land formerly of THOMAS CANWORTHY now of JOHN SEMER, part laid off for PETER BOWER & land formerly of THOMAS DILL (Book C vol. 3 pg 28) ... . Wit: [?], GABRIEL SMITH. Ackn 24 Jun 1772 before JOHN SMITH justice. (E:pg 135)

29 Apr 1772. Deed. WILLIAM THOMAS of Warrington Township, York Co yeoman and ANN his wife for £600 sold to RICCORD HUSSEY of Newberry Township, York Co a 224 ½ a. tr of land ... whereas the Proprietaries by their parent dated at Phila 28 Oct 1762 did grant unto the afsd WILLIAM THOMAS a 224 ½ a. tr of land in Warrington Township adj JAMES LENOX, SAMUEL JAMES, HENRY CLARK & WILLIAM OZBURN (Patent Book AA vol. 4 pg 88) ... . Wit: SAMUEL LEWIS, WILLIAM PENROSE. Ackn 20 Apr 1772 before MATTHEW DILL justice. (E:pg 138)

21 May 1772. Deed. GEORGE NESS of Manchester Township, York Co yeoman and ANNA MARIA his wife for £1021 sold to MARTIN KAP of Heidelberg Township, Lancaster Co yeoman a 159 a. tr of land ... whereas the Proprietaries by their patent dated at Phila 14 Apr 1761 did grant unto the said GEORGE NESS a 159 a. tr of land in Manchester Township adj ANDREW SMITH, GEORGE ERNEST MYER, JACOB RUDISILLY, JOHN WOLF & RYNHART HAMMER (Patent Book AA vol. 1, pg 229) ... . Wit: [GEORGE ?], [CARL ?]. Ackn 21 May 1772 before DAVID JAMESON justice. (E:pg 141)

10 Apr 1772. Deed. THOMAS ARMOR of York Town, York Co surveyor and SARAH his wife for £170 sold to PETER WOLF of Manchester Township, York Co tavernkeeper a 95 a. tr of land ... whereas the Proprietaries by their patent dated at Phila 27 Feb last did grant unto the said THOMAS ARMOR a 95 a. tr of land called *Manchester* adj JACOB ZIEGLER, JACOB WOLF, CHRISTIAN OISTER & PETER WOLF (Patent Book AA vol. 13 pg 47) ... . Wit: GEO EICHELBERGER, THOS ARMOR Junr. Ackn 11 Apr 1772 before JOHN ADLUM esqr justice. (E:pg 143)

2 May 1772. Deed. JOHN JOSEPH of Manheim Township, York Co yeoman and CATHARINE his wife for £550 sold to PETER WOLF of Manchester Township, York Co innkeeper a 284 a. 80 perches tr of land ... whereas in pursuance of two warrants granted to WILLIAM HOFFMAN decd dated at

Phila 6 Aug 1753 and 2 Jun 1762 there was surveyed and laid out unto
GEORGE HENRY JOSEPH a 284 a. 80 perches tr of land adj THOMAS
WILSON, PETER DICK, JACOB STAM, GEORGE LINEWEAVER, & the
heirs of PHILIP HELTZEL, and the said GEORGE HENRY JOSEPH being so
seized in the land died intestate leaving the said JOHN JOSEPH his eldest son
and heir at law, CATHARINA w/o JONAS BOTT, CHRISTENA w/o GEORGE
ODERMAN & MARILLIS JOSEPH, and in pursuance of a petition of the said
JOHN JOSEPH it was ordered by the Court that the tr of land should be divide
amongst the children of the intestate, on 27 Mar last past the freeholders
returned the land could not be divided without spoiling the whole and valued the
land at £400, and the land was allotted unto the said JOHN JOSEPH he paying
the other children their share of the valuation ... . Wit: [?], HENRY MILLER.
Ackn 2 May 1772 before JOHN ADLUM justice. (E:pg 145)

15 Jun 1772. Deed of Mortgage. CHRISTIAN WAMPLER of York Town,
York Co yeoman for better securing the payment of £50 and also 5 shillings sold
to CHARLES BARNETZ of same place brewer two lotts of ground in York
Town, Lot No. 160 on George Street and Lot No. 363 on High Street and the w
side of Codorus Cr ... whereas the said CHRISTIAN WAMPLER standeth
bound unto the said CHARLES BARNETZ for £100 conditioned for the
payment of £50 on 1 Nov next ... provided that if the said CHRISTIAN
WAMPLER shall well and truly pay unto the said CHARLES BARNETZ £50
then this indenture to be void ... . Wit: [?], HENRY MILLER.   Ackn 16 Jun
1772 before JOHN ADLUM justice. (E:pg 148)

4 Apr 1772. Deed. HENRY MOHLER of Berwick Township, York Co yeoman
and CATHARINE his wife for £250 sold to VALENTINE PRIZZLE of same
place yeoman a 90 a. tr of land ... whereas in pursuance of a warrant dated at
Phila 1 Apr 1751 there was surveyed and laid out unto PETER SHUGART a 90
a. tr of land in the township afsd adj CLEMENT STUDEBERGER, Widow
KNIPFER, SARAH PRESSELD & HENRY JACOBS, and the said PETER
SHUGART on 21 May 1763 did sell unto the said HENRY MOHLER the tr of
land (Book B pg 83) ... . Wit: JOS BOUDE, JACOB KOHLER. Ackn 4 Apr
1772 before RD MCALISTER justice. (E:pg 150)

23 May 1772. Deed of Mortgage. VALENTINE PRIZZLE of Berwick
Township, York Co wheelright and MARGARET his wife for better securing
the payment of £63 and also 5 shillings sold to SEBASTIAN OBALT of
Heidleberg Township, York Co yeoman a 77 a. tr of land ... whereas the
Proprietaries by their warrant dated at Phila 14 Mar 1755 did grant unto JOHN
NOEL late of Paradise Township, York Co a 77 a. tr of land in said township
which by a survey since made is bounded by CHRISTIAN BEASER, CONRAD
DOLL, JACOB HIDLER & land late of GOTLEIP PRECHNER ... and the said

JOHN NOEL on 13 Aug 1764 did sell the tr of land unto the afsd VALENTINE PRIZZLE (Book B pg 440), and the said VALENTINE PRIZZLE stands bound unto the said SEBASTIAN OBALT for £126 conditioned for the payment of £63 on 23 May next ensuing ... provided that if the said VALENTINE PRIZZLE shall well and truly pay unto the said SEBASTIAN OBALT £63 then this indenture to be void ... . Wit: JOS BOUDE, RACHEL BOUDE. Ackn 23 May 1772 before RD MCALISTER justice. 6 Jun 1775 SEBASTIAN OBALT discharged mortgage. Wit: SAML JOHNSTON recorder. (E:pg 152)

23 May 1772. Deed of Mortgage. VALENTINE PRIZZLE (PRIZLE) of Berwick Township, York Co wheelwright and MARGARET his wife for better securing the payment of £62 and also 5 shillings sold to SEBASTIAN OBALT of Heidleberg Township, York Co yeoman a 90 a. tr of land ... whereas in pursuance of a warrant dated at Phila 1 Apr 1751 there was surveyed and laid out unto PETER SHUGART a 90 a. tr of land in the township afsd adj CLEMENT STUDEBERGER, Widow KNIPFER, SARAH PRIZZLE & HENRY JACOBS, and the said PETER SHUGART on 21 May 1763 did sell unto the said HENRY MOHLER the tr of land (Book B pg 83), and the said HENRY MOHLER and CATHARINE his wife on 4 Apr last past did convey the land to the afsd VALENTINE PRIZZLE, and the said VALENTINE PRIZZLE stands bound unto the said SEBASTIAN OBALT for £124 conditioned for the payment of £62 on or before 23 May next ensuing ... provided that if the said VALENTINE PRIZZLE shall well and truly pay unto the said SEBASTIAN OBALT £62 then this indenture to be void ... . Wit: JOS BOUDE, RACHEL BOUDE. Ackn 26 May 1772 before RD MCALISTER justice. 6 Jun 1775 SEBASTIAN OBALT discharged mortgage. Wit: SAML JOHNSTON recorder. (E:pg 154)

29 Jun 1772. Deed of Mortgage. JACOB SPOTS of Chanceford Township, York Co yeoman for £41.17.8 sold to MICHAEL WORMS of York Co one red cow, one plow and tacklings, one harrow with iron teeth, one apple mill and all such other goods and household stuff and emplements of household now remaining in the house wherein I now dwell in Chanceford Township together with all the winter and summer grain now in the ground ... if the said JACOB SPOTS shall well and truly pay unto the said MICHAEL WORMS £41.17.8 then this bill of sale to be void ... . Wit: JACOB [?], [?]. Ackn 29 Jun 1772 before THOS MINSHALL justice. (E:pg 157)

9 Jun 1772. Deed. SIMON CRONE of Newberry Township, York Co yeoman for £33 sold to CASPER SEILER of Windsor Township, York Co yeoman a 41 a. 19 perches tr of land in Windsor Township adj MICHAEL PAULUS, GEORGE LEFEVER & ADAM PAULUS, being the same which GEORGE MEYER on 20 Nov 1762 did grant unto the said SIMON CRONE by the name

of SIMON KRONE (Book A pg 622), and afterwards the said SIMON CRONE obtained a warrant dated 3 Dec 1762 and in pursuance of which it was surveyed and laid out for him ... . Wit: [?], JACOB BILLMEYER Junr. Ackn 9 Jun 1772 before JOHN ADLUM justice. (E:pg 158)

9 Jun 1772. Deed. CASPAR SEILER of Windsor Township, York Co yeoman for £44 sold to FREDERICK ZIEBEKNECHT of same place yeoman a 41 a. 19 perches parcel of land in Windsor Township [same as above] ... . Wit: STOPHEL SHLAGLE, JACOB BILLMEYER Junr. Ackn 9 Jun 1772 before JOHN ADLUM esqr. (E:pg 160)

13 Nov 1770. Deed. HENRY STRICKLER of Lancaster Co and JACOB STRICKLER of York Co two of the sons of ULRICH STRICKLER late of York Co yeoman decd for £300 sold to JOHN STRICKLER of Hellam Township, York Co blacksmith another and eldest son and heir at law of the said ULRICH STRICKLER decd a 212 ½ a. tr of land ... whereas SAMUEL BLUNSTON esqr by virtue of power to him granted by the Proprietaries did by licence dated 21 Sep 1734 allow THOMAS DOYLE to settle and improve on 400 a. of land on the w side of Sasquehannah to be surveyed to him, and the said THOMAS DOYLE on 11 Apr 1741 did assign all his right to 200 a. of the same land to WILLIAM JONES who on 11 May 1741 did assign all his right to the 200 a. unto JOHN DAVIS who on 5 May 1742 did assign all his right to the afsd ULRICH STRICKLER (by the name of WOLERY STRECTLER), and the said ULRICH STRICKLER being seized of the 200 a. died leaving issue the afsd HENRY, JACOB and JOHN, and there was surveyed and laid out unto the said HENRY, JACOB and JOHN (as heirs) a 212 ½ a. tr of land in Hellam Township (formerly in Lancaster Co) but now York Co adj DANIEL HARMAN, HENRY KANN (alis COHN), Widow KOONTZ, JOHN TREICHLER, JACOB STRICKLER & road leading from York Town to Wrights Ferry ... . Wit: JACOB [?], JACOB BILLMEYER Junr. Ackn 13 Nov 1770 before MICHAEL SWOOPE esqr justice. (E:pg 163)

31 Mar 1760. Assignment. The subscribers for £12.10 to each of us by BARBARA DREICHLER adminr of JOHN DREICHLER decd have assigned over all our right of a tr of land granted to CHRISTIAN STONMAN 30 Oct 1736 and then signed over to our father MICHEL BIXLER 15 Sep 1737 which said grant and tr of land we assign over to said decd JOHN DRICHLER's children ... [signed] HENRY MEYER & MADLENA his wife, MICHAEL DERSTEIN & BARBARA his wife, FRENA BIXLER & ANNA BIXLER. Wit: HENRY STRICKLER, CHRISTIAN BIXLER. 16 Jun 1772 before JOHN ADLUM esqr justice came HENRY STRICKLER & CHRISTIAN BIXLER on their solemn affirmation did declare they were present & saw the within named HENRY MEYER intermarried with MAUDLENA one of the daus of

MICHAEL BIXLER decd & MICHAEL DERSTEIN & BARBARA his wife & FRENA BIXLER & ANNA BIXLER since decd sign this deed to BARBARA DRECHLER widow. (E:pg 165)

BARBARA TREIGHLER (DREICHLER) for 5 shillings give unto JOHN TREIGHLER (DREICHLER) all my right in the within bill of sale and estate conveyed to me. Wit: MICHAEL MILLER, JOHANNES REIST. Ackn 20 Jun 1772 before JOHN ADLUM justice. (E:pg 166)

21 Apr 1772. Deed of Mortgage. JACOB WILLIAMS of Warrington Township, York Co house carpenter for better securing the payment of £70 and also 5 shillings sold to WILLIAM THOMAS of same place yeoman a 100 a. tr of land in Warrington Township adj JEHU THOMAS, JOSHUA DAVIES, TETER UPPAH, ABRAHAM WILLIAMS & WILLIAM ROSS ... whereas the said JACOB WILLIAMS standeth bound unto the said WILLIAM THOMAS for £140 conditioned for the payment of £70 on 21 Apr 1773 ... provided that if the said JACOB WILLIAMS shall well and truly pay unto the said WILLIAM THOMAS £70 then this indenture to be void ... . Wit: WILLIAM PENROSE, WM MATTHEWS. Ackn 13 May 1772 before WILLIAM RANKIN justice. 7 Jan 1775 WILLIAM PENROSE one of the executors of the will of WILLIAM THOMAS decd discharged mortgage. Wit: SAML JOHNSTON recorder. (E:pg 166)

27 May 1772. Deed of Mortgage. JOHN KREBIL of Donegal Township, Lancaster Co, PA farmer for better securing the payment of £350 and also 5 shillings sold to MICHAEL QUICKEL of Dover Township, York Co farmer a 170 a. tr of land in Manchester Township adj Little Conewago Cr, SEBASTIAN FINK, GEORGE BRIGHTENGROSS, GEORGE SCHNYDER, JACOB GUTWALT, JACOB KINSEL, the heirs of BARNET GEMLING & said MICHAEL QUICKEL ... whereas the afsd JOHN KREBIL by seven obligations dated 26 Nov last stands bound unto the said MICHAEL QUICKEL for £700 conditioned for the payment of £350 in payments before 16 Mar 1779 ... provided that if the said JOHN DREBIL shall well and truly pay unto the said MICHAEL QUICKEL £350 then this indenture to be void ... . Wit: THOS ARMOR, [?]. Ackn before JOHN ADLUM justice. (E:pg 168)

7 Apr 1772. Deed. GEORGE SWOBE of Paradise Township, York Co yeoman and ANNA MARIA his wife for £500 sold to CONRAD GENTZLER of same place yeoman a 196 ¾ a. tr of land ... whereas in pursuance of a warrant dated at Phila 25 Aug 1746 there was surveyed and laid out to the afsd GEORGE SWOBE a 196 ¾ a. tr of land in Paradise Township (late pt/o Lancaster Co) now York Co adj KILLIAN FISSEL, THOMAS WILSON, DETER DICKS &

CHRISTIAN HIRSHY ... . Wit: GEORGE KINTZ, GEORGE LEWIS
LESLER. Ackn 7 Apr 1772 before JOHN ADLUM justice. (E:pg 170)

7 Jul 1772. Deed of Mortgage. PHILIP WEISE of Paradise Township, York,
Co yeoman for better securing the payment of £1220 and also 5 shillings sold to
DANIEL REICHER of Manchester Township, York Co yeoman his messuage
and 272 a. tr of land (being the same tr of land which the said DANIEL
REICHER and CATHARINE his wife day before this date sold to the said
PHILIP WEISE) ... whereas the said PHILIP WEISE by 12 obligations standeth
bound unto the said DANIEL REICHER for £2440 conditioned for the payment
of £1220 in payments before 25 Mar 1783 ... provided that if the said PHILIP
WEISE shall well and truly pay unto the said DANIEL REICHER £1220 then
this indenture to be void ... . Wit: [?], HENRY MILLER. Ackn 7 Jul 1772
before JOS UPDEGRAFF justice. 26 Mar 1774 DANIEL REICHER discharged
mortgage. Wit: SAML JOHNSTON recorder. (E:pg 172)

3 Oct 1769. Deed. JACOB STROMAN of York, York Co for £15 sold to
THOMAS ARMOR of same place surveyor a tr of land adj CHRISTIAN
LANDIS & JOHN HAMIS in Windsor Township which was granted unto me by
an application No. 5584 dated at Phila 28 Aug last for 150 a. ... . Wit: [?],
JOSEPH WALLACE. Ackn 1 Jan 1771 before MICHAEL SWOOPE justice.
(E:pg 174)

8 Jun 17--. Deed. PETER LITTLE of Germany Township, York Co yeoman
and URSULA his wife for £5 sold to MARY COONSE of same place a lot of
ground in the Town of Petersburg in the township afsd pt/o a 311 a. tr of land,
No. 57, on Kings Street leading to York Town and to Frederick Town, MD, in
breadth 66' and in length 264', paying to the said PETER LITTLE the yearly
rent of 7 shillings on 1 May forever ... whereas the Proprietaries by their patent
dated at Phila 18 Sep 1760 did grant unto the said PETER LITTLE a 311 a. tr of
land in Germany Township (Patent Book AA vol. 1 pg 80), and the said PETER
LITTLE hath laid out a town on the tr of land called Petersburg and is desirous
that it be forever called Petersburg ... . Wit: GEO CLARK, [?]. Ackn 8 Jun
1772 before HENRY SLAGLE justice. (E:pg 175)

8 Jun 1772. Deed. PETER LITTLE of Germany Township, York Co yeoman
and URSULA his wife for £[?] sold to JOHN DYER son of JOSEPH of
Frederick Co, MD a lot of ground in the Town of Petersburg pt/o a 311 a. tr of
land, No. 25, bounded by Lot No. 24 & Kings Street leading to York Town and
Frederick Town, MD, in breadth 66' and in length 260', paying to the said
PETER LITTLE the yearly rent of 7 shillings on 1 May forever ... whereas the
Proprietaries by their patent dated at Phila 18 Sep 1760 did grant unto the said
PETER LITTLE a 311 a. tr of land in Germany Township (Patent Book AA vol.

1 pg 80), and the said PETER LITTLE hath laid out a town on the tr of land called Petersburg and is desirous that it be forever called Petersburg ... . Wit: GEO CLARK, MATHIAS BAKER. Ackn 8 Jun 1772 before HENRY SLAGLE justice. (E:pg 178)

8 Jun 1772. Deed. PETER LITTLE of Germany Township, York Co yeoman and URSULA his wife for £6 sold to FREDERICK TRYER (TRYOR) of same place two lots of ground in the Town of Petersburg pt/o a 311 a. tr of land, No. 77 & 78, bounded by Kings Street leading to York Town & to Frederick Town, MD, 66' each and in length 260', paying unto the said PETER LITTLE 7 shillings 6 pence on May 1 forever ... whereas the Proprietaries by their patent dated at Phila 18 Sep 1760 did grant unto the said PETER LITTLE a 311 a. tr of land in Germany Township (Patent Book AA vol. 1 pg 80), and the said PETER LITTLE hath laid out a town on the tr of land called Petersburg and is desirous that it be forever called Petersburg ... . Wit: GEO CLARK, GEORGE KINTZ. Ackn 8 Jun 1772 before HENRY SLAGLE justice. (E:pg 181)

21 May 1771. Deed. JACOB DAUTEL (DOWDALL) of York Town, York Co tanner and ANNA MARIA his wife for £200 sold to GEORGE SLOSSER of the City of Phila merchant ½ of a lot of ground being the same part whereon the said JACOB DAUTEL lately erected a brick dwelling house, 32'6" and in depth 230' ... whereas the Proprietaries by their patent dated at Phila 9 Oct 1764 did grant unto the said JACOB DAUTEL two contiguous lots of ground in the Town of York on the w side of Codorus Cr and s side of High Street, in front each 65' and in depth 230' ... (Patent Book AA vol. 6 pg 1) ... . Wit: JOHN HECKENDORN, WM LEAS. Ackn 21 May 1771 before JOS UPDEGRAFF justice. (E:pg 184)

27 Aug 1772. Deed. THOMAS ARMOR of York Town, York Co surveyor for £15 sold to PETER LICE of Shrewsberry Township, York Co farmer a 158 a. tr of land ... whereas the Proprietaries by their warrant dated at Phila 18 Dec 1751 did grant unto CHRISTIAN EVERHART 50 a. of land adj CHRISTMAN LOW, MICHAEL FOGLE & HANS YERICK MEYER in Codorus Township, which said warrant was by NICHOLAS SCULL esqr surveyor general directed to GEORGE STEVENSON esqr dep surveyor of York Co to be executed by him, and the said GEORGE STEVENSON before the execution of said warrant discovered that the lands mentioned in said warrant were within 7 miles of York Town and therefore reserved and appropriated to the Proprietaries before the said warrant was granted and refused to survey the same to the said CHRISTIAN EVERHART, and on 15 Jun 1754 at York on the application of the said CHRISTIAN EVERHART located the said warrant upon a parcel of vacant unimproved land adj NICHOLAS HUSTER, br of Codorus Cr in Shrewsberry Township, and the said CHRISTIAN EVERHART on 17 Jul 1754

for £10 sold to TOBIAS AMSPOKER the afsd warrant (Book C pg 341), and in pursuance of the afsd warrant there was surveyed & laid out unto the said TOBIAS AMSPOKER a 158 a. tr of land in Shrewsberry Township adj NICHOLAS HUSTER, HENRY WILLHELM, PHILIP HENRY RATS, and the said TOBIAS AMSPOKER on 5 Apr 1764 did convey unto the afsd THOMAS ARMOR the afsd tr of land (Book C pg 191?) ... . Wit: [JOSEPH ?], THOS ARMOR Junr. Ackn 27 Aug 1772 before JOHN ADLUM justice. (E:pg 187)

27 Aug 1772. Deed of Mortgage. JOHN KUMFORT of Hellam Township, York Co yeoman and MARIA ELIZABETH his wife for better securing the payment of £506.1.4 and also 5 shillings sold to JOHN STEWART of York Township, York Co yeoman a 192 a. tr of land in Hellam Township adj HENRY SMITH, BALTZER FRITZ, CHRISTIAN NEWCOMMER, GEORGE SHOLLER & MICHAEL FREEZ ... whereas the said JOHN KUMFORT standeth bound unto the said JOHN STEWART for £912.2.8 conditioned for the payment of £456.1.4 and the said JOHN KUMFORT by one other obligation standeth bound unto the said JOHN STEWART for £100 conditioned for the payment of £50 on 1 Nov 1773 ... provided that if the said JOHN KUMFORT shall well and truly pay unto the said JOHN STEWART £506.1.4 then this indenture to be void ... . Wit: PHILLIP ALBRIGHT, DAVID GRIER. Ackn 27 Aug 1772 before JOHN ADLUM esqr justice. 9 May 1775 JOHN STEWART discharged mortgage. Wit: SAML JOHNSTON recorder. (E:pg 189)

20 Aug 1772. Deed. THOMAS ARMOR of York Town, York Co surveyor for £10 sold to PETER WOLF of Manchester Township, York Co tavernkeeper a 5 a. tr of land ... whereas MARTIN MILLER of Shrewsberry Township, York Co on 28 Mar last did sell unto the afsd THOMAS ARMOR a 5 a. tr of land adj CHRISTIAN OISTER & JACOB ZIEGLER in Manchester Township ... . Wit: [?], RUDIC KAEGGY. Ackn 31 Aug 1772 before JOHN ADLUM esqr justice. (E:pg 190)

28 Mar 1772. Deed. MARTIN MILLER of Shrewsberry Township, York Co farmer about 1755 on vacant land adj CHRISTIAN OISTER and JACOB ZEIGLER in Manchester Township I did grub about 5 a. and plowed and sowed about 3 a. thereof and reaped wheat which can be testified by ELIAS OISTER & others, for £10 sold to THOMAS ARMOR the 5 a. of land ... . Wit: ZAOH SHUGOUT, [?]. Ackn 12 Aug 1772 before JOHN ADLUM esqr justice. (E:pg 191)

1 Jul 1772. Deed of Mortgage. WILLIAM MATTHEWS of York Town, York Co surveyor and HANNAH his wife for better securing the payment of £297.11 1 penny 3 farthings and also 5 shillings sold to WILLIAM WILLIS mason and

HERMAN UPDEGRAFF tanner both of Manchester Township, York Co a 1 ¼ a. tr of land with a corn mill and saw mill on Big Conewago Cr in Dover Township adj DERICK UPDEGRAFF ... whereas the said WILLIAM MATHEWS standeth bound unto the said WILLIAM WILLIS for £142.11.10 conditioned for the payment of £71.5.11 on 17 May 1774 and also standeth bound unto the said HERMAN UPDEGRAFF £92.10.3 conditioned for the payment [?] on 27 May 1774 ... provided that if the said WILLIAM MATTHEWS shall well and truly pay unto the said WILLIAM WILLIS & HERMAN UPDEGRAFF £297.11 1 penny 3 farthings then this indenture to be void ... . Wit: WM KERSEY, JOS UPDEGRAFF. Ackn 14 Sep 1772 before JOSEPH UPDEGRAFF esqr justice. (E:pg 192)

17 Sep 177-. Deed. MARTIN MANSBERGER of Newberry Township, York Co for 5 shillings sold to my son JOHN MANSBERGER a 150 a. tr of land in Newberry Township adj JACOB SHELLY, ALEXANDER ELLIOT, Big Conewago Cr and the Great Road leading from York Town to Noblets Ferry, to include my dwelling house, it being pt/o 300 a. which was granted to me by an application dated 1 Jun 1768, No. 5024 ... . Wit: JOHN UPDEGRAFF, GEO LEWIS LESLER. Ackn before MARTIN EYCHELBERGER justice. (E:pg 194)

1 Jul 1772. Deed of Mortgage. WILLIAM MATTHEWS of York Town, York Co surveyor and HANNAH his wife for better securing the payment of £297.11 1 penny 3 farthings and also 5 shillings sold to WILLIAM WILLIS mason and HERMAN UPDEGRAFF tanner both of Manchester Township, York Co a 1 ¼ a. tr of land with a corn mill and saw mill on Big Conewago Cr in Dover Township adj DERICK UPDEGRAFF ... whereas the said WILLIAM MATTHEWS standeth bound unto the said WILLIAM WILLIS for £142.11.10 conditioned for the payment of £17.5.11 on 17 May 1774 and standeth bound unto the said HERMAN UPDEGRAFF for £119.10.3 ½ penny conditioned for the payment of £59.15 1 penny 3 farthings on 17 May 1774, and standeth bound unto the said WILLIAM WILLIS and HERMAN UPDEGRAFF for £133.0.2 conditioned for the payment of £66.10 1 penny on 17 May 1774 and standeth bound unto the said WILLIAM WILLIS and HERMAN UPDEGRAFF for £200 conditioned for the payment of £100 on 17 May 1774 ... provided that if the said WILLIAM MATTHEWS shall well and truly pay unto the said WILLIAM WILLIS & HERMAN UPDEGRAFF the afsd debts then this indenture to be void ... . Wit: WM KERSEY, JOS UPDEGRAFF. Ackn 14 Sep 1772 before JOSEPH UPDEGRAFF esqr justice. (E:pg 195)

24 Sep 1772. Deed. LEVI STEVENS of [blank] Township, Bedford Co, PA surveyor for £100 sold to THOMAS ARMOR of York Town, York Co surveyor a 60 a. 50 perches tr of land ... whereas the Proprietaries by their patent dated at

Phila 31 Jul 1767 did grant unto the afsd LEVI STEVENS a 60 a. 50 perches tr
of land in Manheim Township called *Irregular Pentagon* adj JOHN DIGGES,
MICHAEL CARTIS, CONRAD VALENTINE & VALENTINE EYLER (Patent
Book AA vol. 10 pg 55) ... . Wit: GEO EICHELBERGER, CHAS LUKENS.
Ackn 24 Sep 1772 before JOHN ADLUM esqr justice. (E:pg 197)

25 Jun 1772. Deed of Mortgage. DOMINICUS HACKH (HAKH) of the Town
of York, York Co surg for better securing the payment of several debts and also
5 shillings sold to GOTLIEB ZIEGEL of same place innkeeper a messuage and
Lot No. 166 on the n side of Phila Street in York Town bounded by PHILIP
ALBRECHT & JACOB WOLF, in breadth 65' and in length 230', it being the
same which CHARLES DIESBY son and heir of SAMUEL DIESBY on 13 Jun
instant did convey to the said DOMINICUS HACKH ... whereas the said
DOMINICUS HACKH standeth bound unto the said GOTLIEB ZIEGEL for
£36.3.4 conditioned for the payment of £18.1.8 on 12 Nov 1773, and the said
GOTLIEB ZIEGEL for the debts of the said DOMINICUS HACKH became
bound unto CHARLES DIESBY of North Town, SC for £30 conditioned for the
payment of £15 on 12 Nov 1773 ... provided that if the said DOMINICUS
HACKH shall well and truly pay unto the said GOTLIEB ZIEGEL the afsd
debts and hold him harmless in the last mentioned debt then this indenture to be
void ... . Wit: MICHAEL BILLMEYER, JACOB BILLMEYER Junr. Ackn 4
Jul 1772 before JOS UPDEGRAFF justice. 22 Oct 1792 FREDERICK YOUCE
surviving executor of the will of GOTLIEB ZIEGEL discharged mortgage. Wit:
J. BARNITZ recorder. (E:pg 199)

8 Oct 1772. Deed. JOHN MATTHEWS of Chanceford Township, York Co
farmer for £22 sold to WILLIAM BUCHANAN taylor a 203 ½ a. tr of land
which was granted unto me by warrant dated at Phila 19 May 1752 in
Chanceford Township adj my other land ... . Wit: FRANCIS GROVE, THOS
ARMOR. Ackn 21 Oct 1772 before JOSEPH UPDEGRAFF esqr justice. (E:pg
202)

26 Oct 1772. Deed. CHARLES THOMPSON of the city of Phila, PA merchant
for £965 sold to JOHN WHITE of said city merchant three trs of land, 182 a.,
128 a. 32 perches & 114 a. 126 perches ... whereas the Proprietaries by their
patent dated 14 Mar 1764 did grant unto DAVID HUNTER a 182 a. tr of land in
Straban Township adj JOSEPH GREEN, PATRICK MONTGOMERY, JOHN
MURPHY, Church land & WILLIAM GUFFY (Patent Book AA vol. 5 pg 499)
... whereas DAVID MCCONAUGHY esqr sheriff of York Co by virtue of
several writs did seize in execution the afsd tr of land with a messuage and on 13
Apr 1768 did sell the land containing in the whole 400 a. (which included all the
vacant land on each side thereof) unto the said CHARLES THOMPSON, but the
said DAVID HUNTER not being contented that the sheriff had a right to seize

34

and sell the vacant land made application to the Land Office (No. 5102) dated 12 Jul 1768 upon which was surveyed unto the said DAVID HUNTER 128 a. 32 perches vacant land thereof by ARCHIBALD MCCLEAN dep surveyor, and the said CHARLES HUNTER to prevent all disputes procured the said DAVID HUNTER by an assignment endorsed on the return of survey dated 15 Sep 1769 to sell all his right in the said 128 a. 32 perches, whereas in consequence of the said application there was granted unto the said CHARLES THOMPSON as assignee of said DAVID HUNTER a warrant dated 28 Sep 1770, in confirmation the Proprietaries by their patent dated 12 Oct 1770 did confirm unto the said CHARLES THOMPSON the 128 a. 32 perches of land (on the s side of the afsd tr of land) called *Forebody* adj JAMES DICKSON, CHARLES THOMPSON, PATRICK MONTGOMERY, ROBERT LATIMORE & FRANCIS CORSART ... whereas SAMUEL DICKSON procured another application (No. 5101) dated 12 Jul 1768 (on the n side of the afsd tr of land) and there was surveyed unto the said SAMUEL DICKSON 114 a. 125 perches of land in Straban Township by the said ARCHIBALD MCCLEAN dep surveyor, and the said CHARLES THOMPSON also procured the said SAMUEL DICKSON, in order to prevent all claims to the said vacant land, by assignment dated 16 Sep 1769 unto the said CHARLES THOMPSON all his right to the land, in consequence there was granted unto the said CHARLES THOMPSON as assignee of the said SAMUEL DICKSON a warrant dated 28 Sep 1770, in confirmation the Proprietaries by their patent dated 12 Oct 1770 did grant unto the said CHARLES THOMPSON a 114 a. 126 perches tr of land in Straban Township called *Tusculum* adj CHARLES THOMPSON, the meeting land, SAMUEL HATLON, SAMUEL THOMPSON, JAMES DICKSON & JOSEPH GREEN (Patent Book AA vol. 11 pg 425) ... . Wit: ANTHONY SEYFERT, WILLIAM PARR. Ackn 28 Oct 1772 before WILLIAM ALLEN justice. (E:pg 203)

19 Aug 1772. Deed of Mortgage. HUGH DANIEL of Paradise Township, York Co weaver and MARY his wife for better securing the payment of £30 and also 5 shillings sold to PATRICK MCSHERRY of Germany Township, York Co innkeeper a 133 a. tr of warranted land in Paradise Township adj MICHAEL UHL, ALEXANDER MCCLEARY & BALTZER YOUNG ... whereas the said HUGH DANIEL standeth bound unto the said PATRICK MCSHERRY for £60 conditioned for the payment of £30 on 19 Aug 1773 ... provided that if the said HUGH DANIEL shall well and truly pay unto the said PATRICK MCSHERRY £30 then this indenture to be void ... . Wit: ABDIEL MCCALISTER, ARCHIBALD MCCALISTER. Ackn 19 Aug 1772 before RD MCALISTER justice. 11 Oct 1773 PATRICK MCSHERRY discharged mortgage. Wit: SAML JOHNSTON recorder. (E:pg 207)

9 Oct 1772. Deed of Mortgage. JOHN MCCONAUGHY yeoman of York Co for better securing the payment of £464 and also 5 shillings sold to JOHN

WILLSON of Lancaster Co yeoman a 233 a. 67 perches tr of land in Manalin
Township adj ROBERT MOOR, JOHN PARKS & EPHRAIM JOHNSTON,
which was granted to ROBERT MCCONAUGHY by warrant dated 23 Oct 1753
and by the heirs of the said ROBERT MCCONAUGHY sold to the afsd JOHN
MCCONAUGHY ... whereas the said JOHN MCCONAUGHY standeth bound
unto the said JOHN WILLSON for £928 conditioned for the payment of £464 on
1 May next ensuing ... provided that if the said JOHN MCCONAUGHY shall
well and truly pay unto the said JOHN WILLSON £464 then this indenture to be
void ... . Wit: JOHN BUCHANAN, SAML MCCONAUGHY. Ackn 20 Oct
1772 before ROBERT MCPHERSON justice. 29 Apr 1775 ROBERT
MCPHERSON of York Co esqr by virtue of a warrant of atty made by JOHN
WILLSON discharged mortgage. Wit: SAML JOHNSTON recorder. (E:pg
209)

8 Jun 1772. Deed. PETER LITTLE of Germany Township, York Co yeoman
and URSULA his wife for £100 sold to JOHN ALSPOAK of same place
yeoman Lot Nos. 82 & 83 in the Town of Petersburg pt/o a 311 a. tr of land adj
JACOB EYLER, Kings Street leading from York Town to Frederick Town, MD
& said PETER LITTLE, in breadth 66' and in length 264' (each lot), paying the
said PETER LITTLE 7 shillings on May 1 forever ... whereas the Proprietaries
by their patent dated at Phila 18 Sep 1760 did grant unto the said PETER
LITTLE a 311 a. tr of land in Germany Township (Patent Book AA vol. 1 pg
80), and the said PETER LITTLE laid out a town which he called Petersburg
and is desirous that the same shall forever be called Petersburg ... . Wit: GEO
CLARK, JOS DYER. Ackn 8 Jun 1772 before HENRY SLAGLE justice.
(E:pg 210)

29 Oct 1772. Deed of Mortgage. PETER WILHELM the farther and JOHN
WILHELM and GEORGE WILHELM his sons of York Township, York Co for
better securing the payment of £65 and also 5 shillings sold to WILLIAM
BAUSMAN of Lancaster Borough, Lancaster Co yeoman two trs of land in
York Township, a 93 a. tr of land adj THEOPHILUS HARTMAN, DAVID
HUNTER, CONRATH REIGHT & JOHN SEGRIST and a 15 a. 61 perches tr
of land adj the afsd tr, being the same which was on 1 Aug last past conveyed by
the said WILLIAM BAUSMAN unto the said PETER WILHELM and his said
two sons ... whereas the said PETER WILHELM, JOHN WILHELM &
GEORGE WILHELM standeth bound unto the said WILLIAM BAUSMAN for
£130 conditioned for the payment of £65 in payments before 1 Nov 1774 ...
provided that if the said PETER WILHELM, JOHN WILHELM & GEORGE
WILHELM shall well and truly pay unto the said WILLIAM BAUSMAN £65
then this indenture to be void ... . Wit: FREDRICK KUHN, [?]. Ackn 29 Oct
1772 before THOS MINSHALL justice. 22 Mar 1794 JACOB HAY atty for
WILLIAM BAUSMAN, JOHN BAUSMAN, GABRIEL [HIRSTER?] &

ANDREW BAUSMAN executors of the will of WILLIAM BAUSMAN decd discharged mortgage. Wit: J. BARNITZ recorder. (E:pg 212)

21 Jul ----. Deed of Gift. PHILIP HELSEL of Manheim Township, York Co farmer for a valuable consideration do give unto my son TOBIAS HELSEL ½ of a 230 a. tr of land surveyed by virtue of a warrant adj CHARLES YOUNG, he is to pay the Proprietaries for the land himself ... . Wit: FRIEDERICK TRANBERG, PHILIP FRIEND. Proved 5 Nov 1772 by PHILIP FRIEND before ROBT MCPHERSON justice. (E:pg 214)

2 Nov 1772. Deed. FELIX HELDEBRAND of Shrewsbury Township, York Co yeoman and ELIZABETH his wife for £270 sold to FREDERICK FISSEL of same place miller a 222 a. 113 perches tr of land pt/o a 251 a. tr of land adj PHILIP SHAFER, BALTZER COLAR & FELIX HELDEBRAND's other land ... whereas in pursuance of a warrant granted to PHILIP SIMON of York Co dated 9 Mar 1753 there was surveyed and laid out for the said PHILIP SIMON a 251 a. tr of land in Shrewsbury Township adj HUMPHREY MONTGOMERY, JACOB WELSHANTZ & DAVID SHAFER, the said PHILIP SIMON being owner of the afsd tr of land with other land adj lately died seized thereof intestate and left a widow named CARTROUL (since his death intermarried with JOHN GOBLE) and lawful issue to survive him, to wit, ELIZABETH since intermarried with FELIX HILDEBRAND his eldest dau, ANNA MARIA, MARELLIS, CATHARINE and ADAM SIMON who since the said intestate's death died intestate unmarried and without issue, and the said FELIX HILDEBRAND and ELIZABETH his wife did on 29 Nov last past prefer a petition to the Orphans Court setting forth that the said PHILIP SIMON had died owner and seized of two trs of land joining each other in Shrewsbury Township, about 300 a., adj DAVID SHAFER, WILLIAM EARHART & VALLENTINE HAMSBAUGHER, pt/o the afsd tr of land, and prayed the Court to make partition of the land, and the freeholders found the land would not divide without spoiling the whole and valued the land at £365, and the Court allotted the land to the said FELIX HELDEBRAND & ELIZABETH his wife (she being the eldest dau of the intestate) they paying the other children their share of the valuation ... . Wit: WM KERSEY, WM MATTHEWS. Ackn 2 Nov 1772 before JOS UPDEGRAFF justice. (E:pg 214)

25 Nov 1772. Deed of Mortgage. TOBIAS HABERSTOCK of Paradise Township, York Co yeoman for better securing the payment of £150 and also 5 shillings sold to HENRY HERRING of same place yeoman a 84 a. tr of land in Paradise Township whereon the said TOBIAS HABERSTOCK now dwells, which the said HENRY HERRING conveyed unto the said TOBIAS HABERSTOCK on 24 Feb 1771 (Book D pg 506) ... whereas by 15 obligations dated 22 Jul 1769 the said TOBIAS HABERSTOCK standeth bound unto the

said HENRY HERRING for £300 conditioned for the payment of £150 in payments before 15 years after the death of the said HENRY HERRING and his wife ... provided that if the said TOBIAS HABERSTOCK shall well and truly pay unto the said HENRY HERRING £150 then this indenture to be void ... . Wit: GEO EICHELBERGER, HENRY MILLER. Ackn 26 Nov 1772 before JOHN ADLUM justice. (E:pg 217)

1 Aug 1768. Deed. RICHARD PETERS of the City of Phila, PA clerk for £817 sold to JOHN PECKER of Reading Township, York Co yeoman two trs of land, 431 a. and 230 a. ... whereas the Proprietaries by their patent dated at Phila 30 Aug 1743 did grant unto MATTHIAS YOUNG of Lancaster Co a 431 a. tr of land in Manchester Township, Lancaster Co (now Reading Township, York Co) adj JACOB KRYTS & DERRICK MUMMER (Patent Book A vol. 11 pg 209), and the said MATTHIAS YOUNG and ANNA MARGARET his wife on 20 Sep 1743 did sell to the said RICHARD PETERS the 431 a. tr of land (Book B pg 119 in Lancaster), and the Proprietaries by their patent dated at Phila 19 Mar 1747 did grant unto the said RICHARD PETERS a 230 a. tr of land on Great Connewago Cr in (then Lancaster Co) now York Co adj JEREMIAH STILLWELL & HANS ULRICH WAGGONER (Patent Book A vol. 14 pg 480) ... . Wit: ABBY WILLING, JOSEPH SHIPPEN. Ackn 1 Aug 1768 before THOMAS WILLING esqr justice. (E:pg 220)

1 Oct 1772. Deed of Mortgage. SIMON KOPPENHEFFER of Manchester Township, York Co yeoman for better securing the payment of £700 and also 5 shillings sold to GEORGE ERNST MEYER of same place yeoman a 230 a. tr of land ... whereas the Proprietaries by their patent dated 26 Jun last past did grant unto the said GEORGE ERNST MEYER a 230 a. tr of land called *Sinking Valley* in Manchester Township adj ANDREW SMITH, PETER SCHULTZ, JACOB RUDISILLY & GEORGE NARR (Patent Book A vol. 13 pg 169), and the said GEORGE ERNST MEYER on 1 Oct 1772 sold the afsd tr of land to the said SIMON KOPPENHEFFER ... the said SIMON KOPPENHEFFER on 15 Nov last past became bound unto the said GEORGE ERNST MEYER for £1400 conditioned for the payment of £700 in payments before 10 May 1782 ... provided that if the said SIMON KOPPENHEFFER shall well and truly pay unto the said GEORGE ERNST MEYER £700 then this indenture to be void ... . Wit: [?], [?]. Ackn 1 Oct 1772 before MARTIN EICHELBERGER justice. 11 May 1789 BALTZER RUDISIL & VALENTINE SHULTZ executors of the will of GEORGE ERNST MEYER decd discharged mortgage. Wit: J. BARNITZ recorder. (E:pg 222)

3 Dec 1772. Deed. HENRY SCHENCK of Codorus Township, York Co yeoman and ANNA his wife for £650 sold to JACOB SCHNELLBECHER of Dover Township, York Co yeoman a 253 a. tr of land ... whereas the

Proprietaries by their patent dated at Phila 26 Mar 1756 granted unto the said
HENRY SCHENCK a 253 a. tr of land in Dover Township formerly in
Lancaster Co now in York Co (Patent Book A pg 173) ... . Wit: [GEORGE
MEYER?], GEO LEWIS LESLER. Ackn 3 Dec 1772 before MARTIN
EICHELBERGER justice. (E:pg 224)

1 Dec 1772. Deed of Mortgage. HENRY SPENGLE of York Co yeoman and
CATHARINE his wife for better securing the payment of £373 and also 5
shillings sold to CHRISTIAN WAMPLER of York Township, York Co yeoman
a 41 a. tr of land ... whereas the said HENRY SPENGLE standeth bound unto
the said CHRISTIAN WAMPLER for £746 conditioned for the payment of £373
on 1 Dec next ... the said HENRY SPENGLE obtained a patent dated 21 Jan
1767 for a 41 a. tr of land in Windsor Township adj a tr of land patented under
MD to STEPHEN ONION called *Canhoda*, JOHN MEYER, *Bonds Manor*
patented under MD, *Smiths Choice* & ADAM IMMEISER (Patent Book AA vol.
8 pg 171) ... provided that if the said HENRY SPENGLE shall well and truly
pay unto the said CHRISTIAN WAMPLER £373 then this indenture to be void
... . Wit: [?], HENRY MILLER. Ackn 1 Dec 1772 before MARTIN
EICHELBERGER justice. (E:pg 226)

3 Dec 1770. Deed of Mortgage. JACOB SCHNELLBECKER of Dover
Township, York Co yeoman and CATHARINE his wife for better securing the
payment of £450 and also 5 shillings sold to HENRY SCHENCK of Codorus
Township, York Co yeoman a 253 a. tr of land ... whereas the Proprietaries by
their patent dated at Phila 26 Mar 1756 granted unto the said HENRY
SCHENCK a 253 a. tr of land in Dover Township formerly in Lancaster Co now
in York Co (Patent Book A pg 173), and the said HENRY SCHENCK did sell
the tr of land unto the afsd JACOB SCHNELLBECKER [*see E 224*] ... whereas
the said JACOB SCHNELLBECKER by nine obligations dated 16 Nov last past
became bound unto the said HENRY SCHENCK for several sums conditioned
for the payment of £450 in payments before 15 May 1782 ... provided that if the
said JACOB SCHNELLBECKER shall well and truly pay unto the said HENRY
SCHENCK £450 then this indenture to be void ... . Wit: [HENRY KINTZ?],
GEORGE [?]. Ackn 5 Dec 1772 before MARTIN EICHELBERGER justice.
(E:pg 229)

22 Mar 1756. Deed. JOHN ROHRER of Baltimore Co, MD yeoman and
CATHARINE his wife for £185.7 sold to CONRAD HOLSBAM of York Co
miller a messuage and 180 a. tr of land on a br of Little Codorus now in the
occupation of JACOB JONES adj BALSAR SPANGLER, JACOB HESTANT
& the said CONRAD HOLSBAM ... whereas the Proprietaries by their patent
dated 30 Oct 1736 did grant unto MICHAEL MILLER a 200 a. tr of land within
the *Mannor of Springetsbury* on the w side of Sasquehanna then in Lancaster Co

but now in York Co, and the said MICHAEL MILLER on 4 Apr 1746 sold unto JOHN ROHRER & ULRICK WISLAR for £130 all that improvement on Little Codoras, and the said ULRICK WISLAR on 12 Jun 1749 sold unto the said JOHN ROHRER all his right in the improvement and tr of land for £121 ... . Wit: [?], JAMES SMITH. Ackn 23 Mar 1756 before HAR UPDEGRAFF justice. (E:pg 231)

13 Oct 1772. Quit Claim. JOHN HENTHORN of Red Stone in [*blank*] and [*blank*] his wife for 10 shillings quit claim unto MICHAEL SMYSER of Manchester Township, York Co yeoman a 10 ½ a. piece of land pt/o a tr of land adj MATTHIAS SMYSER, line of Providence & JACOB HOKE ... whereas the Proprietary of MD by his patent dated 1 Oct 1735 did grant unto JOHN LOW a 372 a. tr of land then in Baltimore Co, MD now in Manchester Township, York Co adj the Great Road leading to Minochasy (Patent in Lib ETN fol. 11 in Baltimore Co), and the said JOHN LOW on 21 May 1740 conveyed unto the afsd JOHN HENTHORN the 372 a. tr of land (Lib ETW 3 fol. 135 in Baltimore Co), and the said JOHN HENTHORN on 3 May 1745 did convey unto MATTHIAS SMYSER a 272 a. tr of land pt/o the afsd tr (Liber TBNC fol. 60-69 in Baltimore Co) ... and by a survey the last mentioned tr of land does not contain 272 a., and leaveth out a 10 ½ a. piece between this 261 ½ and the other pt/o 100 a. granted unto JACOB HOKE ... . Wit: JOHN HOKE, JACOB SMYSER, [?]. Proved by JOHN HOKE & JACOB SMYSER 30 Oct 1772 before JOHN ADLUM justice. (E:pg 233)

4 Jul 1772. Deed. JOHN YODER Senr of Oley Township, Berks Co, PA for £65 sold to DANIEL YODER of Reading Township, York Co yeoman two trs of land, a 119 a. 114 perches tr of land (in pursuance of a warrant granted to LEONHARD OX 21 Apr 1758 there was surveyed unto the said JOHN YODER unto whom said OX conveyed 18 Apr 1763) called *Yoders Land* in Reading Township, York Co adj JOHN HUNT (HONT), NICHOLAS DETTER, JOHN LEASE & JOHN YODER's other land, and in pursuance of a warrant dated 7 May 1767 there was surveyed for the said JOHN YODER a 83 a. 143 perches tr of land called *Yeoders Addition* in Reading Township adj JOHN HUNT, the afsd tr of land, Reverend Mr. THOMPSON & NICHOLAS BOSHOY, which the Proprietaries by their patent dated 24 Jun 1772 did grant unto the afsd JOHN YODER (Patent Book AA vol. 13 pg 167 in Phila) ... . Wit: CONRAD SHEFFER, WILLIAM REESE. Ackn 16 Nov 1772 before THOMAS WILLING esqr justice. (E:pg 236)

21 Dec 1772. Deed of Mortgage. DANIEL YODER of Reading Township, York Co yeoman for better securing the payment of £100 and also 5 shillings sold to HENRY SELL of Berwick Township, York Co yeoman two trs of land [*same as above*] ... whereas the said DANIEL YODER standeth bound unto the

said HENRY SELL for £200 condition for the payment of £100 on 21 Dec 1776 ... provided that if the said DANIEL YODER shall well and truly pay unto the said HENRY SELL £100 then this indenture to be void ... . Wit: JOHN MORRIS, JOHN FRANKEBERGER. Ackn 22 Dec 1772 before JOSEPH UPDEGRAFF esqr justice. 2 May 1788 HENRY SELLY discharged mortgage. Wit: J. BARNITZ recorder. (E:pg 238)

30 Oct 1765. Deed. JOHN GALBRAITH of Straban Township, York Co yeoman for £105 sold to ROBERT GALBRAITH of the City of Phila a 150 a. tr of land in Straban Township adj WILLIAM MCCREARY, Levingtons Path, SAMUEL HAYS, JOHN ANDERSON, the Great Road leading to York, Rock Cr & MARGARET PATTERSON, which was purch by the said JOHN GALBRAITH from MICHAEL LYNCH 11 Mar 1754 ... . Wit: JAMES JACKS, JOHN WILLSON. Ackn 30 Oct 1765 before HENRY SLAGLE justice. (E:pg 241)

29 Jun 1755. Power of Atty. ALLEN ROBINETT of York Co yeoman appoint my trusty & well beloved friend WILLIAM COPELAND of Newbury Township, York Co my atty to sue for, recover & receive all sums of money as are now due and owing unto me, and to convey my lands, goods & chattels whatsoever in York Co, particularly a 200 a. plantation in the township afsd adj RICHARD ASTON & JOSEPH WILLIAMS, surveyed to me in pursuance of a warrant ... . JOSEPH ADLUM, JOHN ALUM Junr. Proved by JOSEPH ADLUM 4 Jan 1773 before JOHN ADLUM justice. (E:pg 242)

6 Aug 1771. Deed. DIETERICK (DETERICK) (DETRICK) FAHNSTICK Senr of Cocalleco Township, Lancaster Co yeoman and MARGARETHA his wife for £100 sold to TORRIS FAHNSTICK of Manchester Township, York Co (son of said DIETERICK FAHNSTICK) miller a 100 a. parcel of land in Manchester Township adj Bermudian Cr, mill tr & land of BENJAMIN FAHNSTICK, being pt/o a 400 a. tr of land granted to EDWARD SMOUT decd by patent dated 12 Apr 1751 (Patent Book A vol. 15 pg 602 in Phila), and the said EDWARD SMOUT departed this life having first made his will dated 20 Jun 1751 and did direct his executors (to wit) ELIZABETH SMOUT, MARCUS YOUNG & JOHN HOBSON to sell the land, and ELIZABETH SMOUT, MARCUS YOUNG & JOHN HOBSON on 27 Nov 1755 sold the tr to JAMES MORE, and the said JAMES MORE on 28 Nov 1759, sold the same to the afsd DEITERICK FAHNSTICK ... . Wit: GEO GARBER, PETER MILLER. Ackn 8 Aug 1771 before JOSEPH UPDEGRAFF justice. (E:pg 243)

13 Dec 1772. Deed. JACOB KEGY of Hidelberg Township, York Co farmer for £4 sold to THOMAS ARMOR of York Town, York Co surveyor all my right in a warrant for 50 a. of land adj my other land & others in Hidelberg Township

granted unto me by the Proprietaries 19 Oct 1765 ... . Wit: LAWRENCE
MCMULLAN, THOMAS ARMOR Junr. Ackn 31 Dec 1772 before RICHD
MCCALISTER (MCALLISTER) justice. (E:pg 245)

15 Oct 1772. Articles of Agreement. Between JACOB SHNEIDER
(SCHNEIDER) of Manchester Township, York Co yeoman and SOPHIA
FRANK (FRANCK) of same place widow ... whereas the said SOPHIA
FRANK is seized of tr of land in Manchester Township being the 1/3 pt/o said tr
which was the real estate of GEORGE PHILIP FRANCK decd who died
intestate, and the marriage is shortly intended to be had between the said JACOB
SHNEIDER and SOPHIA FRANK, it is agreed between the parties that she shall
keep and enjoy the thirds of said decd's estate both real and personal to her own
proper use ... and the said JACOB SHNEIDER is not at present seized of an
estate sufficient for the said SOPHIA FRANCK equivalent to her fortune, the
said JACOB SHNEIDER agrees with the said SOPHIA FRANK that in case the
intended marriage shall take effect and the said JACOB SHNEIDER should
happen to die in the lifetime of the said SOPHIA then the said SOPHIA
FRANK will stand seized of all such of his estate both real & personal whereof
the said JACOB shall die seized ... if the said SOPHIA FRANK should die in
the lifetime of the said JACOB without leaving any issue begotten by the said
JACOB then it shall be lawful for the said JACOB shall stand seized of all such
estate both real and personal of the said SOPHIA, but in case of any issue by the
said JACOB then it shall be divided by the father JACOB and the said issue ... .
Wit: [?], WALTER MCFARLAND, GEO LEWIS LESLER. Ackn 15 Oct 1772
before JOHN ADLUM justice. (E:pg 246)

24 Dec 1772. Deed of Mortgage. JACOB SIDLER of Donegal Township,
Lancaster Co, PA yeoman for better securing the payment of £115 and also 5
shillings sold to JAMES MCCOLLOUGH of Hopewell Township, York Co
cooper a messuage and 185 a. tr of land in Hopewell Township adj ANDREW
FINLEY, WILLIAM GAMMELL, WILLIAM EDIE & others ... whereas the
afsd JACOB SIDLER standeth bound unto the said JAMES MCCOLLOUGH
for £230 conditioned for the payment of £115 in payments before 1 Apr 1780 ...
provided that if the said JACOB SIDLER shall well and truly pay unto the said
JAMES MCCOLLOUGH £115 then this indenture to be void ... . Wit: JOHN
[?], DAVID GRIER. Ackn 27 Jan 1773 before JOHN ADLUM justice. 15 Aug
1788 JAMES MCCOLLOUGH discharged mortgage. Wit: J. BARNITZ
recorder. (E:pg 247)

28 Jul 1772. Deed. HENRY FERNSLER of the Town of Hanover, Heidleberg
Township, York Co hatter and ELIZABETH his wife for £145 sold to JACOB
MILLER of Frederick Co, MD brewer Lot No. 7 in the Town of Hanover ...
whereas RICHARD MCCALISTER esqr on 6 Jan 1769 did sell unto the afsd

HENRY FERNSLER a lott of ground in the Town of Hanover, No. 7, in breadth 57'6" and in length 230', bounded by Frederick Street & Lot No. 8, being pt/o a tr of land called *Digges' Choice* which the said RICHARD MCCALISTER holds in right of JOHN DIGGES decd ... . Wit: JOSEPH BOUDE, [?] BURYER. Ackn 28 Jul 1772 before RD MCALLISTER justice. (E:pg 249)

16 Feb 1748/9. Deed. ALEXANDER MCCANLIS of Fawn Township, Lancaster Co, PA yeoman for £25 sold to THOMAS STEEL of same place yeoman a 100 a. tr of land pt/o a 200 a. tr of land in Fawn Township w side of the State Ridge where JAMES ANDREWS decd formerly presumed to settle which I claim by virtue of a warrant for £200 of land from the Land Office to be surveyed which land on 15th instant divided between the said THOMAS STEEL and JAMES ANDREWS Junr by a line made by ANDREW ROWAN, HUGH WHITEFORD & SAMUEL GORDEN ... . Wit: ISAAC SANDERS, SAMUEL STEEL, ANDREW ROWAN. Proved 5 Aug by ISAAC SANDERS 1772 before SAML JOHNSTON justice. (E:pg 251)

28 May 1772. Deed. WILLIAM JONES of Newberry Township, York Co yeoman for £148 sold to JAMES RANKIN of same place yeoman a 148 ½ a. tr of land ... whereas the Proprietaries by their patent dated at Phila 22 Jun 1770 did grant unto the said WILLIAM JONES a 148 ½ a. tr of land in Newberry Township called *Booth Bounded* adj GEORGE ASHBUDGE, SAMUEL JONES, Widow VANE & RICHARD PETERS esqr (Patent Book – vol. 11 pg 353) ... . Wit: RICHARD CASPER, JOHN RANKIN. Ackn 28 May 1772 before WILLIAM RANKIN justice. (E:pg 252)

10 Feb 1773. Deed of Mortgage. ROBERT JONES of Manchester Township, York Co yeoman for better securing the payment of £80 and also 5 shillings sold to JACOB KERN of York Town, York Co taylor a 211 ¾ a. tr of land in Manchester Township whereon the said ROBERT JONES now dwells adj GEORGE STEVENSON, WILLIAM WILLIS & Big Codorus Cr (subject to a mortgage to GEORGE ERNST MEYER to secure the payment of £100) ... whereas the said ROBERT JONES standeth bound unto the said JACOB KERN for £160 conditioned for the payment of £80 on 1 Feb next ensuing ... provided that if the said ROBERT JONES shall well and truly pay unto the said JACOB KERN £80 then this indenture to be void ... . Wit: [?], JACOB BILLMEYER Junr. Ackn 10 Feb 1773 before JOHN ADLUM esqr justice. 30 Jan 1776 JACOB KERN discharged mortgage. Wit: SAML JOHNSTON. (E:pg 255)

8 Oct 1772. Deed of Mortgage. SIMON COPPENHEFFER of Manchester Township, York Co yeoman for better securing the payment of £800 and also 5 shillings sold to CHARLES MEREDITH of the City of Phila merchant a messuage and 230 a. tr of land called *Sinking Valley* in Manchester Township

adj ANDREW SMITH, PETER SHULTS, JACOB RUDISILLY & GEORGE
NAARS ... whereas JOHN WEAVER of Heydelberg, Lancaster Co yeoman,
PHILIP HAUTZ of Bethel, Berks Co & HENRY HAUTZ of Bethel Township,
Lancaster Co yeoman by eight obligations dated 13 & 14 May 1772 stand bound
unto the said SIMON COPPENHEFFER for £1600 conditioned for the payment
of £800 in payments before 1781, and the said SIMON COPPENHEFFER on 21
May last past did assign over all the said bonds unto the said CHARLES
MEREDITH, and the said SIMON COPPENHEFFER by a bond stands bound
unto the said CHARLES MEREDITH as further security for the payment of the
said bonds of £1600 conditioned for the payment of £800 in payments afsd ...
provided that if the said SIMON COPPENHEFFER shall well and truly pay unto
the said CHARLES MEREDITH £800 then this indenture to be void ... . Wit:
JNO ORD, THOS SMITH. Ackn 8 Oct 1772 before SAMUEL JOHNSTON
esqr justice. 7 Jun 1788 by virtue of a letter of atty to GEORGE LEWIS
LESLER from MARY MEREDITH executrix of the will of CHARLES
MEREDITH decd discharged mortgage. Wit: J. BARNITZ recorder. (E:pg
257)

3 Mar 1769. Deed. HENRY LEINBACHER of Dover Township, York Co
yeoman for £100 sold to his son CONRAD LEINBACHER of same place
yeoman a messuage and a 190 a. tr of land in Dover Township whereon the said
HENRY LEINBACHER now dwells adj PETER CRONEBACH, FELIX
LEINBACHER & JACOB WEYMER, which was granted to the said HENRY
LEINBACHER by warrant dated 30 May 1744 ... . Wit: [?], JACOB
BILLMEYER Junr. Ackn 4 Mar 1769 before JOHN ADLUM esqr justice.
(E:pg 259)

12 Jan 1773. Deed of Mortgage. JOHN BERKMAN of Dover Township, York
Co yeoman and CHRISTINA his wife for better securing the payment of £14.7
and also 5 shillings sold to JACOB MAY and GERHARD GREFF of same
place yeomen a lott of ground in Dover Town, Dover Township, No. 29, adj the
Great Road leading from York Town to Carlisle now called York Street, Lot No.
30 & JACOB YONER, in breadth on said street 60' and in depth 297' which
was granted unto the said JOHN BERKMAN by the said JACOB YONER and
CHRISTINA his wife on 20 Sep 1771 ... whereas the said JOHN BERKMAN
standeth bound unto the said JACOB MAY and GERHARD GREFF for £29.14
conditioned for the payment of £14.17 before 1 May next ... provided that if the
said JOHN BERKMAN shall well and truly pay unto the said JACOB MAY and
GERHARD GREFF £14.7 then this indenture to be void ... . Wit:
FREDERICK HOUSMAN, HENRY MILLER. 12 Jan 1773 before DAVID
JAMESON esqr justice. (E:pg 261)

8 Jun 1772. Deed. PETER LITTLE of Germany Township, York Co yeoman and URSULA his wife for £6 sold to JACOB GRAY of same place two lotts of ground in the Town of Petersburg pt/o a 311 a. tr of land, Lot Nos. 3 & 4, adj Kings Street leading to York Town & Frederick Town, MD, 66' each in front and in length each 264' paying unto the said PETER LITTLE on 1 May every year forever the rent of £7.6 each ... whereas the Proprietaries by their patent dated at Phila 18 Sep 1760 did grant unto the said PETER LITTLE a 311 a. tr of land in the said township (Patent Book AA vol. 1 pg 80), and the said PETER LITTLE hath laid out a town which he called Petersburg and is desirous that the same shall hereafter be called by the name of Petersburg ... . Wit: GEO CLARK, JOS DYER. Ackn 8 Jun 1772 before HENRY SLAGLE justice. (E:pg 263)

16 Oct 1772. Bond. SAMUEL EDIE & ROBERT MCPHERSON esqrs of Cumberland Township, York Co and DAVID MCCONAUGHY esqr of Menallen Township, York Co are firmly bound unto GEORGE the Third King for £2000 ... the condition of this obligation is such that the said SAMUEL EDIE esqr on 1 Oct instant was elected sheriff of York Co and by an indenture recorded at Phila between JOSEPH ADLUM coroner of York Co on the one part and MATHEW DILL esqr, THEOBALT SHOLLAS, HUGH DUNWOODIE, JOHN MICHAEL Junr, PHILIP ROTHROCK & JACOB SHUPE assistant judges and WILLIAM MCCANDLYS, STEPHEN MCKINLEY, JOHN THOMPSON, JOSEPH LOURY, JONATHAN MARSH & ROBERT BLACK inspectors freeholders of the other part, now if the said SAMUEL EDIE esqr shall well and truly serve and execute all the Kings writs and process to him directed without delay then this obligation to be void ... . Wit: SAML JOHNSTON recorder, JOHN CLARK Junr. (E:pg 267)

5 Oct 1772 at Phila. Commission. To SAMUEL EDIE of York Co esqr greeting, know that reposing special trust and confidence in your loyalty, integrity & ability we have appointed you to be sheriff of York Co ... . [signed] RICHD PENN. (E:pg 268)

5 Oct 1772 at Phila. Writ of Assistance. To all judges, justices, magistrates and other offices and other persons whatsoever in York Co greeting, whereas by a commission [see above] we have granted unto SAMUEL EDIE esqr the office of sheriff of York Co ... we require and command you that to the said SAMUEL EDIE you be aiding and assisting in all things that to the office of sheriff do or may in any wise belong ... . [signed] RICHARD PENN esqr by virtue of a commission from THOMAS PENN & JOHN PENN esqrs Proprietaries. (E:pg 269)

29 Jan 1773. Deed. SAMUEL EDIE esqr high sheriff of York Co for £20 sold a
20 a. tr of land to WILLIAM MCLEARY ... whereas in a Court of Common
Pleas SAMUEL GETTYS lately recovered against NATHAN HARKNESS late
of York Co yeoman otherwise called NATHANIEL HARKNESS a debt of
£32.15, and 45 shillings 6 pence damages ... the sheriff seized in execution a 20
a. tr of land in Cumberland Township, York Co of the said NATHAN
HARKNESS adj THOMAS DOUGLAS, ROBERT WORK & WILLIAM
MCCLEARY and exposed the land to public vendue on 14 Nov and sold the
land to WILLIAM MCCLEARY of Cumberland Township yeoman for £20 he
being the highest bidder ... . Wit: DAVID GRIER, THOS SMITH. Ackn 29
Jan 1773. (E:pg 270)

26 May 1772. Deed. SAMUEL EDIE esqr high sheriff of York Co for £176.6 1
penny sold to SAMUEL HADDON a 271 a. tr of land ... whereas in a Court of
Common Pleas ANDREW MAYES lately recovered a debt of £70, and 89
shillings 6 pence damages
against MICHAEL DRUMGOLD of Strabann Township yeoman & HANCE
HAMILTON of Cumberland Township esqr both of York Co ... whereas
DAVID MCCONAUGHY then high sheriff seized in execution a messuage and
a 271 a. tr of land of the said MICHAEL DRUMGOLD adj SAMUEL
DICKSON, NATHAN PETTERSON, SAMUEL THOMPSON & JAMES
DICKSON, and exposed to sale at public vendue and the same sold to SAMUEL
HADDON for £176.6 1 penny he being the highest bidder ... afterwards before
any deed was executed to the said SAMUEL HADDON the time for which the
said DAVID MCCONAUGHY held the office of sheriff expired and the said
SAMUEL EDIE was elected ... . Wit: THOMAS SMITH, DAVID GRIER.
Ackn 17 Aug 1772. (E:pg 273)

6 Jul 1763. Deed. ARTHUR SMITH of York Co for £7.10 sold to JAMES
SMITH of the Town of York, York Co a 150 a. tr of land in Newbery Township
which was granted to me by warrant dated 2 Jun 1762 ... . Wit: JNO MEEM,
JOHN ADLUM Junr. Ackn 6 Jul 1763 before JOHN ADLUM justice. (E:pg
276)

5 Feb 1773. Deed. JAMES SMITH of York Town, York Co atty at law for
£140 sold unto JAMES RANKIN of Newbery Township, York Co yeoman a
143 a. tr of land in Newbery Township adj the road from Rankins Ferry to
Carlise, ENOS ROGERS, JAMES NAILER & ARTHER SMITH, pt/o a greater
tr of land granted unto ARTHER SMITH by warrant dated at Phila 2 Jun 1762,
which was granted by the said ARTHER SMITH on 6 Jul 1763 unto the said
JAMES SMITH [see above] ... . Wit: THOS ARMOR, JOHN RANKIN.
Ackn 5 Mar 1773 before WILLIAM RANKIN justice. (E:pg 277)

18 Apr 1761. Deed. ROBERT VALE of Warrington Township, York Co for £30 sold to PETER MARSH of same place a 133 a. tr of land ... whereas in pursuance of a warrant there was surveyed on 9 Oct 1744 unto the said ROBERT VALE a 133 a. tr of land in Warrington Township adj MOSES MAPPIN ... PETER MARSH is to pay all the arrears that is due & to become due to the Proprietors of said tr forever ... . Wit: WILLIAM NEVITT, JOHN MCMULLAN. Proved 8 Dec 1762 by JOHN MCMILLAN of Warrington Township yeoman before WM COLEMAN esqr justice. (E:pg 279)

18 Dec 1772. Deed of Mortgage. HERMAN WERKING of York Co yeoman for better securing the payment of £75.2 and also 5 shillings sold to JACOB SHERMAN of York Co inn holder a messuage and 40 a. tr of land in Manheim Township whereof JACOB WERKEN lately died owner of & was valued and ordered to the grantor eldest son of said decd ... whereas the said HERMAN WERKING standeth bound unto the said JACOB SHERMAN for £150.4 conditioned for the payment of £75.2 in one year ... provided that if the said HERMAN WERKING shall well and truly pay unto the said JACOB SHERMAN £75.2 then this indenture to be void ... . Wit: JAMES SMITH, DAVID MCMECHEN. Proved 23 Mar 1773 by JAMES SMITH before MARTIN EICHELBERGER esqr justice. (E:pg 280)

17 Mar 1773. Deed. WILSON BUCKMASTER of Cesal Co, MD for £10 sold to JOHN FLOWERS of Shrowsbry Township, York Co a messuage and 234 a. parcel of land in Shrowsbry Township adj MICHEL CAVERICK, JOHN HELLER & EGNATIOUS DAVIS ... . Wit: WILLIAM SMITH, ISABEL MITCHEL. Ackn 17 Mar 1773 before WILLIAM SMITH justice. (E:pg 282)

11 Mar 1773. Deed. THOMAS GRAY of Berwick Township, York Co farmer for £3.5 sold to THOMAS ARMOR of York Township, York Co all my right to that warrant dated 2 Oct last granted unto me for 30 a. of land adj my other land & others in Berwick Township ... . Wit: WILLIAM GRAY, ENOCH HAWKSWORTH. Ackn 11 Mar 1773 before JOHN ADLUM esqr justice. (E:pg 283)

26 Mar 1773. Deed. ANDREAS HOKE of Manchester Township, York Co yeoman and BARBARA his wife for 5 shillings sold to JOHN HOKE and PETER HOKE of same place yeomen a 30 a. 107 perches tr of land ... whereas the Proprietaries by their patent dated at Phila 27 Nov 1771 did grant unto JACOB YONER a 30 a. 107 perches tr of land called *Yonersberg* adj CONRAD MILLER, said JOHN & PETER HOKE (Patent Book AA vol. 11 pg 602), and the said JACOB YONER & CHRISTINA his wife on 9 Jun last did sell unto the said ANDREAS HOKE the afsd land ... . Wit: JACOB [?], HENRY MILLER. Ackn 26 Mar 1773 before HENRY SLAGLE justice. (E:pg 284)

2 Jan 1773. Deed. SAMUEL HOLDSWORTH of York Co yeoman for £400 sold to JAMES DIXON (DIXSON) of York Co shoemaker a messuage and 170 a tr of land pt/o the tr of land whereon the said SAMUEL HOLDSWORTH now dwells being the n pt/o the whole tr in Straban Township adj JOHN GALBREATH, JOHN FLEMING & WILLIAM BIGGAR ... . Wit: DAVID MCMECHEN, LEWIS BUSH. Ackn 4 Feb 1773 before DAVID MCCONAUGHY justice. (E:pg 286)

26 Sep 1763. Deed. NATHANAEL (NATHANIEL) LIGHTNER of Leacock Township, Lancaster Co yeoman and MARGARET his wife for love and regard and £60 sold to their son WILLIAM LIGHTNER of same place yeoman a 204 a. tr of land ... whereas JOHN TODD of Chester Co, PA and SARAH his wife on 28 Jun 1760 did grant to ROBERT TODD his son of Huntington Township, York Co a 204 a. tr of land in Huntington Township adj JOSUA HENWORTH, HENRY WEIDEBACK, GEORGE STALL, THOMAS POWEL & WILLIAM WEYERMAN, and the said ROBERT TODD and HANNAH his wife on 12 Apr 1763 did grant the 204 a. tr of land unto the said NATHANAEL LIGHTNER ... . Wit: MICHAEL LIGHTNER, ADAM LIGHTNER. Ackn 26 Nov 1771 before JOHN ADLUM justice. (E:pg 287)

9 Jun 1772. Deed. JACOB YONER of Dover Township, York Co yeoman and CHRISTINA (CHRISTING) his wife for £103.2.6 sold to ANDREW HOKE of Manchester Township, York Co yeoman two trs of land called the *Overplus* & *Yonerburg*, in the whole 79 a. 56 perches ... whereas the Proprietaries by their patent dated at Phila 27 Nov 1771 did grant unto the said JACOB YONER two trs of land in Manchester Township as pt/o the original purch of 5000 a. made by the late WILLIAM PENN esqr decd by ADRIA VROOEZEN in any pt/o the province, one of them called the *Overplus* a 48 a. 198 perches tr of land adj ANDREW HOKE, MATHIAS SMYER & CONRAD MILLER and a 30 a. 107 perches tr of land called *Yonerburg* adj CONRAD MILLER, PETER HOKE & JOHN HOKE (Patent Book AA vol. 11 pg 602) ... . Wit: JAMES SMITH, DAVID MCMECHEN. Ackn 9 Jun 1772 before MARTIN EICHELBERGER justice. (E:pg 290)

9 Apr 1773. Deed. JAMES BANKS of Windsor Township, York Co husbandman & ANN his wife for £100 sold to SAMUEL RICHEY of York Co yeoman a messuage and a 303 a. tr of land called *Mulberry Tree* in Windsor Township adj Fishing Cr on which the said JAMES now dwells, 260 a. of it was surveyed and laid out in pursuance of Application No. 390 dated 14 Jan 1767 and 40 a. of it including the houses by virtue of a warrant dated 18 Feb 1773, both surveyed and made to the said THOMAS BANKS [*sic*] who bought the right to said place from SAML RICHY who bought his right from WILLIAM

MERNS ... . Wit: GEO HENRY Junr, CONRAD STOWSEBEROG. Ackn Apr 1773 before JOHN ADLUM justice. (E:pg 292)

17 Apr 1773. Deed. PHILIP JACOBS of York Co yeoman and SUSANNA his wife for £300 sold to GEORGE JACOBS of Cumni Township, Berks Co, PA yeoman a 112 a. tr of land ... whereas the Proprietaries by their patent dated at Phila 18 Dec 1749 did grant unto HENRY JACOBS 461 a. of land on Beaver Cr a br of Conawago formerly in Lancaster Co but now in York Co (Patent Book A vol. 14 pg 343), and the said HENRY JACOBS on 3 Jul 1761 did convey unto the said PHILIP JACOBS (his son) a 112 a. tr of land pt/o the afsd tr in Paradise Township adj GEORGE JACOBS ... . Wit: THOS HARLEY, SAML JACOBS. Ackn 17 Apr 1773 before JOHN ADLUM justice. (E:pg 293)

24 Nov 1772. Deed of Mortgage. ROBERT WHITE of the Town of Hanover, York Co merchant for better securing the payment of £850 and also 5 shillings sold to CHARLES THOMPSON (THOMSON) of the City of Phila, PA merchant three trs of land in Straban Township, a 182 a. tr of land adj JOSEPH GREEN, PATRICK MONTGOMERY, JOHN MURPHY, the Church land & WILLIAM GUFFY, a 128 a. 32 perches tr of land called *Fore Body* adj JAMES DICKSON, CHARLES THOMPSON, PATRICK MONTGOMERY, ROBERT LATIMORE & FRANCIS CORSART and a 114 a. 126 perches tr of land called *Tusculum* adj CHARLES THOMPSON, the meeting land, SAMUEL HADDON, SAMUEL THOMSON, JAMES DICKSON & JOSEPH GREEN, which three trs of land CHARLES THOMPSON on 26 Oct last past did grant unto JOHN WHITE, and the said JOHN WHITE on this date did grant unto the said ROBERT WHITE ... whereas RICHARD MCCALISTER [sic]of the Town of Hanover by eight obligations standeth bound unto the said CHARLES THOMPSON (in payments) before 29 Nov 1780 ... provided that if the said ROBERT WHITE shall well and truly pay unto the said CHARLES THOMPSON £850 then this indenture to be void ... . Wit: ARCHD MCCLEAN, DAVID LEITCH. Ackn 24 Nov 1772 before WILLIAM ALLEN esqr chief justice. 5 Dec 1772 JANE WHITE w/o ROBERT WHITE for 5 shillings release unto CHARLES THOMPSON all my right of dower in the three trs of land provided as within provided. Wit: ARCHD MCCLEAN, ABDUL MCCALISTER. Ackn 5 Dec 1772 before RICHARD MCCALISTER justice. 14 Jul 1787 CHAS THOMSON discharged mortgage. Wit: JACOB BARNITZ recorder. (E:pg 296)

23 Nov 1772. Deed. JOHN WHITE of the City of Phila, PA merchant for £965 sold to ROBERT WHITE of the Town of Hanover, York Co merchant three trs of land [same as above] ... whereas on 26 Oct now last past CHARLES THOMSON of the City of Phila merchant sold to JOHN WHITE three adj trs of

land (Book E pg 203) ... . Wit: ARCHIBALD MCCLEAN, DAVID LEITCH.
Ackn 24 Nov 1773 before WILLIAM ALLEN esqr chief justice. (E:pg 300)

31 Oct 1772. Deed. SAMUEL EDIE esqr high sheriff of York Co for £550 sold
to HARMAN UPDEGRAFF a 211 a. tr of land in Newberry Township ...
whereas in a Court of Common Pleas HENRY KEPPELE, LODWIG
LAUMAN, HENRY KEPPELE the younger & PAUL ZANTZINGER executors
of the will of MICHAEL GROSS decd recovered against JACOB YONER late
of York Co yeoman otherwise called JACOB YONER of Leacock Township,
Lancaster Co yeoman a debt of £1000 and 51 shillings 6 pence damages ... the
sheriff seized in execution as the estate of the afsd JACOB YONER a 200 a. tr
of land in Dover Township adj JACOB LAMBERT, JACOB MAY,
NICHOLAS YONER & others which remained in my hands for want of buyers
... and seized in execution one other 211 a. tr of land in Newberry Township adj
HENRY ENSMINGER, SAMUEL JOHN & others and exposed to public
vendue and the 211 a. tr of land sold to HARMAN UPDEGRAFF of Manchester
Township, York Co tanner for £550 he being the highest bidder ... . Wit:
THOMAS SMITH, JOHN CLARK Junr. Ackn 17 Apr 1773. (E:pg 303)

14 Dec 1772. Deed. ROBERT GORDEN (GORDON) of Baltimore Co, MD
for £40 sold to THOMAS COOPER of York Co a 42 a. tr of land adj *Coopers
Prospect* ... whereas JAMES CROMEY obtained a warrant dated in Phila 18
Nov 1748 which was executed on land adj the old temporary line which was
sold by the said CROMEY to JAMES THOMPSON on 4 Mar 1764 and by the
said THOMPSON sold to the said ROBERT GORDEN on 5 Jun 1770 ... . Wit:
WILLIAM ROWAN, JOHN WALLACE. Ackn 14 Dec 1772 before WILLIAM
SMITH justice. (E:pg 306)

1 Apr 1773. Deed. PHILIP HUFF of Cumberland Township, York Co farmer
for £45 sold to BENJAMIN MCKINLEY of Frederick Co, MD a 200 a. tr of
land adj CHARLES VANCE & others in the Proprietaries *Mannor of Mask*
which was granted unto me by an order of survey dated 15 Jun last ... . Wit:
THOS ARMOR, GILBERT MCADAMS. Ackn 29 Apr 1773 before THOMAS
MINSHALL esqr justice. (E:pg 307)

28 Apr 1773. Deed of Mortgage. ERNST RALFSNEIDER of Windsor
Township, York Co yeoman for better securing the payment of £92.4 and also 5
shillings sold to HENRY SELEY of Berwick Township, York Co yeoman a
messuage and 131 a. 110 perches tr of land in Windsor Township adj JOHN
SMITH, MICHAEL ZIMMERMAN, CASPER RUBY & others, it being the
same which was granted unto the said ERNST RALFSNEIDER by the said
HENRY SELEY on 21 Jan 1771 and whereon the said ERNST RALFSNEIDER
now lives ... whereas the said ERNST RALFSNEIDER standeth bound unto the

said HENRY SELEY for £184.8 conditioned for the payment of £92.4 on 1 May 1777 ... provided that if the said ERNST RALFSNEIDER shall well and truly pay unto the said HENRY SELEY £92.4 then this indenture to be void ... . Wit: JACOB MILLER, HENRY MILLER. Ackn 28 Apr 1773 before JOS UPDEGRAFF justice. (E:pg 308)

14 Apr 1773. Deed of Mortgage. ADAM GREVER of Manheim Township, York Co yeoman for better securing the payment of £122 and also 5 shillings sold to RUDOLPH NAFTZINGER of same place yeoman a 167 a. tr of land in Manheim Township adj JACOB LICHTY & JOHN SUMMERS ... whereas the said ADAM GREVER stands bound unto the afsd RUDOLPH NAFTZINGER for £122 to be paid in payments before 1 Nov 1776 ... provided that if the said ADAM GREVER shall well and truly pay unto the said RUDOLPH NAFTZINGER £122 then this indenture to be void ... . Wit: JOS BOUDE, POLLY MCCALISTER. Ackn – Apr 1773 before RD MCCALISTER justice. 14 Dec 1779 RUDOLPH NOFTZGAR discharged mortgage. Wit: ARCHD MCCLEAN recorder. (E:pg 309)

14 Apr 1773. Deed. RUDOLPH NAFTZINGER of Manheim Township, York Co yeoman for £190 sold to ADAM GREVER of York Co yeoman a 167 a. tr of land ... whereas the Proprietaries by their warrant dated at Phila 18 Apr 1750 granted unto PHILIP THOMAS of Helm Township a 100 a. tr of land adj JACOB LICHTEY & JOHN SUMMERS and by a survey since contains 167 a., and the said PHILIP THOMAS on 28 Apr 1767 did sell unto the said RUDOLPH NAFTZINGER the afsd tr of land ... . Wit: JOS BOUDE, POLLY MCCALISTER. Ackn 14 Apr 1773 before RD MCCALISTER justice. (E:pg 311)

28 Apr 1767. Deed. PHILIP THOMAS of Helm Township, York Co taylor for £47 sold to RUDY NAFTZINGER of Manheim Township, York Co farmer a 100 a. tr of land in Manheim Township near CHRISTIAN HOCKSTATER about a mi from Little Conewago on the Long Run, which was granted unto me by warrant dated at Phila 18 Apr 1750 ... . Wit: [?], GEO EICHELBERGER. Ackn 28 Apr 1767 before HENRY SLEGLE esqr justice. (E:pg 312)

7 Apr 1773. Deed of Mortgage. GEORGE BLINSINGER of the Town of Hanover, York Co taylor and MAUDALENA his wife for better securing the payment of £22 and also 5 shillings sold to CASPAR REINICKER of same place innholder a house and lot of ground on Carlisle Street in the Town of Hanover wherein the said GEORGE BLINSINGER now dwells, No. 24 ... whereas the said GEORGE BLINSINGER stands bound unto the said CASPAR REINICKER for £44 conditioned for the payment of £22 on 10 May next ensuing ... provided that if the said GEORGE BLINSINGER shall well and

truly pay unto the said CASPAR REINICKER £22 then this indenture to be void
... . Wit: [?], JOS BOUDE. Ackn 27 Apr 1773 before RD MCCALISTER
justice. 1 May 1790 CASPER REINECKER discharged mortgage. Wit: J.
BARNITZ recorder. (E:pg 313)

22 May 1773. Deed of Mortgage. JACOB GOCHONOVER of Manheim
Township, York Co yeoman and MARIA his wife for better securing the
payment of £150 and also 5 shillings sold to CASPAR REINICKER of York Co
innholder a 276 a. tr of land in Manheim Township adj DEWALT SNYDER,
CHRISTOPHER RHINEMAN, HENRY HARTMAN & CHRISTIAN
HOSTETTER ... whereas the said JACOB GOCHONOVER stands bound unto
the said CASPAR REINICKER for £300 conditioned for the payment of £150
on or before 24 May instant ... provided that if the said JACOB
GOCHONOVER shall well and truly pay unto the said CASPAR REINICKER
£150 then this indenture to be void ... . Wit: ARCHD MCCLEAN, JOS
BOUDE. Ackn 22 May 1773 before RD MCALISTER justice. 3 May 1774
CASPER RENACKER discharged mortgage. Wit: SAML JOHNSTON
recorder. (E:pg 314)

1 Sep 1769. Deed. JOSEPH WALLACE of York Town, York Co cordwainer
for £15 sold to THOMAS ARMOR of same place surveyor a 100 a. tr of land
adj JOHN MCMULLEN, THOMAS ATHERTON & WILLIAM GRIFFITH in
Warrington Township which was granted unto me by Application No. 5524
dated at Phila 19 Jun last ... . Wit: JACOB STROMAN, [?]. Ackn 1 Nov
1770 before JOHN POPE esqr justice. (E:pg 316)

16 Mar 1773. Deed of Mortgage. FREDERICK HUBER of York Town, York
Co blacksmith for £23 sold to BALTZER SPANGLER of same place 1 anvil, 1
bellows, 3 vices, 3 hammers, 1 screw plate, 3 hand vices, 2 pick irons, 3 bench
hammers, 1 ladle hammer, all the tongs in my shop and all other tools belong to
my shop ... provided that if the said FREDERICK HUBER shall well and truly
pay unto the said BALTZER SPANGLER £23 on 15 Apr next then this bill of
sale to be void ... . Wit: DANIEL SPANGLER, HENRY MILLER. Ackn 16
Mar 1773 before [*blank*]. (E:pg 317)

27 Apr 1773. Deed of Mortgage. JACOB SHIVE of York Town, York Co
cooper for £7.17 sold to CHARLES BARNET of same place brewer several
coopers tools, 1 iron pott, 1 iron scilit, 1 tea kettle, 2 pewter plates, 1 dough
drought, 1 feather bed and bed cloaths, 1 round table, 2 cheers, 1 washing tub, 1
pickling tub & 1 watering pann ... provided that if the said JACOB SHIVE shall
well and truly pay unto the said CHARLES BARNET £7.17 on or before 1 Oct
next then this bill of sale to be void ... . Wit: SARAH MILLER, HENRY
MILLER. Ackn 27 Apr 1773 before HENRY SLAGLE justice. (E:pg 318)

8 Feb 1773. Deed of Mortgage. WILLIAM WIDROW of Manoughan Township, York Co for better securing the payment of £50 and also 5 shillings sold to MATTHEW DILL esqr of same place a messuage and 200 a. tr of land made over to the said WILLIAM WIDROW on 6 Apr 1772 by HENRY WERSLOV adj JOHN GLEN, WILLIAM PORTER, SAMUEL COOK & BALSLER MOUDEY ... whereas the said WILLIAM WIDROW by three obligations dated 5 Dec 1767 stands bound unto JOHN KENNADY for £60 conditioned for the payment of £30, and the said JOHN KENNADY assigned the afsd obligations unto ROBT STEVENSON, and the said STEVENSON assigned all his right of the afsd obligations unto the afsd MATTHEW DILL ... and the said WILLIAM WIDROW stands bound unto the said MATTHEW DILL for £40 conditioned for the payment of £20 on 9 Jan 1773 ... provided that if the said WILLIAM WIDROW shall well and truly pay unto the said MATTHEW DILL £50 then this indenture to be void ... . Wit: LEWIS WILLIAMS, MARY DILL. Proved 5 May 1773 by LEWIS WILLIAMS & MARY DILL before ARCHIBALD MCGREW justice. (E:pg 319)

16 Dec 1772. Deed. ANDREW ROWAN of Faun Township, York Co yeoman for £110 sold to WILLIAM ROWAN yeoman of same place yeoman a 245 a. tr of land pt/o a resurvey of a parcel of land made in pursuance of a 300 a. application in the Land Office in Phila dated 4 Mar 1768 in said township ... . Wit: MATHEW MCCALL, JAMES MCCALL. Ackn 16 Dec 1772 before CUNINGHAM SEMPLE justice. (E:pg 320)

30 Apr 1773. Quit Claim. MICHAEL SMYSER of Manchester Township, York Co tavernkeeper and MARGARET his wife for 5 shillings quit claim unto JOHN HOKE of same place farmer a messuage and 114 a. 55 perches tr of land whereon the said JOHN HOKE now lives in Manchester Township adj PETER HOAK, the beginning of the original tr granted by LORD BALTIMORE, other pt/o original tr in possession of the said MICHAEL SMYSER, the Great Road & JOHN HOAK's other land ... . Wit: WM LEAS, HENRY MILLER. Ackn 3 Jun 1773 before JOS UPDEGRAFF justice. (E:pg 321)

13 Sep 1765. Deed. GEORGE STEVENSON of York Town, York Co gent for £100 sold to GEORGE LEGATE of Shrewsbury Township, York Co weaver a 325 ½ a. tr of land in the township afsd (late pt/o York Township), which was surveyed to me 12 Apr 1752 in pursuance of a warrant dated 18 Dec 1751 and the same whereon the said GEORGE LEGATE now dwells ... . Wit: JOHN BOYD, WILLIAM PATTERSON. Ackn 2 Jun 1773 before WILLIAM SMITH justice. (E:pg 323)

24 May 1773. Deed of Mortgage. SEBASTIAN HARLEYMAN of Codorus Township, York Co farmer for better securing the payment of £181 and also 5

shillings sold to PETER SPRENKLE of York Co yeoman a 213 a. tr of land whereon the said SEBASTIAN HARLEYMAN now dwells in Codorus Township adj JOHN BOYER, JOHN HOKE, PETER HOKE, FELIX MILLER, JAMES SMITH, DAVID GRIER, ANDREW SHETLER, MICHAEL HOSTLER & HENRY SUMMERAUR ... whereas the said SEBASTIAN HARLEYMAN standeth bound unto the said PETER SPRENKLE for £362 conditioned for the payment of £181 on 1 Jun 1775 ... provided that if the said SEBASTIAN HARLEYMAN shall well and truly pay unto the said PETER SPRENKLE £181 then this indenture to be void ... . Wit: DAVID GRIER, MICHL HAHN. Ackn 24 May 1773 before JOS UPDEGRAFF justice. 30 May 1782 PETER SPRENKLE discharged mortgage. Wit: ARCHD MCCLEAN recorder. (E:pg 324)

9 Apr 1773. Deed of Mortgage. NICHOLAS YOUNG of Winsor Township, York Co yeoman for better securing the payment of £250 and also 5 shillings sold to JOHN CRONE of same place yeoman a 202 a. tr of land in Winsor Township adj LAURENCE HORSHNER, CHRISTOPHER HELTZEL, BALTZER SHANEBERGER, JACOB LEVER & PETER AUTTICK, which in pursuance of a warrant dated at Phila 31 May 1762 was granted unto the said JOHN CRONE [sic] ... whereas the said NICHOLAS YOUNG by 13 obligations dated 9 May 1772 standeth bound unto the said JOHN CRONE for £500 conditioned for the payment of £250 in 12 payments of £80 on 4 May until paid ... provided that if the said NICHOLAS YOUNG shall well and truly pay unto the said JOHN CRONE £250 then this indenture to be void ... . Wit: JOHN MORRIS, [?]. Ackn 9 Apr 1773 before JOSEPH UPDEGRAEF esqr justice. (E:pg 325)

16 Jun 1773. Deed of Mortgage. JACOB BLAWSER of Manchester Township, York Co yeoman as well for indemnifying and saving harmless DANIEL PIETLER from the payment of an obligation and also 5 shillings sold to the said DANIEL PIETLER of Hellam Township, York Co yeoman a 100 a. tr of land in Manchester Township adj PHILIP JACOB KING, land late of MARTIN CRONEMILLER decd & Codorus Cr ... whereas at the special instance and request of the afsd JACOB BLAWSER the afsd DANIEL PIETLER together with the said JACOB BLAWSER stand bound unto JACOB AMENT for £200 conditioned for the payment of £100 that they will well and truly save harmless the said JACOB AMENT from all mortgages, judgments & incumbrances whatsoever which were at that time on a house and lot of ground in Freys Town which said JACOB BLAWSER did convey unto the said JACOB AMENT, also at the instance and request of the said JACOB BLAWSER the said DANIEL PIETLER together with the said JACOB BLAWSER stand bound unto JACOB KERN for £126 conditioned for the payment of £63 and unto GEORGE THRONE for £100 conditioned for the payment of £50 ... provided that if the

said JACOB BLAWSER shall well and sufficiently save harmless and keep indemnified the afsd DANIEL PIETLER from the payment of the afsd debts then this indenture to be void ... . Wit: [?], HENRY MILLER. Ackn 16 Jun 1773 before JOHN ADLUM justice. (E:pg 327)

28 Apr 1772. Deed. JOHN FRANKELBERGER of Berwick Twnship, York Co yeoman & BARBARA his wife for £76.8.9 sold to JACOB MILLER of same place cooper a 6 ¾ a. tr of land pt/o a 186 a. tr of land adj Conewago Cr, town land of Berlin, ... whereas the Proprietaries by their patent dated at Phila 26 Dec 1764 did grant unto the afsd JOHN FRANKELBERGER a 186 a. tr of land in Berwick Twnship adj Conewago Cr, JOHN LEHN, JACOB SARBACH & PETER LEHN (Patent Book A vol. 6 pg 89) ... . Wit: JOHN MICKLE, FRANCIS BEATY. Ackn 28 May 1772 before JNO POPE justice. (E:pg 329)

23 Feb 1773. Deed. JACOB MILLER of Berwick Township, York Co cooper & SOPHIA his wife for £83 sold to ROBERT JOHNSTON CHESTER of same place inn keeper a 6 ¾ a. tr of land in Berwick Township ... whereas the Proprietaries by their patent dated at Phila 26 Dec 1764 did grant unto JOHN FRANKEBERGER of Paradise Township, York Co yeoman a 186 a. tr of land in Berwick Township adj Canewago Cr, JOHN LANE, JACOB SORBOUGH & PETER LANE (Patent Book AA vol. 6 pg 87), and the said JOHN FRANKEBERGER & BARBARA his wife did grant unto the said JACOB MILLER 6 ¾ a. pt/o the 186 a. tr of land [see above] ... . Wit: FRANCIS BEATTY, ALEX MCGREW. Ackn 27 Mar 1773 before JOHN POPE esqr justice. (E:pg 331)

8 Jun 1773. Deed. ADAM GARDNER of York Town, York Co innkeeper and CATHARINE AMENT of Hellam Township, York Co widow executors of the will of GEORGE AMENT late of Hellam Township, York Co decd for £1306 sold to MARTIN HUBER of Hellam Township, York Co yeoman a 198 a. tr of land ... whereas the said GEORGE AMENT in his lifetime was possessed of a tr of land in Hellam Township but died seized thereof without having received a patent for the same, the said GEORGE AMENT made his will dated 10 Sep 1770 and did will that his tr of land whereon he then dwelt should be sold at public vendue, and did appoint his son in law ADAM GARDNER and his wife CATHARINE the executors, and the said ADAM GARDNER & CATHARINE AMENT on 13 Feb 1771 did obtain a warrant for surveying and laying out the said tr of land in order they that they might on return of survey have a patent of confirmation for the same in trust for the use of the said GEORGE AMENT decd's estate, in pursuance of said warrant a 198 a. tr of land called *Mount Airy* was surveyed and laid out adj CONRAD or GEORGE DEETS, HENRY SMITH, HENRY MESSERSMITH, Grist Cr, WILLIAM MORGAN,

NICHOLAS KIPE & land formerly of PHILIP BENTZ ... the Proprietaries by their patent dated 11 Mar 1772 did grant unto the said ADAM GARTNER & CATHARINE AMENT the 198 a. of land, in trust for uses mentioned in the afsd will of the said GEORGE AMENT (Patent Book AA vol. 12 pg 40) ... the said ADAM GARDNER & CATHARINE AMENT in pursuance of the directions of the will on 20 Apr last past exposed to public sale the afsd tr of land and sold to the said MARTIN HUBER for £1306 he being the highest bidder ... . Wit: WM LEAS, JOHN CLARK Junr. Ackn 8 Jun 1773 before JOHN ADLUM esqr justice. (E:pg 333)

11 Jun 1773. Deed. JACOB SCHNELBECKER & KATHRINA his wife of Dover Township, York Co farmer for £37.15.6 sold to FREDERICK ICHOLTZ of same place farmer a 18 a. 111 perches tr of land pt/o a 250 a. tr of land adj the tr called *Poplar* & the said FREDERICK ICHOLTZ ... whereas the Proprietaries by their patent dated at Phila 26 Mar 1756 did grant unto HENRY SCHENK a 250 a. tr of land in Dover Township (Patent Book A vol. 19 pg 173), and the said HENRY SCHENK & ANNA his wife on 3 Dec last did convey unto the said JACOB SCHNELBECKER the 250 a. tr of land (Book E pg 224) ... . Wit: THOS ARMOR, THOS ARMOR Junr. Ackn 15 Jun 1773 before JOHN ADLUM esqr justice. (E:pg 336)

12 Mar 1773. Deed. MICHAEL EBERT of Manchester Township, York Co yeoman and EVA MARGARETA his wife for £18 sold to JOSEPH WELSHANCE of York Township, York Co gun smith Lot No. 4 ... whereas the Proprietaries by their patent dated at Phila 17 Oct 1766 did grant unto JOHN HAHN and MICHAEL HAHN by the name of JOHN HAAN and MICHAEL HAAN a 233 a. tr of land in York Township called *Bingen* adj Codorus Cr, GEORGE STEVENSON, NICHOLAS DIEHL, the Great Road & land formerly MAUL's but now JOHN HAYS (Patent Book AA vol. 8 pg 45), and the said JOHN HAHN on 4 Nov 1766 did sell unto his brother the said MICHAEL HAHN all his right in the afsd tr of land, and MICHAEL HAHN and ELIZABETH his wife on 20 Nov 1766 did convey the tr of land unto MATTHIAS SITTLER, who together with CATHARINA his wife on 15 May 1767 did sell unto the said MICHAEL EBERT a lot of ground in York Township, Lot No. 4, pt/o the 233 a. tr of land, in breadth 65' and in length 460' bounded by HENRY WALTER, said MATTHIAS SITLER (now of GEORGE BENTZ) & JOHN HAY (Book C pg 288) ... . Wit: [?], JACOB BILLMEYER Junr. Ackn 12 Mar 1773 before JOHN ADLUM justice. (E:pg 337)

5 Jun 1773. Deed of Mortgage. PETER GASHAW of Germany Township, York Co innkeeper and BARBARA his wife for better securing the payment of £120 and also 5 shillings sold to Reverend NICHOLAS KURTZ of the Town of York, York Co (Minister of the Gospel) several lots of ground in the Town of

Petersburg, Germany Township, (Nos. 40,41,42,43,44&67) in front 66' and in length 264' bounded by King Street leading to York Town & Frederick Town, MD, purch from PETER LITTLE and URSELLA his wife on 11 Apr 1769 and 8 Jun 1772, each subject to the yearly rent of 7 shillings 6 pence unto the said PETER KLEIN [*sic*] ... whereas the said PETER GASHAW standeth bound unto the said NICHOLAS KURTZ for £240 conditioned for the payment of £120 on 5 Jun next ensuing ... provided that if the said PETER GASHAW shall well and truly pay unto the said NICHOLAS KURTZ £240 [*sic*] then this indenture to be void ... . Wit: [BROWG KINTZ?], JOHN MORRIS. Ackn 7 Jun 1773 before JOHN ADLUM justice. (E:pg 340)

9 Feb 1773. Deed of Mortgage. DAVID EVANS and THOMAS EVANS each of Dover Township, York Co yeomen for better securing the payment of £42.15.9 and also 5 shillings sold to PHILIP BENTZ of same place yeoman a 130 a. tr of land in Dover Township which in pursuance of an application No. [*blank*] from the Proprietaries unto the said DAVID EVANS was surveyed and laid out adj the heirs of JACOB OBB decd, PHILIP KAUFF, PETER BRUMBAGH, LUDWICK SPIECE & PHILIP WOOLF ... whereas the said DAVID EVANS and THOMAS EVANS standeth bound unto the said PHILIP BENTZ for £85.11.6 conditioned for the payment of £42.15.9 on 9 Feb 1775 ... provided that if the said DAVID EVANS and THOMAS EVANS shall well and truly pay unto the said PHILIP BENTZ £42.15.9 then this indenture to be void ... . Wit: JOHN MORRIS, MICHAEL HAHN. Ackn 9 Feb 1773 before JOSEPH UPDEGRAFF esqr justice. (E:pg 342)

17 Jun 1773. Deed of Mortgage. JOHN MAULSBY of Newberry Township, York Co yeoman for better securing the payment of £105 and also 5 shillings sold to PHILIP BENTZ of Dover Township, York Co a messuage and a 200 a. tr of land in Newberry Township adj JAMES FISHER, BENJAMIN ELLIOT, JAMES NAILOR & land late of JAMES SMITH, being pt/o the tr of land which the said JOHN MAULSBY lately purch from DAVID COPELAND and the same whereon the said MAULSBY now lives ... whereas the said JOHN MAULSBY standeth bound unto the said PHILIP BENTZ for £210 conditioned for the payment of £105 on 16 Jun next ... provided that if the said JOHN MAULSBY shall well and truly pay unto the said PHILIP BENTZ £105 then this indenture to be void ... . Wit: SARAH MILLER, HENRY MILLER. Ackn 17 Jun 1773 before JOHN ADLUM justice. 6 Feb 1775 PHILIP BENTZ discharged mortgage. Wit: SAML JOHNSTON recorder. (E:pg 343)

24 Jun 1773. Deed. DAVID STEWTHEBAKER of Paradise Township, York Co joiner for £30 sold to MELCHAR WEAVER of Reading Township, York Co weaver an undivided pt/o a tr of land in Berwick & Paradise Townships adj JOHN LANE, JACOB SORBAUGH & SAMUEL JACOBS, which is his share

of the land as eldest son of CLEMENTS STEWTHEBAKER decd (the said CLEMENTS STEWTHEBAKER held the said tr by warrant dated in Phila in the office book and having died intestate the said DAVID STEWTHEBAKER as eldest son became possessed of the whole until the dividing of the same) ... . Wit: ABRAHAM SWIGART, ROBERT JOHNSTON CHESTER. Ackn 7 Aug 1773 before JOHN SMITH justice. (E:pg 345)

18 Aug 1773. Deed. MARTIN EICHELBERGER, FREDERICK EICHELBERGER & ELIZABETH HOLTZINGER all of York Co executors of the will of BARNET HOLTZINGER late of Baltimore Co, MD decd for £394 sold to THOMAS HARTLEY of York Town, York Co atty at law Lot No. 89 in the Town of York ... whereas the Proprietaries by their patent dated at Phila 31 Oct 1752 did grant unto the said BARNET HOLTZINGER (by the name of BERNHART HOLTZINGER of the Town of York, York Co yeoman) a lot of ground (No. 89) in the Town of York on the s side of High Street, in breadth 65' and in length 230', bounded by Lot No. 90 & Lot No. 76 (Patent Book A vol. 18 pg 100), and the said BARNET HOLTZINGER afterward died owner and seized of the afsd lot of ground having made his will and did appoint the said FREDERICK EICHELBERGER, MARTIN EICHELBERGER & ELIZABETH HOLTZINGER (his wife) executors and did direct them to sell all his houses, lots & lands in MD and PA and the money arising to be distributed as in the said will which was proved in MD and a copy recorded in Phila, PA ... . Wit: GEO EICHELBERGER, GEORGE STAKE. Ackn 18 Aug 1773 before JOHN ADLUM justice. (E:pg 347)

17 Aug 1773. Deed. MARTIN EICHELBERGER esqr of Manchester Township, York Co, FREDERICK EICHELBERGER of same place farmer and ELIZABETH HOLTZINGER of York Town, York Co widow executors of the will of BARNET HOLTZINGER decd for £241.10 sold to THOMAS HARTLEY of York Town, York Co atty at law a 11 a. tr of land and 1 a. tr of land ... whereas the Proprietaries by their patent dated at Phila 17 Oct 1766 did grant unto MICHAEL HAHN and JOHN HAHN a 233 a. tr of land in York Township (Patent Book AA vol. 8 pg ---), and the said JOHN HAHN on 4 Nov 1766 did sell unto the said MICHAEL HAHN all his right in the tr of land, and the said MICHAEL HAHN and ELIZABETH his wife on 20 Nov 1766 sold the tr of land to MATHIAS SITLER, and the said MATHIAS SITLER and CATHARINA his wife on 21 Dec 1766 sold 11 a. pt/o the tr of land to BARNET HOLTZINGER adj Codorus Cr, MOUL's land (now of JOHN HAY) & the Great Road that leads from York Town to Stevenson's Mill, and the said BARNET HOLTZINGER for £9 bought of GEORGE BENTZ a 1 a. tr of land in York Township pt/o the afsd tr (which the said GEORGE BENTZ had bought from the said MATHIAS SITLER), and the said BARNET HOLTZINGER afterward died owner and seized of the afsd trs of land having made his will and

did appoint the said FREDERICK EICHELBERGER, MARTIN
EICHELBERGER & ELIZABETH HOLTZINGER (his wife) executors and did
direct them to sell all his houses, lots & lands in MD and PA and the money
arising to be distributed as in the said will which was proved in MD and a copy
recorded in Phila, PA ... . Wit: GEO EICHELBERGER, GEORGE STAKE.
Ackn 18 Aug 1773 before JOHN ADLUM justice. (E:pg 349)

18 Aug 1773. Deed. THOMAS HARTLEY of York Town, York Co atty at law
for £541.10 sold to ELIZABETH HOLTZINGER of same place widow a 11 a. tr
of land and 1 a. tr of land [*same as above*] ... . Wit: GEORGE STAKE, GEO
EICHELBERGER. Ackn 18 Aug 1773 before MARTIN EYCHELBERGER
justice. (E:pg 352)

18 Aug 1773. Deed of Release. GEORGE BENTZ of York Township, York Co
yeoman for 5 shillings released unto ELIZABETH HOLTZINGER of York
Town, York Co widow a 1 a. tr of land [*same as above*] ... whereas the said
GEORGE BENTZ some time ago in the lifetime of BARNET HOLTZINGER
did sell unto the said BARNET HOLTZINGER for £9 (which the said GEORGE
did receive) a 1 a. piece of land in York Township adj the road leading from
York Town to Stephensons Mill, Codorus Cr & other land of the said BARNET
HOLTZINGER ... . Wit: GEO EICHELBERGER, THOS HARTLEY. Ackn
18 Aug 1773 before MARTIN EYCHELBERGER justice. (E:pg 355)

10 Aug 1773. Deed of Mortgage. HENRY SHAFFER of the Town of Hanover,
York Co yeoman and ELIZABETH his wife for better securing the payment of
£127.10 and also 5 shillings sold to CASPER REINICKER of same place
innholder Lot No. 42 in the Town of Hanover, in breadth 57'6" and in length
220', bounded by York Street & Lot No. 109, being pt/o a larger tr of land called
Digges' Choice which RICHARD MCCALISTER esqr holds in right of JOHN
DIGGES decd who on 7 Sep 1763 did grant the lott of ground unto ANDREW
FREDERICK of York Co yeoman, who on the day before this date did convey
the lott of ground unto the said HENRY SHAFFER ... whereas the said HENRY
SHAFFER stands bound unto the said CASPER REINICKER for £255
conditioned for the payment of £127.10 on 1 May next ensuing ... provided that
if the said HENRY SHAFFER shall well and truly pay unto the said CASPER
REINICKER £127.10 then this indenture to be void ... . Wit: JOS BOUDE,
CHARLES WILDBAHNE. Ackn 15 Sep 1773 before RD MCALISTER
justice. 30 Apr 1784 CASPER REINECKER discharged mortgage. Wit:
ARCHD MCCLEAN recorder. (E:pg 357)

17 May 1773. Deed of Mortgage. JOHN PARK of Hellam Township, York Co
yeoman for better securing the payment of £120 and also 5 shillings sold to
SAMUEL PARK of Dunigall Township, Lancaster Co yeoman a 224 a. tr of

land in Hellam Township adj VALENTINE HIGHER & Stony Hill, which was granted unto the said JOHN PARK by ROBERT SMITH ... whereas the said JOHN PARK standeth bound unto the said SAMUEL PARK for £240 conditioned for the payment of £120 on 1 Nov next ensuing ... provided that if the said JOHN PARK shall well and truly pay unto the said SAMUEL PARK £120 then this indenture to be void ... . Wit: SAMUEL THOMPSON, ISABELA PARK. Ackn 31 May 1773 before JOHN ADLUM justice. (E:pg 359)

20 Sep 1773. Deed of Mortgage. PETER BRANDON of Manheim Township, York Co yeoman and MARGARET his wife for better securing the payment of £66 and also 5 shillings sold to JACOB SHERMAN of same place yeoman a 200 a. tr of land in Manheim Township adj JACOB BOWMAN, ADAM POTTENFIELD & others, which GEORGE EICHELBERGER esqr late sheriff of York Co on 6 Sep 1771 did convey unto the said JACOB SHERMAN, who did convey the tr of land unto the said PETER BRANDON ... whereas the said PETER BRANDON standeth bound unto the said JACOB SHERMAN for £132 conditioned for the payment of £66 on or before 20 Jul next ensuing ... provided that if the said PETER BRANDON shall well and truly pay unto the said JACOB SHERMAN £66 then this indenture to be void ... . Wit: JOS BOUDE, HENRY SIMUND. Ackn 20 Sep 1773 before RD MCALISTER justice. (E:pg 361)

3 Apr 1773. Deed of Mortgage. MARTIN LONG and FREDRICK LONG both of Manheim Township, York Co yeomen for better securing the payment of £107.6 and also 5 shillings sold to JACOB SHEARMAN of same place yeoman a 200 a. tr of land in Manheim Township adj PETER DICKS, ADAM FORNEY, Plumb Cr & Little Canawaga, and two black mares, one back mare colt, three cows, three heifers ... whereas the said MARTIN & FREDRICK LONG standeth bound unto the said JACOB SHEARMAN for £214.12 conditioned for the payment of £107.6 on or before 3 Apr next ensuing ... provided that if the said MARTIN & FREDRICK LONG well and truly pay unto the said JACOB SHEARMAN £107.6 then this indenture to be void ... . Wit: HENRY SIMUND, [?]. Ackn 3 Apr 1773 before RICHARD MCCALISTER esqr justice. 24 Feb 1803 JACOB SHERMAN discharged mortgage. Wit: J. BARNITZ recorder. (E:pg 362)

2 May 1771. Deed. GEORGE EICHELBERGER esqr high sheriff of York Co for £400 sold to NICHOLAS BEDINGER a 200 a. tr of land ... whereas JACOB OYSTER in the Court of Common Pleas recovered against ABRAHAM HOUSEWORTH late of York Co yeoman damages of £499.8.6 which he sustained by reason of not performing certain promises and assumptions made to the said JACOB OYSTER by the said ABRAHAM HOUSEWORTH ... the

sheriff seized in execution a tr of land in Berwick Township adj PHILIP
SCHNELL, FREDERICK WOLFF, JOHN LARIMORE & JOST NOLL, and on
26 Dec last past exposed to sale by public vendue and the same sold to
NICHOLAS BEDINGER of Berwick Township, York Co innkeeper for £400 he
being the highest bidder ... . Wit: ANDREAS BILLMEYER, JACOB
BILLMEYER Junr. Ackn 13 Aug 1771. SAML JOHNSTON prothy. (E:pg
364)

27 Nov 1772. Deed. ROBERT DONALD (DONNALD) (DONNEL) of Faun
Township, York Co yeoman for £1050 sold to JOHN SAMPLE of same place
yeoman a 492 a. 111 perches tr of land in Faun Township adj THOMAS
BUCHANNON, THOMAS STEEL, JAMES EDGAR & JAMES
BUCHANNON and a 76 ½ a. tr of land adj afsd tr, THOMAS BUCHANNON
& DANIEL KENLEY ... whereas DANIEL MCCONNEL on 22 Jun 1762 did
convey unto the said ROBERT DONALD a tr of land in Faun Township
(formerly in Lancaster Co) on the brs of Indian Rock Run held by DANIEL
MCCONNEL by two Proprietary warrants dated 16 Oct 1741 and one dated 4
Jan 1749 ... . Wit: WILLIAM ROWAN, SAMUEL MORRISON, ISAAC
SANDERS. Ackn 6 Oct 1773 before JOHN ADLUM justice. (E:pg 366)

17 Jun 1772. Deed. JACOB SCHWARTZ of York Town, York Co labourer for
£63 sold to PETER SCHWARTZ of same place clock maker Lot No. 14 in York
Town ... whereas JOST FRYMILLER on 15 Dec 1752 entered his name on the
plan of York Town for a lot of ground, No. 14, to beholden of the Proprietaries
upon certain conditions which the said JOST FRYMILLER hath not complied
with, and by consent there was laid out on 23 Jun 1750 unto JACOB
SCHWARTZ the afsd Lot No. 14 which expressed certain conditions relating to
said lot under the hand of GEORGE STEVENSON esqr, which lot is bounded
by Queen Street, Lot No. 13 & Lot No. 15, in front 65' and in length 230' ... .
Wit: JACOB [RNUN?], GEO LEWIS LESLER. Ackn 22 Jun 1772 before
MARTIN EICHELBERGER justice. (E:pg 369)

9 Oct 1773. Deed of Mortgage. PETER BRANDON of Manheim Township,
York Co yeoman and MARGARET his wife for better securing the payment of
£117.1.2 and also 5 shillings sold to GEORGE SEIVERT of the Town of
Hanover, York Co merchant a 270 a. 101 perches tr of land ... whereas by order
of survey No. 4945 dated 5 Apr 1768 there was surveyed unto JAMES HALL of
York Co yeoman a 270 a. 101 perches tr of land in Manheim Township adj the
road leading from Hanover Town towards Baltimore, PHILIP POTTERFIELDT,
ADAM POTTERFIELDT, JACOB BOWMAN & HENRY DEWALT ...
whereas GEORGE EICHELBERGER esqr late high sheriff of York Co on 26
Sep 1771 for the payment and satisfaction of the debts of the said JAMES
HALL exposed to sale by public vendue the afsd tr of land and sold the same

unto JACOB SHERMAN of York Co yeoman, and the said JACOB SHERMAN did sell the afsd tr of land unto the said PETER BRANDON, and the said PETER BRANDON stands bound unto the said GEORGE SEIVERT for £234.2.4 conditioned for the payment of £117.1.2 on or before 9 Oct 1774 ... provided that if the said PETER BRANDON shall well and truly pay unto the said GEORGE SEIVERT £117.1.2 then this indenture to be void ... . Wit: JOS BOUDE, CONRAD FOX. Ackn 9 Oct 1773 before HENRY SLAGLE justice. (E:pg 370)

2 Jul 1773. Deed of Mortgage. NICHOLAS SHADON of Manahan Township, York Co yeoman for better securing the payment of £30 and also 5 shillings sold to HENRY LOHMAN of Warrington Township, York Co yeoman a 50 a. tr of land in Manahan Township pt/o a greater tr of land adj LEWIS WILLIAMS & DITRICK KEISER ... whereas the said NICHOLAS SHADON standeth bound unto the said HENRY LOHMAN for £60 conditioned for the payment of £30 on 2 Jul 1777 ... provided that if the said NICHOLAS SHADON shall well and truly pay unto the said HENRY LOHMAN £30 then this indenture to be void ... . Wit: [?], BENJ COBLE. Ackn 2 Jul 1773 before JOHN SMITH justice. (E:pg 374)

9 Feb 1773. Deed of Mortgage. JAMES PATTERSON of Chanceford Township, York Co yeoman for £58.11.9 sold to JOHN JORDON of same place a 116 a. tr of land in Chanceford Township adj THOMAS SCOT & MOSES WOLLOE, which was granted to SAMUEL REED by warrant dated at Phila 14 Jun 1762 ... provided that if the said JAMES PATTERSON shall well and truly pay unto the said JOHN JORDON £58.11.9 on or before 1 May 1775 then this indenture to be void ... . Wit: JOHN MCDOWEL, MARGARET MCDOWELL. Ackn 3 Jun 1773 before JOHN ADLUM justice. (E:pg 375)

16 Oct 1773. Deed of Mortgage. JOHN MEYER of Codorus Township, York Co yeoman for better securing the payment of £125 and also 5 shillings sold to HENRY WOLFF executor of the will of JOHN WOLFF late of York Co yeoman decd a 226 a. tr of land called *Cleared Valley* in Codorus and Manheim Townships adj said MOYER's other land, HENRY DANNER & JACOB EVERSOLE, as by a patent granted to the said JOHN MEYER (Patent Book AA vol. 13 pg 580 in Phila) ... whereas the said JOHN MEYER standeth bound unto the said HENRY WOLFF for £250 conditioned for the payment of £125 on 16 Oct next ... provided that if the said JOHN MEYER shall well and truly pay unto the said HENRY WOLFF £125 then this indenture to be void ... . Wit: THOS HARTLEY, JNO CLARK Junr. Ackn 16 Oct 1773 before SAMUEL JOHNSTON esqr justice. 9 May 1785 HENRY WOLFF mortgage discharged. Wit: ARCHD MCCLEAN recorder. (E:pg 377)

16 Aug 1763. Deed. EDWARD RYAN (RYANY) now of Hidelberge Township, York Co yeoman for £300 sold to PATRICK MCSHERY of Mountpleasant Township, York Co an improvement and 300 a. tr of land in Mountpleasant Township adj ANDREW HARRIER, HENRY GRIFFE & LUDWICK SCHRIVER ... . Wit: PETER YOUNG, DAVID YOUNG. Proved 16 Oct 1773 by PETER YOUNG before HENRY SLAGLE justice. (E:pg 379)

11 Jun 1766. Deed. JAMES WELCH of Manchester Township, York Co esqr and MARGARET his wife for £245 sold to PHILIP ETTINGER and ANTHONY RODE of York Co yeomen a tr of land in Manchester Township adj the land formerly of JOHN CONNOLLY, AARON BROOK, land formerly belonging to JAMES MORROW & JACOB HAGER ... . Wit: MARTIN EYCHELBERGER, JOSEPH ROSE. Ackn 11 Jun 1766 before MARTIN EYCHELBERGER justice. (E:pg 381)

5 Nov 1773. Deed. MARTIN EBERT of Manchester Township, York Co yeoman and EVA BARBARA his wife for £1500 sold to MICHAEL EBERT of same place yeoman a 331 a. tr of land ... whereas the Proprietaries by their patent dated 29 Sep 1760 did grant unto the said MARTIN EBERT a 331 a. tr of land in Manchester Township adj Codorus Cr, ISAAC STONER & MICHAEL EBERT (Patent Book AA vol. 2 pg 53 in Phila) ... . Wit: [?], HENRY MILLER. Ackn 5 Nov 1773 before MARTIN EICHELBERGER justice. (E:pg 383)

7 Nov 1760. Deed. ARCHIBALD MCCALISTER of Cumberland Co, PA and JANE his wife for £147 sold to ISAAC EVERITT of Frederick Co, MD yeoman a 157 a. tr of land pt/o a 433 a. tr of land on Burmudian Cr in Huntington Township adj JACOB BENTZ & WILLIAM COX ... whereas the Proprietaries by their patent dated 9 Jul 1743 did grant unto WILLIAM LOGAN a 433 a. tr of land on Burmudian Cr formerly in Lancaster Co but now in York Co adj BRICE BLAIR (Patent Book A vol. 11 pg 160), and the said WILLIAM LOGAN on 15 Jul 1743 did sell the tr of land unto RICHARD PETERS of the City of Phila esqr (Book B pg 11 in Lancaster), and the said RICHARD PETERS on 29 Mar 1749 did sell the tr of land unto the afsd ARCHIBALD MCALISTER ... . Wit: HENRY STEVENSON, JOHN BOYD. Ackn 7 Nov 1760 before JOHN ADLUM justice. (E:pg 385)

1 Aug 1773. Bill of Sale. WILLIAM FLYNN of Monaghan Township, York Co for £70 sold to ELIZABETH FLYNN my dau 1 grey horse, 1 bay mare, 1 young cow, 1 yellow & white cow, 1 brindled heifer, 1 flecked heifer, 1 red & white heifer, 13 sheep, 14 hogs, 2 small butts of unthreshed wheat, a parcel of flax unbroken, about 200 bushels of potatoes, about 50 bushels of turneps, about

60 bushels of corn in the ears, 1 pot, 1 grid iron, 1 chest, 2 beds & bedcloaths & about 5 a. of rye in the ground ... . Wit: JAMES COULTER, CHARLES LOGAN. Ackn 15 Nov 1773 before WILLIAM RANKIN justice. (E:pg 388)

8 Jun 1773. Deed. JOHN HILL of Chanceford Township, York Co for £240 sold to JOHN REED of same place a 123 a. tr of land in Chanceford Township pt/o a greater tr of land originally surveyed and laid out for WILLIAM ANDERSON (General Surveyors Office Phila) adj ROGER WILLIAMS, JOHN MCDOWEL & GERRARD BRANNER ... . Wit: CUNINGHAM SEMPLE, WILLIAM CURVEY. Ackn 8 Jun 1773 before CUNINGHAM SEMPLE justice. (E:pg 389)

15 Nov 1773. Deed of Mortgage. JACOB MINICH of Manheim Township, York Co yeoman for better securing the payment of £47.7.2 and also 5 shillings sold to MICHAEL BEALER of York Co yeoman two trs of land in Manheim Township, a 127 a. tr of land adj HENRY HEARING, CHRISTOPHER SNIDER, TOBIAS STYER & LODWICK SOLOMON MILLER, which was surveyed to GEORGE HATTRUP (Application No. 5541) and a 50 a. tr of land adj TOBIAS STYER & others, which was surveyed to the said JACOB MINICH by warrant dated 20 Mar 1773 ... whereas the said JACOB MINICH stands bound unto the said MICHAEL BEALER for £95.14.4 conditioned for the payment of £47.7.2 on or before 15 Nov 1775 ... provided that if the said JACOB MINICH shall well and truly pay unto the said MICHAEL BEALER £47.7.2 then this indenture to be void ... . Wit: JOS BOUDE, [?]. Ackn 15 Nov 1773 before RD MCALISTER justice. 1 Jun 1775 MICHAEL BEALER discharged mortgage. Wit: SAML JOHNSTON recorder. (E:pg 391)

26 Jul 1773. Deed of Mortgage. LAWRENCE CRONE of Paradise Township, York Co yeoman for better securing the payment of £50 and also 5 shillings sold to GEORGE ODERMAN of same place yeoman a 113 a. tr of land in Paradise Township adj JOHN HERSHEY, TOBIAS HELFEL & others, whereon the said LAWRENCE CRONE now dwells ... whereas the said LAWRENCE CRONE standeth bound unto the said GEORGE ODERMAN for £100 conditioned for the payment of £50 on 1 Jan next ... provided that if the said LAWRENCE CRONE shall well and truly pay unto the said GEORGE ODERMAN £50 then this indenture to be void ... . Wit: [?], HENRY MILLER. Ackn 27 Jul 1773 before JOHN ADLUM justice. (E:pg 393)

16 Aug 1773. Quit Claim. JOHN SMYSER of Dover Township, York Co one of the sons of the within named GEORGE SMYSER the testator decd for £100.6.8 quit claim unto JOHN MYER all my right in a tr of land ... . Wit: MICHL SWOOPE, JACOB BILLMEYER Junr. Ackn 16 Aug 1773 before MARTIN EICHELBERGER justice. (E:pg 395)

9 Mar 1773. Deed. THOMAS ARMOR of York Town, York Co surveyor for
£20 sold to JOHN MORRISON of Chanceford Township, York Co farmer a 50
a. tr of land ... whereas the Proprietaries by their warrant dated 1 Apr 1751 did
grant unto JAMES MORRISON of Chanceford Township 50 a. of land
including his improvement in said town, and the said JAMES MORRISON on 2
Oct 1761 did sell unto the said THOMAS ARMOR the 50 a. tr of land (Book D
pg 468) ... . Wit: WM MORRISON Junr, THOS ARMOR Junr. Ackn 9 Mar
1773 before JOHN ADLUM esqr justice. (E:pg 397)

3 Jun 1773. Deed. JOHN MORRISON of Chanceford Township, York Co
executor of JAMES DICKSON late of same place decd for £180 sold to
ROBERT LEMON of same place a 141 ½ a. tr of land adj land formerly of
ALEXANDER MCCANLESS ... whereas JAMES DICKSON dyed seized in a
tr of land in Chanceford Township which he held in pursuance of a warrant
dated 24 Aug 1744, and the said JAMES DICKSON by his will dated 12 Feb
1768 did ordain that the said tr of land should be sold by his executor ... . Wit:
JOHN SEMPLE, JOHN MACKMULLON. Ackn 3 Aug 1773 before
CUNNINGHAM SEMPLE justice. (E:pg 398)

10 Dec 1773. Deed. GEORGE SMITH of Hellam Township, York Co yeoman
for £325 sold to GEORGE DEETS of same place, HENRY LIEBHART of
Windsor Township, York Co yeoman & JACOB HERBAUGH of Frederick Co,
MD yeoman a 168 a. tr of land being the same tr of land HENRY SMITH decd
devised to his son the said GEORGE SMITH ... whereas in pursuance of a grant
from the Proprietaries dated 30 Oct 1736 there was surveyed and laid out unto
HENRY SMITH a 168 a. tr of land on the w side of Susquehannah formerly in
Lancaster Co but now in Hellam Township, York Co adj Widow
MESSERSMITH, GEORGE AMENT, CONRAD DEETS, JOHN DAVIS,
JOHN FURREY & LEONARD COMFORT, and the said HENRY SMITH
being so seized died having first made his will dated 25 Jun 1771 (to wit) "after
my wife's death I give and bequeath unto my son GEORGE SMITH the
plantation whereon I now live in consideration of £800 whereof my son
GEORGE shall have £50 and pay immediately after my wife's death £200 which
shall be divided in seven parts, between my son GEORGE, my dau ROSENA
w/o LORENTZ CRONE, my dau CATHARINA w/o ANTHONY OLER, my
dau ELIZABETH w/o FRANTZ BISHOF, my dau BARBARA w/o HENRY
LIPHARD, my dau MARGRET w/o JACOB HERBAUGH & my dau
MAGDALENA w/o GEORGE DEATS ... and MARGARET SMITH widow of
the said HENRY SMITH decd since his death also died ... . Wit: THOS
HARTLEY, HENRY MILLER. Ackn 10 Dec 1773 before JOS UPDEGRAFF
justice. (E:pg 401)

2 Sep 1773. Deed of Mortgage. WILLIAM UPDEGRAFF of the Town of York, York Co yeoman & SARAH his wife for better securing the payment of £450 and also 5 shillings sold to ABRAHAM UPDEGRAFF of same place yeoman a 102 a. tr of land in Newberry & Manchester Townships ... whereas the said WILLIAM UPDEGRAFF standeth bound unto the said ABRAHAM UPDEGRAFF for £900 conditioned for the payment of £450 to be paid yearly in payments before 10 Aug 1783 ... provided that if the said WILLIAM UPDEGRAFF shall well and truly pay unto the said ABRAHAM UPDEGRAFF £450 then this indenture to be void ... . Wit: WM MATTHEWS, JOHN MORRIS. Ackn 2 Sep 1773 before JOS UPDEGRAFF justice. (E:pg 405)

11 Sep 1773. Deed. ARTHER GREER (GRIER) of York Town, York Co yeoman for £8 sold to GEORGE IRWIN of same place merchant a 100 a. tr of land ... whereas in pursuance of a warrant dated 5 Aug 1773 there was surveyed to the said ARTHER GREER 100 a. of land adj the West Br of Susquehannah & Black Pole Cr in Northumberland Co ... . Wit: DAVID GRIER, JOHN RUTHERFORD. Ackn 15 Dec 1773 before SAMUEL JOHNSTON esqr justice. (E:pg 407)

4 Dec 1773. Deed of Mortgage. ADAM HOFFMAN of York Town, York Co yeoman for better securing the payment of £600 and also 5 shillings sold to CHRISTINA HOFFMAN of same place widow and relict of HENRY HOFFMAN decd two trs of land, a 156 a. 29 perches tr of land in Windsor Township adj GEORGE WAMBACH, JACOB SHANE, PETER REISINGER & PHILIP MILLHOFF and a 28 a. 109 perches tr of land adj GEORGE WAMBACH, PETER WAMBACH, PHILLIP MILLHOFF & the afsd tr of land ... whereas ADAM HOFFMAN standeth bound unto the said CHRISTINA HOFFMAN for £1200 conditioned for the payment of £600 payable on 2 May 1775 ... provided that if the said ADAM HOFFMAN shall well and truly pay unto the said CHRISTINA HOFFMAN £600 then this indenture to be void ... . Wit: [?], JOHN MORRIS. Ackn 24 Dec 1773 before SAMUEL JOHNSTON esqr justice. 8 May 1775 CHRISTINA HOFFMAN discharged mortgage. Wit: SAML JOHNSTON recorder. (E:pg 409)

15 Dec 1773. Deed of Mortgage. JACOB COCHONOVER of Manheim Township, York Co miller for £30.18 sold to HENRY FITE of York Co 1 good wagon, 4 horses, 6 cows, 3 sheep, 1 plough and irons, 1 harrow & 12 hogs ... provided that if the said JACOB COCHONOVER shall well and truly pay unto the said HENRY FITE £30.18 then this bill of sale to be void ... . Wit: JOS BOUDE, [?]. Ackn 15 Dec 1773 before RD MCALISTER justice. (E:pg 411)

27 Oct 1767. Deed. JACOB SPITLER Senr of York Township, York Co yeoman for £50 sold to JACOB SPITLER Junr of same place yeoman a 100 a. tr

of land ... whereas the Proprietaries by their warrant dated at Phila 24 Sep 1762 did grant unto the said JACOB SPITLER Senr by the name of HANS SPITTLE 100 a. of land in Shrewsburry Township adj CHRISTIAN MEYER, ULRICK LIEB & his other land ... . Wit: JOHN WAGNER, FRANCIS KOONS. Ackn 27 Oct 1767 before MICHAEL SWOOPE justice. (E:pg 413)

27 Oct 1767. Deed. JACOB SPITLER Senr of York Township, York Co yeoman for £50 sold to JACOB SPITLER Junr of same place yeoman a 50 a. tr of land in York Township adj JOHN MEYER, ULRICK LIEB & CHRISTIAN MEYER ... whereas PHILIP HEBEISEN by the name of PHILIP HEIRSE lodged 50 shillings in the hands of EDMUND PHYSICK by the hands of GEORGE STEVENSON in pt/o 50 a. of land adj JOHN MEYER in York Township for the Proprietaries by a receipt under the hand of the said EDMUND PHYSICK dated at Phila 11 Jun 1762, and the said PHILIP HEBEISEN on 25 May 1767 did sell the 50 a. unto the afsd JACOB SPITLER Senr ... . Wit: JOHN WAGNER, FRANCIS KOONS. 37 Oct 1767 before MICHAEL SWOOPE justice. (E:pg 415)

13 Sep 1773. Deed of Mortgage. ANDREAS WALTER of Codorus Township, York Co yeoman for better securing the payment of £42.1 and also 5 shillings sold to JACOB BIGLER of Dover Township, York Co yeoman a lot of ground in Dover Town, Dover Township, No. 29, in breadth 65' and in length 297', adj York Street, JACOB YONER, Lot No. 30 & Lot No. 28 (other land of JACOB YONER) ... whereas the said ANDREAS WALTER standeth bound unto the said JACOB BIGLER for £84.2 conditioned for the payment of £42.1 on 13 Sep next ensuing ... provided that if the said ANDREAS WALTER shall well and truly pay unto the said JACOB BIGLER £42.1 then this indenture to be void ... . Wit: JOHN MORRIS, MATHIAS HENRICH. Ackn 13 Sep 1773 before JOSEPH UPDEGRAFF esqr justice. (E:pg 418)

22 Dec 1773. Deed of Mortgage. BALTZER ZUMWALT of York Township, York Co yeoman for better securing the payment of £115 and also 5 shillings sold to JACOB AMENT of the Town of Hanover, York Co saddler a lot of ground in breath 130' and in depth 460' in York Township bounded by the Great Road leading from York Town to Wrights Ferry, MATHIAS SITLER & HENRY SPICKARD ... whereas the said BALTZER ZUMWALT standeth bound unto the said JACOB AMENT for £230 conditioned for the payment of £115 in payments before 22 Dec 1776 ... provided that if the said BALTZER ZUMWALT shall well and truly pay unto the said JACOB AMENT £115 then this indenture to be void ... . Wit: FRANCIS FORDINE, DAVID GRIER. Ackn 22 Dec 1773 before JOSEPH UPDEGRAFF esqr justice. (E:pg 420)

16 Aug 1773. Deed. SAMUEL EDIE esqr high sheriff of York Co for £171 sold to GEORGE ERNSTMEYER Lot No. 160 in the Town of York ... whereas JOHN ROTHROCK lately in the Court of Common Pleas recovered against CHRISTIAN WAMPLER a debt of £83.13.8 and 51 shillings 6 pence damages ... the sheriff seized in execution as the estate of the said CHRISTIAN WAMPLER a lott of ground with a stone dwelling house on the e side of George Street and n side of Phila Street in the Town of York, No. 160, in breath 65' and in length 230' and exposed to public vendue and the same sold unto GEORGE ERNSTMEYER for £171 he being the highest bidder ... . Wit: THOS HARTLEY, HENRY MILLER. Ackn 2 Dec 1773. SAML JOHNSTON proth. (E:pg 423)

22 Dec 1773. Deed. JAMES AMENT of the Town of Hanover, York Co saddler and ANNA MARIA his wife for £115 sold to BALTZER ZUMWALT of York Township, York Co innholder a lot of ground in York Township ... whereas the Proprietaries by their patent dated 17 Oct 1766 did grant unto JOHN HAHN & MICHAEL HAHN a 230 a. tr of land in York Township called *Bingen* (Patent Book AA vol. 8 pg 45), and the said JOHN HAHN on 4 Nov 1766 did sell unto the said MICHAEL HAHN his right in the land, and the said MICHAEL HAHN and ELIZABETH his wife on 20 Nov 1766 did sell unto MATTHIAS SITTLER the afsd tr of land, and the said MATHIAS SITLER and CATHARINA his wife on 10 May 1769 did sell to JOSEPH SMITH a lot of ground in York Township on the n side of the Great Road leading from York Town to Rights Ferry bounded by other lands of the said MATHIAS SITLER & HENRY SPICKART, in breadth 130' and in depth 460' it being pt/o the 230 a. tr of land, and the said JOSEPH SMITH and BARBARA his wife did sell unto JACOB BLASSER the afsd lot of ground 28 Dec 1772, and the said JACOB BLASSER and BARBARA his wife on 10 Jun 1773 did sell unto the afsd JACOB AMENT the afsd lot of ground ... . Wit: FRANCIS JORDENE, DAVID GRIER. Ackn 22 Dec 1773 before JOSEPH UPDEGRAFF esqr justice. (E:pg 426)

18 Feb 1770. Deed. ISRAEL MORRIS of the City of Phila, PA yeoman for £211.5 sold to ROBERT JONES of Manchester Township, York Co farmer a 211 ¼ a. tr of land ... whereas the Proprietaries by their patent dated at Phila 21 Aug 1772 did grant unto the said ISRAEL MORRIS a 211 ¼ a. tr of land called *Cedar Spring* in Manchester Township adj Big Codorus Cr, GEORGE STEVENSON & WILLIAM WILLIS (Patent Book AA vol. 13 pg 201) ... . Wit: GEO ROSS, WM MATTHEWS. Ackn 18 Feb 1770 before THOS WILLING justice. (E:pg 429)

7 Apr 1773. Deed. PETER LITTLE of Frederick Co, PA [*sic*] yeoman for £80 sold to LODWICK LITTLE of York Co pt/o a 19 a. 19 perches tr of land in

Germany Township adj JOSEPH FLOAT, ABRAHAM KING & JOHN KNOFF ... . Wit: GEO CLARK, DANIEL HECK. Proved by DANIEL HECK 12 Oct 1773 before RD MCALISTER justice. (E:pg 433)

10 Oct 1771. Articles of Agreement. CONRAD HOLTZBAUM of York Township, York Co yeoman for £14.4 sold to JOHN STEWART of same place yeoman pt/o a messuage & 1 ½ perch in breadth piece of land in York Township e side of Little Codorus Cr adj GEORGE STEVENSON & said JOHN STEWART, for said JOHN STEWART to make a water course to convey the water of the said cr to the land of the said JOHN STEWART with liberty of making a dam or pond across said cr ... to the true performance of the agreements the parties bind themselves either to the other in the penal sum of £100 ... . Wit: DANL EVANS, DAVID GRIER. Ackn 12 Jan 1774 before SAML JOHNSTON justice. (E:pg 434)

29 Dec 1770. Deed. JOHN PETER REISINGER of Windsor Township, York Co yeoman and EVE his wife for £6 sold to CHRISTIAN SLIMMER of same place yeoman a 4 a. 12 perches tr of land ... whereas the Proprietaries by their patent dated at Phila 20 Feb 1767 did grant unto the said JOHN PETER REISINGER a 4 a. 12 perches tr of land in Windsor Township called *Reissinger's Pleasure* adj *Smith's Choice*, *Buford* MD patent, CHRISTIAN SLIMMER & *Bond Mannor* (Patent Book AA vol. 8 pg 227) ... . Wit: [?], WM LEAS. Ackn 29 Dec 1770 before MICHAEL SWOOPE justice. (E:pg 436)

1 May 1773. Deed of Mortgage. JAMES HANCOCK of Newberry Township, York Co yeoman and ELIZABETH his wife for better securing the payment of £62 and also 5 shillings sold to GEORGE FISHER of Lower Paxtang Township, Lancaster Co yeoman a 100 a. tr of land in Newberry Township adj WILLIAM WILSON, JAMES EWING, NEAL DEVENNY, WILLIAM GARRETSON, PETER HOFF & JOSEPH TAYLOR, which was surveyed to THOMAS PUGH in pursuance of his application dated 19 Jan 1757, who on 19 Aug 1767 granted the same to the said JAMES HANCOCK ... whereas the said JAMES HANCOCK standeth bound unto the said GEORGE FISHER for £62 conditioned for the payment of £31 on 1 May 1774 ... provided that if the said JAMES HANCOCK shall well and truly pay unto the said GEORGE FISHER £31 then this indenture to be void ... . Wit: WM RANKIN, JOHN PUGH. Ackn 8 May 1773 before WM RANKIN esqr justice. (E:pg 440)

24 Dec 1773. Deed of Mortgage. MICHAEL FULWILLER of Warrington Township, York Co potter for better securing the payment of £100 and also 5 shillings sold to GEORGE MILEY and HENRY LOHMAN both of township afsd yeomen a 50 ¾ a. tr of land in Warrington Township adj JOHN FULWILLER, JACOB HOLL & ISAAC HOLL ... whereas MICHAEL

FULWILLER standeth bound unto the said GEORGE MILEY and HENRY LOHMAN for £200 conditioned for the payment of £100 on 24 Dec 17-7 ... provided that if the said MICHAEL FULWILLER shall well and truly pay unto the said GEORGE MILEY & HENRY LOHMAN £100 then this indenture to be void ... . Wit: GABRIEL SMITH, JOHN SMITH. Ackn 24 Dec 1773 before JOHN SMITH justice. 16 Nov 1783 FREDERICK REIDER executor of the will of HENRY LOHMAN decd discharged mortgage. Wit: ARCHD MCCLEAN recorder. (E:pg 442)

27 Aug 1773. Deed of Mortgage. JOHN SAMPLE (SEMPLE) of Faun Township, York Co yeoman for better securing the payment of several debts and also 5 shillings sold to CUNINGHAM SEMPLE of same place esqr a 492 a. 111 perches tr of land in said township adj THOMAS BUCKANON, THOMAS STEEL, JAMES EDGAR & JAMES BUCHANON also a 76 ½ a. tr of land adj THOMAS BUCKANON & DANIEL KINLEY, both surveys 569 a. 31 perches of land the said JOHN SAMPLE holds by deed from ROBERT DONALD dated 27 Nov 1772 ... whereas the said CUNINGHAM SEMPLE by a note and several bonds together with the said JOHN SAMPLE (as JOHN SAMPLE's proper debt) stand bound unto ROBERT DONALD of Fawn Township, York Co yeoman (dated 27 Nov 1772) conditioned for the payment of £1050 in payments before 1 Oct 1780 ... provided that if the said JOHN SAMPLE shall well and truly pay unto the said CUNINGHAM SEMPLE the several debts then this indenture to be void ... . Wit: JAMES RAMSEY, ISAAC SANDERS. Proved by JAMES RAMSEY 27 Jan 1774 before DAVID JAMESON justice. 28 Apr 1790 CUNINGHAM SAMPLE esqr discharged mortgage. (E:pg 444)

21 May 1763. Deed. WILLIAM HARRIS of East Pennsborough Township, Cumberland Co, PA yeoman and MARGARET his wife for £350 sold to JOHN HARRIS of Paxton Township, Lancaster Co yeoman a 210 a. tr of land being his share of a 420 a. tr of land ... whereas the Proprietaries by their patent dated 17 Mar 1737 did grant unto JOHN HARRIS (father of the said JOHN HARRIS & WILLIAM HARRIS) a 820 a. tr of land on the w side of Sasquehanna River then in Pennsbury Township, Lancaster Co but now in Newbury Township, York Co adj DAVID PRIEST & AARON PRICE (Patent Book A vol 1 pg 69 in Phila), and the said JOHN HARRIS (the father) died seized in the tr of land and by his will dated 22 Nov 1746 did devise to his sons JOHN and WILLIAM 420 a. pt/o his tr of 1020 a. which the afsd tr is part on the w side of River Sasquehannah in Newbury Township ... in pursuance of the will 420 a. have been surveyed and laid off to the said JOHN HARRIS and WILLIAM HARRIS adj land formerly of DAVID PRIEST but now of MICHAEL TEASE & the said river ... the said JOHN HARRIS and WILLIAM HARRIS have by consent caused partition to be made between them ... . Wit: JAMES HENDRICKS, ANN NOBLIT. Wit for MARGRAT HARRIS: WM RANKIN, AARON

WRIGHT. Ackn 21 May 1763 before ABRAHAM NOBLIT justice. Ackn by
MARGARET HARRIS 23 Sep 1773 before WM RANKIN justice. (E:pg 448)

1 Sep 1773. Deed of Release. GEORGE SHITZ of Northern Liberties of the
City of Phila, PA husbandman (being the son and residuary heir of MATTHIAS
SHITZ decd) for 5 shillings release unto MICHAEL CARLE Junr of Mannheim
Township (formerly in Lancaster Co) now York Co blacksmith a tr of land
(formerly in Lancaster Co) which by virtue of a warrant to my late father
MATHIAS SHITZ decd for 200 a. at Conewaga adj HANS ADAM FURNEY,
DERRICK YOUNGBLOOD, PETER REYSHER & NICHOLAS FURNEY,
dated 6 Oct 1738, was surveyed to my said father containing 162 a. .... Wit:
NICHOLAS FISHER, CONRAD FELTE, CHRISTIAN LEHMAN. Proved 24
Nov 1773 by NICHOLAS FISHER & CONRAD FELTE before HENRY
SLAGLE justice. (E:pg 453)

14 Sep 1773. Deed of Mortgage. EAVIN MINSHALL of Manoughan
Township, York Co for better securing the payment of £120 and also 5 shillings
sold to ISAAC LEREW of same place a 150 a. tr of land in Manoughan
Township adj ROBT ROSBROUGH, SAMUEL NELSON, DANIEL
WILLIAMS & JOHN WILLIAMS, being held by virtue of a warrant granted to
JOHN GILES 4 Apr 1751 ... whereas the said EAVIN MINSHALL stands
bound unto the said ISAAC LEREW for £240 conditioned for the payment of
£120 ... provided that if the said EAVIN MINSHALL shall well and truly pay
unto the said ISAAC LEREW £120 then this indenture to be void .... Wit:
JOSHUA WILLIAMS, [?]. Ackn 25 Sep 1773 before MATTHEW DILL
justice. 14 Mar 1786 by virtue of a letter of atty to GODFREY LENHART of
York Town from ISAAC LERUE, GODFREY LENHART discharged
mortgage. Wit: JACOB BARNITZ recorder. (E:pg 454)

8 Dec 1773. Deed of Mortgage. JOHN KAUFFMAN of Mannor Township,
Lancaster Co yeoman and BARBARA his wife for better securing the payment
of £804.14 and also 5 shillings sold to HENRY WOLFF of York Town, York
Co innkeeper executor of the will of JOHN WOLFF late of York Co yeoman
decd a 213 a. tr of land in Manchester Township adj ISRAEL PEMBERTON,
JOHN SMITH, PETER WOLF, VALENTINE GRANTZ, NICHOLAS KING &
GEORGE NEES, which was granted to the said JOHN KAUFFMAN by the said
HENRY WOLFF as executor of the said JOHN WOLFF decd this day ...
whereas the said JOHN KAUFFMAN standeth bound unto the said HENRY
WOLFF for £1604.14 conditioned for the payment of £804.14 in payments
before 1 Jul 1780 ... provided that if the said JOHN KAUFFMAN shall well and
truly pay unto the said HENRY WOLFF £804.14 then this indenture to be void
.... Wit: JNO CLARK Junr, HENRY WOLFE Junr. Ackn 8 Dec 1773 before

WM RANKIN justice. 24 Apr 1786 HENRY WOLFF discharged mortgage.
Wit: JACOB BARNITZ recorder. (E:pg 455)

2 Dec 1771. To JOHN LUKENS surveyor general: Whereas ZACHARIAS
NORDON Senr of York Co hath requested the Proprietaries would allow him to
take up 40 a. of land adj GEORGE HUBERT, NICHOLAS KLAPSADDLE &
NICHOLAS GROUSE in Mountpleasant Township, York Co (provided the land
does not lay in or interfere with our *Manor of Maske* or any other four manors or
appropriated trs) ... these are to authorize and require you to survey unto the
said ZACHARIAS NORDON at the place afsd 40 a. of land ... . [*signed*]
RICHARD PENN. To ARCHIBALD MCCLANE dep surveyor: execute this
warrant and make return of survey. Signed for JOHN LUKENS by JUDAH
LUKENS. (E:pg 458)

27 Oct 1773. Quit Claim. ZACHARIAS NORDON of Mountpleasant
Township, York Co sends greetings, whereas it appears by the books of the dep
surveyor wherein the within mentioned land doth lye, that there is not vacant
land there the same having been surveyed divers years past unto GEORGE
HUBERT by a warrant dated 10 Jun 1762. In consideration thereof I do hereby
release and quit claim the within warrant unto the Proprietaries ... . Ackn 27
Oct 1773 before RD MCALESTER justice. (E:pg 458)

2 Jan 1772. To JOHN LUKENS surveyor general: Whereas ZACHARIAS
NORDON hath requested that the Proprietaries would allow him to take up 40 a.
of land adj GEORGE HUBERT, NICHOLAS KLAPSADDLE and NICHOLAS
GROUSE in Mountpleasant Township, York Co (provided the land does not lay
in or interfere with our *Manor of Maske* or any other four manors or
appropriated trs) ... these are to authorize and require you to survey unto the
said ZACHARIAS NORDON at the place afsd 40 a. of land ... . [*signed*]
RICHARD PENN. To ARCHIBALD MCCLEAN dep surveyor: execute this
warrant and make return of survey. Signed for JOHN LUKENS by ROBERT
DILL. (E:pg 459)

31 May 1773. Deed. LEWIS BUSH of York Town, York Co yeoman for £5
sold to THOMAS ARMOR of same place surveyor a 30 a. tr of land adj
HENRY FERREE & others in Shrewsberry Township which was granted unto
me by warrant dated at Phila 24 May instant ... . Wit: DAVID MCMECHEN,
THOS ARMOR Junr. Ackn 1 Jun 1773 before WM RANKIN justice. (E:pg
460)

15 Dec 1773. Deed. LEWIS BUSH of York Town, York Co yeoman for £5.10
sold to THOMAS ARMOR of same place a 50 a. tr of land adj land surveyed for
the Meeting House in Newberry Township, which was granted unto me by

warrant dated 9 Oct last ... . Wit: JNO CLARK Junr, DAVID MCMECHEN. Ackn 26 Jan 1774 before WM RANKIN justice. (E:pg 460)

27 Jan 1774. Deed. CATHARINE LEBENSTEIN and JACOB LEBENSTEIN (executors of the will of GEORGE LEBENSTEIN late of Manchester Township, York Co yeoman decd) for £1400 sold to CASPER KNAB of same place yeoman a 193 ¾ a. tr of land ... whereas the Proprietaries by their patent dated 20 Jan 1764 did grant unto the said GEORGE LEBENSTEIN a 193 ¾ a. tr of land in Manchester Township adj Codorus Cr, CHRISTIAN BIXLER & JACOB FLETCHER, and the said GEORGE LEBENSTEIN being so seized of the tr of land afterwards died having first made his will dated 17 May 1771 part whereof, to wit, "I devise unto CATHARINA my wife my dwelling house together with all the goods, chattels and house hold furniture and husbandry whatsoever during the time as she continueth a widow under my name, if she should alter her state of living a widow and intermarry then it is my will that my plantation shall be sold by public auction granting my wife full power to vend and expose the same to raise money for several purposes in said will mentioned" and did appoint his wife CATHARINE and his son the said JACOB LEBENSTEIN executors ... and the executors did on 20 Nov last past sold the land to the said CASPER KNAB for £1400 he being the highest bidder ... . Wit: SARAH MILLER, HENRY MILLER. Ackn 27 Jan 1774 before JOSEPH UPDEGRAFF justice. (E:pg 461)

28 Jan 1774. Deed of Mortgage. CASPER KNAB of Manchester Township, York Co yeoman for better securing the payment of £1400 and also 5 shillings sold to CATHARINE LEBENSTEIN and JACOB LEBENSTEIN executors of the will of GEORGE LEBENSTEIN late of Manchester Township, York Co yeoman decd a 193 ¾ a. tr of land adj HENRY BOYER, PHILIP JACOB KING, CHRISTIAN PIXLER & others [same as above] ... whereas the said CASPER KNAB standeth bound unto the said CATHARINE LEBENSTEIN and JACOB LEBENSTEIN for £2800 conditioned for the payment of £1400 in payments before 1 Apr 1785 ... . Wit: SARAH MILLER, HENRY MILLER. Ackn 28 Jan 1774 before JOSEPH UPDEGRAFF justice. 14 Sep 1785 JACOB LEBENSTEIN surviving mortgagee discharged mortgage. Wit: ARCHD MCCLEAN recorder. (E:pg 464)

10 Feb 1774. Deed of Mortgage. HENRY ALDT of Shrewsberry Township, York Co yeoman for better securing the payment of £250 and also 5 shillings sold to WILLIAM TROREBOUGH of same place yeoman a 210 ¾ a. tr of land in Shrewsberry Township adj WILLIAM SPRINGLE, CONRAD CURTZ, WILLIAM PETERS & ADAM TROREBOUGH ... whereas the said HENRY ALDT standeth bound unto the said WILLIAM TROREBOUGH for £500 conditioned for the payment of £250 in payments before 1 Apr 1783 ... provided

that if the said HENRY ALDT shall well and truly pay unto the said WILLIAM
TROREBOUGH £250 then this indenture to be void ... . Wit: JOSEPH
GARRETSON, WM KERSEY. Ackn 20 Feb 1774 before JOSEPH
UPDEGRAFF justice. (E:pg 465)

16 Apr 1764. Deed. JACOB SHELLEY of Newbery Township, York Co
yeoman and MARY his wife for £100 sold to DANIEL SHELLEY of same
place yeoman a 97 a. tr of land pt/o a 141 a. tr of land ... whereas the
Proprietaries by their patent dated at Phila 19 Aug 1752 did grant unto
CORNELIUS LANE of York Co a 141 a. tr of land in Newbery Township on
the w side of Susquehannah River, together with an island in said river
containing 37 a. (Patent Book A vol. 16 pg 242), and CORNELIUS LANE and
ELISABETH his wife on 14 Nov 1758 did sell the afsd tr of land and island (in
the whole 178 a.) unto the said JACOB SHELLEY and DANIEL SHELLEY
(Book C vol. 3 pg 19) ... . Wit: JAMES WELCH, PETTER SHELLEY. Ackn
16 Apr 1765 before JAMES WELCH justice. (E:pg 467)

3 Oct 1769. Deed. JOSEPH WALLACE of York, York Co cordwainer for £35
sold to THOMAS ARMOR of same place surveyor a 150 a. tr of land adj
HENRY SEVRID & WILLIAM WYERMAN in Huntington Township which
was granted unto me by an application No. 5523 dated at Phila 19 Jun last ... .
Wit: JACOB STROMAN, [?]. Ackn 1 Nov 1770 before JNO POPE esqr
justice. (E:pg 470)

5 May 1773. Deed. JACOB GROVE of Manchester Township, York Co farmer
for £10 sold to THOMAS ARMOR of York Town, York Co surveyor a warrant
for 20 a. of land ... whereas the Proprietaries by their warrant dated 18 Dec 1749
did grant unto WILLIAM ROBB 20 a. of land in Chanceford Township, and the
said WILLIAM ROBB on 26 Jul 1763 did convey the 20 a. of land unto the said
JACOB GROVE, HENRY GROVE & JOHN GROVE, and the said HENRY
GROVE and MARY his wife & HANS URIE GROVE & MARY his wife on 3
Aug 1771 did release all their right to the 20 a. of land unto the said JACOB
GROVE ... . Wit: [?], THOS ARMOR Junr. Ackn 29 Oct 1773 before
WILLIAM RANKIN esqr justice. (E:pg 470)

31 Mar 1774. Deed of Mortgage. MICHAEL DAUTEL of the Town of York,
York Co tanner for better securing the payment of £200 and also 5 shillings sold
to RICHARD HOCKLEY of the City of Phila esqr a messuage and lot of ground
on the n side of High Street and w side of Cadoras Cr in the Town of York, in
breath 221' and in length 230' adj HERMAN OPDEGRAFF, which the
Proprietaries on 9 Mar instant did grant unto the said MICHAEL DAUTEL ...
whereas the said MICHAEL DAUTEL standeth bound unto the said RICHARD
HOCKLEY for £400 conditioned for the payment of £200 on 31 Mar next

ensuing ... provided that if the said MICHAEL DAUTEL shall well and truly pay unto the said RICHARD HOCKLEY £200 then this indenture to be void ... . Wit: PETER MILLER, ABRM SHOEMAKER. Ackn 1 Apr 1774 before WILLIAM ALLEN esqr chief justice. 19 Jun 1776 by virtue of a letter of atty to JAMES RANKIN from WILLIAM BRANDON HOCKLEY sole executor and devisee of RICHARD HOCKLEY decd, JAMES RANKIN discharged mortgage. Wit: SAML JOHNSTON recorder. (E:pg 472)

17 Mar 1774. Deed of Mortgage. CHRISTIAN GROVE of Newberry Township, York Co yeoman and ELIZABETH his wife for better securing the payment of £60 and also 5 shillings sold to JACOB KERN of York Township, York Co taylor a 200 a. tr of land in Newberry Township adj JACOB MYERS, PETER RODE, JAMES WELCH, ANN NOBLIT & the Susquehanna River (whereon the said CHRISTIAN GROVE now dwells) ... whereas the said CHRISTIAN GROVE standeth bound unto the said JACOB KERN for £120 conditioned for the payment of £60 on 11 Mar 1776 ... provided that if the said CHRISTIAN GROVE shall well and truly pay unto the said JACOB KERN £60 then this indenture to be void ... . Wit: JOHN GILLILAND, WM RANKIN. Ackn 17 Mar 1774 before WILLIAM RANKIN esqr justice. 1 Mar 1777 JACOB KERN discharged mortgage. Wit: SAML JOHNSTON recorder. (E:pg 473)

9 Apr 1774. Deed of Mortgage. HENRY NEASS of Schrewsberry Township, York Co yeoman for better securing the payment of £70 and also 5 shillings sold to JACOB NEASS of York Co yeoman a 100 a. tr of land in Schrewsberry Township adj JOHN FACKLER, JAMES MARSHALL, JACOB HIVELY & others, which the said HENRY NEASS purch from ADAM LUCAS and whereon he now lives ... whereas the said HENRY NEASS standeth bound unto the said JACOB NEASS for £140 conditioned for the payment of £70 in payments before 1 Apr 1776 ... provided that if the said HENRY NEASS shall well and truly pay unto the said JACOB NEASS £70 then this indenture to be void ... . Wit: SARAH MILLER, HENRY MILLER. Ackn 9 Apr 1774 before SAMUEL JOHNSTON esqr justice. 17 Oct 1774 JACOB NEASS discharged mortgage. Wit: SAML JOHNSTON recorder. (E:pg 475)

24 Mar 1772. Deed. PHILIP UNGEFEAR of York Co yeoman one of the sons and devisees of GEORGE UNGEFEAR late of Heidleberg Township, York Co yeoman decd for £230 sold to ANDREW ETZLER of same place yeoman a 64 a. tr of land ... whereas JOHN DIGGES late of MD gent decd on [blank] did convey unto the afsd GEORGE UNGEFEAR a 64 ½ a. tr of land (by a later survey found to have 64 a.) pt/o a larger tr of land called *Digges' Choice* adj land late of PETER NOPHSINGER now of BASTIAN OBATTS, land late of GEORGE SCHRYER but now of JOHN SHURP & land of PHILIP FORNEY,

and the said GEORGE UNGEFEAR being so seized departed this life having first made his will dated 7 Jan 1764 and did devise unto his son the afsd PHILIP UNGEFEAR the afsd tr of land, to wit, my son PHILIP shall have 64 a. which lies between PETER NAPHSINGER, GEORGE SCHRYER & PHILIP FORNEY for which he shall give £200 of which the said PHILIP shall keep £100 for his portion of the said land, he shall not take the land in possession until he is of age and when he is age 23 then shall give to the other heirs yearly £25 till the £100 are paid ... . Wit: GEORGE RANIKAR (RANICAR), JOS BOUDE. Ackn 24 Mar 1772 before RD MCALISTER justice. (E:pg 476)

20 Jun 1768. Quit Claim. SAMUEL MORTHLAND of Warrington Township, York Co and SUSANNA (SUSANNAH) his wife for 5 shillings quit claim unto WILLIAM MORTHLAND of same place a 90 a. tr of land ... whereas the Proprietaries by their patent dated 6 Aug 1747 did grant unto HUGH MORTHLAND a 270 a. tr of land in Warrington Township (then pt/o Lancaster Co now York Co) adj JACOB WAGNER (Patent Book A vol. 12 pg 503 in Phila), and the said HUGH MORTHLAND died seized of the 270 a. of land having first made his will dated 12 Aug 1754 and did bequeath (to wit) to my son WILLIAM MORTHLAND 1/3 pt/o my land lying upon Burmudian adj JOHN MARSH and to my two sons CHARLES & SAMUEL MORTHLAND the remainder pt/o all my lands ... in pursuance of said will a 90 a. tr of land was laid off for the said WILLIAM MORTHLAND adj GEORGE MCMULLEN ... . Wit: JOHN THOMAS, CHRISTIAN NEWCOMER. Ackn 20 Jun 1768 before JOHN SMITH justice. (E:pg 478)

6 Apr 1774. Deed. CHRISTOPHER KREISER of York Township, York Co farmer and CHRISTINA his wife for £1300 sold to MICHAEL KURTZ of Tolphenkacken Township, Berks Co, PA yeoman a 316 a. 28 perches tr of land ... whereas the Proprietaries by their patent dated at Phila 11 Jun 1767 did grant unto ISRAEL MORRIS a 316 a. 28 perches tr of land in York Township called *Stone Pulput* adj Codorus Cr, CASPER KEEFER & HERMAN YOUNKIN (Patent Book AA vol. 8 pg 349 or 379), and the said ISRAEL MORRIS and PHEBE his wife on 21 Jul 1767 did sell the tr of land unto GEORGE ADAM GOSSLER (Book D pg 70), and the said GEORGE ADAM GOSSLER and ELIZABETH his wife on 5 Nov 1767 did sell the tr of land unto the afsd CHRISTOPHER KREISER (Book D pg 19) ... . Wit: GEO EICHELBERGER, WM LEAS. Ackn 6 Apr 1774 before MARTIN EYCHELBERGER justice. (E:pg 480)

20 Jul 1773. Quit Claim. ELIAS OYSTER and ANNA MARIA his wife, MICHAEL LOW and ANNA MARIA his wife & PETER LOW and SUSANNA his wife all of York Co for £420 quit claim unto CASPER KERVER of York Co yeoman a 80 a. tr of land ... whereas CHRISTMAN LOW lately died owner of a

messuage and 80 a. tr of land in Manchester Township adj his other land &
MICHAEL LOW, called his *Mill Place* and left issue to survive him (to wit)
PHILIP LOW, PETER LOW, the said MICHAEL LOW, ANNA MARIA w/o
the said ELIAS OYSTER & MARIA MAGDALENA w/o the said CASPER
KERVER ... . Wit: [?], HENRY MILLER. Ackn 2 Aug 1773 before MARTIN
EYCHELBERGER justice. (E:pg 483)

16 Apr 1774. Deed of Mortgage. CONROD KISSINGER of York Township,
York Co brick maker for better securing the payment of £130 and also 5
shillings sold to MARTIN DANNER of York Town, York Co tobacconist a 7 a.
parcel of land in York Township adj the Great Road leading from York Town to
Susquehannah, KILLIAN SMALL & said MARTIN DANNER, being pt/o a 233
a. tr of land originally granted to JOHN HAAN by patent dated at Phila 17 Nov
1766 (Patent Book AA vol. 8 pg 45) ... whereas the said CONROD
KISSINGER stands bound unto the said MARTIN DANNER for £260
conditioned for the payment of £130 on 16 Apr 1777 ... provided that if the said
CONROD KISSINGER shall well and truly pay unto the said MARTIN
DANNER £130 then this indenture to be void ... . Wit: JACOB DAÜTTOL,
WM LEAS. Ackn 16 Apr 1774 before JOS UPDEGRAFF justice. 16 Mar 1784
MARTIN DANNER discharged mortgage. Wit: ARCHD MCCLEAN recorder.
(E:pg 484)

7 Dec 1773. Deed of Mortgage. JOHN FRENCH of Chanceford Township,
York Co farmer for better securing the payment of £207 and also 5 shillings sold
to JOSEPH JACKSON of same place yeoman a 338 a. 144 perches tr of land in
Chanceford Township adj JACOB STALY ... whereas the said JOHN FRENCH
standeth bound unto the said JOSEPH JACKSON for £414 conditioned for the
payment of £207 in payments before 1 Apr 1781 ... provided that if the said
JOHN FRENCH shall well and truly pay unto the said JOSEPH JACKSON
£207 then this indenture to be void ... . Wit: HENRY LONG, GEO ELDER.
Ackn 19 Jan 1774 before WILLIAM SMITH esqr justice. (E:pg 485)

15 Apr 1774. Deed. SAMUEL BELL of Straban Township, York Co weaver
and MARTHA his wife for £525 sold to HENRY JONES of St. Georges
Hundred, New Castle Co, DE innholder a 450 a. tr of land ... whereas the afsd
Proprietaries by their patent dated at Phila 13 Apr 1772 did grant unto the afsd
SAMUEL BELL a 450 a. tr of land called *Belmont* in Straban Township in the
Manor of Maske adj Rock Cr, DAVID DUNWOODY, Colonel HANCE
HAMILTON (in right of WALTER CARSON), Colonel HANCE HAMILTON
(in right of WILLIAM MILLER), JOHN SEMPLE, NATHANIEL MCCOSS &
STEPHEN GIFFING (Patent Book AA vol. 12 pg 85) ... . Wit: JOHN CLARK
Junr, THOS HARTLEY. Ackn 15 Apr 1774 before SAMUEL JOHNSTON esqr
justice. (E:pg 487)

15 Apr 1774. Deed of Mortgage. HENRY JONES of St. Georges Hundred, New Castle Co, DE innholder for better securing the payment of £325 and also 5 shillings sold to ADAM WITMAN of the Town of Reading, Berks Co, PA merchant a 450 a. tr of land called *Bellmont* [*same as above*] ... whereas the said HENRY JONES standeth bound unto the said ADAM WITMAN for £650 conditioned for the payment of £325 in payments before 15 Apr 1778 ... provided that if the said HENRY JONES shall well and truly pay unto the said ADAM WITMAN £325 then this indenture to be void ... . Wit: DAVID CANDLERG, THOS HARTLEY. Ackn 27 Apr 1774 before MATTHEW DILL esqr justice. 3 Jul 1777 ADAM WITMAN discharged mortgage. Wit: ARCHD MCCLEAN recorder. (E:pg 488)

20 Apr 1774. Deed. MARCUS HAINES of York Township, York Co yeoman and ELIZABETH his wife for £1600 sold to JACOB KELLER of same place yeoman a 293 a. tr of land ... whereas the Proprietaries on 30 Oct 1736 did grant unto JOHN CASPER KERBER a 300 a. tr of land on Codorus Cr and w side of Susquehanna River (formerly pt/o Lancaster Co), and the said JOHN CASPER KERBER being possessed of the land died intestate seized thereof without having received any patent for the same, leaving issue (to wit) CASPER KERBER his eldest son and heir at law, EVA w/o GEORGE WELLER, BARBARA w/o GEORGE MYER, EVA BARBARA w/o MARTIN EBERT, WALBURGH w/o PETER PAUFF & ELIZABETH w/o the said MARCUS HAINES, and the 300 a. tr of land descended to the said children, and the said GEORGE WELLER & EVA his wife, GEORGE MEYER & BARBARA his wife, MARTIN EBERT & EVA BARBARA his wife & PETER PAUFF and WALBURG his wife on 9 Aug 1758 did sell unto the said MARCUS HAINES (by the name of MARCUS HAINS) the a 150 a. tr of land whereon the said MARCUS HAINES now dwells in York Township between the lands of the afsd GEORGE WELLER & JOHN HECKENDORN and adj Codorus Cr and also 150 a. of land, ½ of the grant afsd by the Honorable THOMAS PENN to the afsd JOHN CASPER KERBER (Book A pg 305), and the said CASPER KERBER eldest son and heir at law of the said JOHN CASPER KERBER decd on 13 Mar 1760 did sell the 150 a. tr of land unto the said MARCUS HAINES (by the name of MARCUS HAINS) whereon the said MARCUS HAINES now dwells (Book A pg 396) ... by consent and direction of the Proprietaries on 20 Sep 1755 a survey was made for the said MARCUS HAINES on a tr of land in York Township pt/o the *Manor of Springetsbury* (part formerly granted by licence to the afsd JOHN CASPER KERBER) whose children and heirs sold to the said MARCUS HAINES ... in pursuance of a warrant dated 14 Aug 1766 there was surveyed 293 a., and the Proprietaries by their patent dated at Phila 16 Aug 1766 did grant unto the afsd MARCUS HAINES the 293 a. tr of land (Patent Book AA vol. 7 pg 136) ... . Wit: JOHN CLARK Junr, PHILIP RATHROCK. Ackn 20 Apr 1774 before JOSEPH UPDEGRAFF esqr justice. (E:pg 490)

20 Apr 1774. Deed of Mortgage. JACOB KELLER of York Township, York Co yeoman and CATHARINA his wife for better securing the payment of £1000 and also 5 shillings sold to MARCUS HAINES of same place a 293 a. tr of land adj Codorus Cr & GEORGE WELLER, which was granted to the said JACOB KELLER by the said MARCUS HAINES and ELIZABETH his wife [*see above*] ... whereas the said JACOB KELLER standeth bound unto the said MARCUS HAINES for £2000 conditioned for the payment of £1000 in payments before 20 Apr 1784 ... provided that if the said JACOB KELLER shall well and truly pay unto the said MARCUS HAINES £1000 then this indenture to be void ... . Wit: JOHN CLARK Junr, PHILIP ROTHROCK. Ackn 20 Apr 1774 before JOSEPH UPDEGRAFF esqr justice. 25 May 1793 PHILIP ROTHROCK atty for MARCUS HAINES discharged mortgage. Wit: J. BARNITZ recorder. (E:pg 493)

26 Apr 1774. Quit Claim. Whereas ISAAC DROGGET of the Town of Hanover, York Co tobacconist became indebted unto CASPER REINICKER for £50 for which he obtained his obligation and warrant of atty dated 13 Apr 1771 and for better securing the payment the said ISAAC DROGGET did by indenture of mortgage convey unto the said CASPER REINICKER a messuage and corner lot in the Town of Petersburgh, Germany Township, Lot No. 18 (Book D pg 411) ... on 1 Oct 1772 the said ISAAC DROGGET did sell the messuage and lot of ground unto JOHN MEYERS without discovering that the same was subject to the mortgage, who also on 27 Feb 1773 conveyed the same to WILLIAM GETTYS, both were at the time made acquainted with the mortgage ... CASPER REINICKER of Hanover Township, York Co innholder having been paid the whole of the mortgage and also 5 shillings quit claim unto WILLIAM GETTYS all my right in the messuage and lot of ground ... . Wit: [?], ARCHD MCCLEAN. Ackn 27 Apr 1774 before RD MCALESTER justice. (E:pg 496)

22 Dec 1769. Deed. JAMES MCCRAKEN of York Township, York Co miller for £15 sold to ANDREW FINLEY of Shrewsberry Township, York Co yeoman a 300 a. tr of land between JOHN HARNESS & JOHN YOUNG on the head waters of Grist Cr in York and Windsor Townships which was granted unto me by an application No. 5459 dated at Phila 9 May last ... . Wit: JAMES PATTERSON, THOS ARMOR. Ackn 13 May 1772 before JOHN ADLUM esqr justice. (E:pg 497)

30 Oct 1772. Deed. GEORGE SCHÜLE of York Township, York Co farmer for £68 sold to ANDREW FINLY of Hopewell Township, York Co yeoman a 99 a. tr of land adj MICHAEL LONG, STOFET WOLFART & others in York Township whereon I now dwell, which was surveyed and laid out unto me by an order of survey made by RICHARD HOCKLEY dated 2 Apr 1770 ... . Wit:

THOS ARMOR, THOS ARMOR Junr. Ackn 30 Oct 1772 before THOMAS MINSHALL esqr justice. (E:pg 498)

26 Apr 1774. Quit Claim. PATRICK GALLAGHER of Berwick Township, York Co for £4 quit claim unto the Proprietaries all my right in a tr of land ... whereas a warrant was granted unto me 28 Dec 1772 for the taking up 50 a. of land adj my other land (granted 19 May 1752) & FRANCIS CLAPSADDLE in Berwick Township, which was directed unto ARCHIBALD MCCLEAN or CHARLES LUKINS surveyors to execute, who found that the land had been surveyed 28 Dec 1756 in pursuance of a warrant granted to ADAM DEGOMA dated 28 Feb 1755 ... . Wit: GEORGE EGE, ARCHD MCCLEAN. Ackn 27 Apr 1774 before RD MCALISTER justice. (E:pg 499)

14 Apr 1774. Deed of Mortgage. ANDREW GORDON of Cicell Co, MD for better securing the payment of £1000 and also 5 shillings sold to JOHN HAMILTON of York Co yeoman a 600 a. tr of land in Cumberland Township now in the occupation of the said ANDREW GORDON adj JAMES MCCLURE, ROBERT BLACK, JAMES RIDDLE, JAMES PARKER, JOHN MCNUTT, GEORGE LIVINGSTON & SAMUEL BELL ... whereas the said ANDREW GORDON standeth bound unto the said JOHN HAMILTON for £1000 to be paid in five sundry payments ... provided that if the said ANDREW GORDON shall well and truly pay unto the said JOHN HAMILTON £1000 then this indenture to be void ... . Wit: ROBERT MCPHERSON, WILLIAM CATHCART. Ackn 14 Apr 1774 before ROBERT MCPHERSON justice. (E:pg 500)

30 Apr 1774. Deed of Mortgage. DANIEL EVANS of Manchester Township, York Co blacksmith and CATHARINE his wife for better securing the payment of £50 and also 5 shillings sold to JACOB MEYER of York Co yeoman a 57 a. tr of land in Manchester Township adj MICHAEL KINDER, MICHAEL QUIGLE & others, which the said DANIEL EVANS purch at sheriffs sale as the estate of BARNET GEMLING day before these presents and whereon the said DANIEL EVANS now lives ... whereas the said DANIEL EVANS standeth bound unto the said JACOB MEYER for £100 conditioned for the payment of £50 on or before 29 Apr next ... provided that if the said DANIEL EVANS shall well and truly pay unto the said JACOB MEYER £50 then this indenture to be void ... . Wit: GEO EICHELBERGER, HENRY MILLER. Ackn 30 Apr 1774 before WILLIAM DELAP esqr justice. 25 Aug 1779 CHRISTIAN LIPE one of the executors of the will of JACOB MEYER decd discharged mortgage. Wit: ARCHD MCCLEAN recorder. (E:pg 501)

22 May 1762. Deed. RICHARD PETERS of the City of Phila, PA esqr for £167.10 sold to JOHN KENNAN of Newberry Township, Cumberland Co, PA

yeoman two trs of land, 167 a. and 83 a., in the whole 250 a. ... whereas the Proprietaries by their patent dated 12 Sep 1748 did grant unto the said RICHARD PETERS two trs of land on Yellow Breeches Cr then in Lancaster Co now in York & Cumberland Cos which are divided by said cr, one a 167 a. tr of land in Cumberland Co adj JAMES HUNTER and the other a 83 a. tr of land in York Co (Patent Book A vol. 17 pg 259 in Phila) ... . Wit: SAM CAMPBELL, JOHN KEBLE. Ackn 22 May 1762 before WM COLEMAN esqr justice. (E:pg 502)

2 May 1774. Deed of Mortgage. JOHN LONG of York Township, York Co yeoman for better securing the payment of £100 and also 5 shillings sold to MICHAEL LONG of same place yeoman a 136 a. 115 perches tr of land called *Huntsmans Hall* in York Township originally surveyed and laid out to PHILIP BENTZ Junr in pursuance of a warrant dated at Phila 29 Oct 1771, and by divers conveyances have since been vested in right of the said JOHN LONG ... whereas the said JOHN LONG standeth bound unto the said MICHAEL LONG for £200 conditioned for the payment of £100 on 2 May next ensuing ... provided that if the said JOHN LONG shall well and truly pay unto the said MICHAEL LONG £100 then this indenture to be void ... . Wit: JOHN MORRIS, FREDERICK YOUCE. Ackn 2 May 1774 before WILLIAM SCOTT esqr justice. 20 Nov 1779 MICHAEL LONG discharged mortgage. Wit: ARCHD MCCLEAN recorder. (E:pg 504)

28 Apr 1774. Deed. JOHN HAY of the Town of York, York Co joiner and JULIANA his wife for £1528.10.9 sold to the Honourable THOMAS PENN and JOHN PENN esqrs Proprietaries a 145 a. 93 perches tr of land pt/o a 250 a. tr of land adj Codorus Cr & the town land (excepting Lot No. 90 and house thereon in which the said JOHN HAY now resideth) ... whereas THOMAS PENN on 13 Oct 1736 granted to MARTIN FRY 250 a. of land in York Township, and the right of the said MARTIN FRY to the 250 a. of land is now by virtue of divers conveyances become vested in the said JOHN HAY ... . Wit for JOHN HAY: REUBEN HAINES, DAVID KENNEDY. Wit for JULIANA HAY: JOHN CLARK Junr, R. [NARNAN?]. Ackn 28 Apr 1774 before SAMUEL JOHNSTON esqr justice. Ackn 29 Apr 1774 before THOMAS WILLING esqr judge of the Supreme Court. (E:pg 505)

20 Jul 1773. Deed. SAMUEL EDIE esqr high sheriff of York Co for £162 sold to GEORGE EICHELBERGER and CHRISTIAN STONER a 100 a. tr of land ... whereas JOHN HAY lately in the Court of Common Pleas obtained judgment against JOHN SCHALL for a debt of £69.16 and 51 shillings 6 pence damages ... the sheriff seized in execution as the estate of the said JOHN SCHALL a 100 a. tr of land with a merchant mill in Windsor Township adj DAVID ARCHIBALD & JAMES MCCLELLAND and on 16 Jun last past exposed the

land to sale at public vendue and sold to GEORGE EICHELBERGER and
CHRISTIAN STONER for £162 they being the highest bidders ... . Wit:
BALTZER SPANGLER, MARTIN [?]. Ackn 31 Jul 1773 in open court.
SAML JOHNSTON prothy. (E:pg 507)

24 May 1774. Articles of Agreement. Between MATHEW NEELS of
Monaghan Township, York Co yeoman, SALOME SHULL of same place
widow and MATHIAS DETTER of York Town, York Co innholder ... whereas
FREDERIC SHULL late of York Co yeoman decd by his will dated 28 Mar
1774 did bequeath to his wife the said SALOME £50 to be paid in 4 years after
his death and did allow her to take her choice of one cow for her thirds and did
allow her to receive £4 yearly for 4 years for the maintenance of his youngest
child ... the said MATHEW NEELS doth agree with the said MATHIAS
DETTER his executors and administrators that it shall be lawful for the said
SALOME at any time to ask for the £50 for her now use and all the sums of
money or legacies payable to her for the use of her or any of her children ... the
said MATHEW NEELS doth promise with the said MATHIAS DEETER that
they will at any time release the said £50 or any other legacy given which the
said SALOME or any of her children may be entitled ... the said MATHEW
NEELS & MATHIAS DEETER for the performance of the several articles and
agreements bind themselves in the penal sum of £500 ... . Wit: ANN WOOD,
MARTIN [?]. Ackn 24 May 1774 before WM LEAS justice. (E:pg 510)

29 Jan 1774. Deed. SAMUEL EDIE esqr high sheriff of York Co for £100 sold
to SAMUEL JOHNSTON esqr a 100 a. tr of land in Codorus and Schrewsberry
Townships ... whereas HENRY KEPPELE Junr lately in the Court of Common
Pleas obtained judgment against GEORGE STEVENSON for a debt of £6640
and 51 shillings 6 pence damages ... the sheriff seized in execution as the estate
of the said GEORGE STEVENSON a 70 a. tr of land formerly the plantation of
TOBIAS AMSPOKER decd on Middle Br of Codorus Cr with a dwelling house
and on 8 Dec last past sold at public vendue to SAMUEL JOHNSTON esqr for
£100 he being the highest bidder ... . Wit: DAVID GRIER, THOS
HARTLEY. Wit: to receipt: RN CARNAN. Ackn 29 Jan 1774 in open court.
SAML JOHNSTON recorder. (E:pg 511)

30 May 1774. Deed. CHRISTOPHER PRONK of the Colony of VA yeoman
for £25 sold to JOHN BACKENSTOUS & CHRISTIAN SHEARTZ of Middle
Town, Lancaster Co, PA a 25 a. tr of land in Newberry Township ... whereas
the Proprietaries by their patent dated at Phila 23 Jul 1762 did grant unto the said
CHRISTOPHER PRONK two trs of land, a 25 a. tr of land in Newberry
Township adj Susquehanna River, RICHARD PETERS esqr & JOHN HARRIS
and a 25 a. tr of land in Hellam Township (Patent Book AA vol. 4 pg 8) ... .

Wit: WILLIAM BAILEY, HENRY MILLER. Ackn 30 May 1774 before WM BAILEY justice. (E:pg 513)

30 Apr 1773. Deed. RICCORD HUSSEY of Warrington Township, York Co yeoman and MERIAM his wife and JEDAIAH HUSSEY of Reading Township, York Co and JANE his wife for £400 sold to HENRY MATTHIAS of Newberry Township, York Co taylor a 161 ½ a. tr of land pt/o a 323 a. tr of land ... whereas the Proprietaries by their patent dated 23 Feb last past did grant unto the afsd RICCORD HUSSEY and JEDAIAH HUSSEY a 323 a. tr of land called *Small Gain* in Newberry & Manchester Townships adj Little Conewago Cr, land late of JOHN HUSSEY decd, ROBERT HODGEN, DARBY CONRY & DANIEL MCLOUGHRY (Patent Book AA vol. 13 pg 405) ... . Wit: HANNAH MATTHEWS, WM MATTHEWS. Ackn 30 Apr 1773 before JOS UPDEGRAFF justice. (E:pg 515)

4 Jun 1772. Deed. Reverend RICHARD PETERS of the City of Phila, PA clerk for £222.5 sold to EDWARD JONES of Newberry Township, York Co yeoman a 177 a. tr of land ... whereas the Proprietaries by their patent dated 30 Aug 1748 did grant unto EDWARD SHIPPEN esqr a 177 a. tr of land in Newberry Township then in Lancaster Co but now in York Co adj CALVIN COOPER (Patent Book A vol. 14 pg 80), and the said EDWARD SHIPPEN & MARY his wife on the day after date of patent sold unto the said RICHARD PETERS the tr of land (Book A pg 58) ... . Wit: ALEXR STUART, BEN DAVIS Junr. Ackn 24 Nov 1772 before WILLIAM ALLEN esqr chief justice. (E:pg 517)

27 Apr 1774. Deed of Mortgage. GEORGE DRESSLER of Paradise Township, York Co yeoman for better securing the payment of £50 and also 5 shillings sold to CHRISTIAN WHIEST of York Co yeoman a 95 a. tr of land in Paradise Township whereon the said GEORGE DRESSLER now lives adj LAWRENCE SWISEGOOD, HENRY HERRING & others ... whereas the said GEORGE DRESSLER standeth bound unto the said CHRISTIAN WHIEST for £100 conditioned for the payment of £50 on or before 1 Apr 1777 ... provided that if the said GEORGE DRESSLER shall well and truly pay unto the said CHRISTIAN WHIEST £50 then this indenture to be void ... . Wit: JOHN MUSSEY, HENRY MILLER. Ackn 27 Apr 1774 before JOHN POPE esqr justice. 6 Feb 1782 CHRISTIAN WIEST discharged mortgage. Wit: ARCHD MCCLEAN recorder. (E:pg 519)

2 Nov 1768. Deed. THOMAS SLEMENS of Salsberry Township, Lancaster Co yeoman for £400 sold to ROBERT SLEMENS of Cumberland Township, York Co yeoman a 192 a. tr of land ... whereas there was a warrant granted to the said THOMAS SLEMENS dated 12 Aug 1765 for a 192 a. tr of land in Cumberland Township adj SAMUEL EDIE esqr, MYLES SWENEY,

EDWARD HALL & JAMES BOYD, being the tr of land which the said
THOMAS SLEMENS purch of JOHN PARK & DAVID PARK ... . Wit:
JOHN SLEMENS (SLEMONS), MARGRAT SLEMONS. Ackn 2 Nov 1768
before ROBT MCPHERSON justice. (E:pg 521)

3 Apr 1773. Quit Claim. CHRISTIAN HOOVER of Heidleberg Township,
York Co yeoman for £26 quit claim unto JACOB WINE of York Co yeoman a 5
a. lot of ground in Heidleberg Township, No. 19, bounded by Lot No. 20, Lot
No. 18 & *Digges' Quarter*, pt/o a larger tr of land called *Digges' Choice* which
the said CHRISTIAN HOOVER holds in right of JOHN DIGGES decd and to
him conveyed on 14 Nov 1763 ... . Wit: MICHAEL DANNER, JOS BOUDE.
Ackn 3 Apr 1773 before RD MCALLESTER justice. (E:pg 522)

23 Jun 1774. Deed of Release. JAMES WRIGHT of Hempfield Township,
Lancaster Co, PA esqr and RHODA his wife for 5 shillings release unto JOHN
WRIGHT of Hellam Township, York Co gent two trs of land, a 55 a. tr of land
pt/o a 278 a. tr of land adj NICHOLAS BUT, heirs of FRANCIS WORLEY
decd and a 83 a. 29 perches tr of land pt/o the original tr adj DANIEL
WORLEY, JACOB DOUDLE & WILLIAM WILLIS ... whereas the
Proprietaries by their patent dated at Phila 7 Apr 1752 did grant unto JOHN
WRIGHT (late of Hellam Township decd), the said JAMES WRIGHT &
WILLIAM WILLIS a 480 a. tr of land in Manchester Township adj Codoras Cr,
town land, NICHOLAS BUT, FRANCIS WORLEY, JOHN SMITH &
CHARLES JONES (Patent Book A vol. 16 pg 146), after obtaining the patent it
was mutually agreed that the said JOHN WRIGHT the elder and JAMES
WRIGHT should receive for their 2/3 shares a 278 a. tr of land pt/o the 480 a. tr
of land, and the said JOHN WRIGHT the elder is since dead but made his will
dated 3 Dec 1753 and did order that his real and personal estate to be valued and
divided into six shares, to his wife one share, his two sons ROBERT & JOHN
three shares to include the plantation on which he lived & two daus each one a
share and impowered his executors to sell any other of his lands they should
think proper, the plantation on which he lived excepted, and appointed his wife
ELEANOR WRIGHT and the said JAMES WRIGHT executors, and the said
WILLIAM WILLIS and BETTY his wife on 25 Feb 1767 did release their right
in the afsd 278 a. tr of land unto the said JAMES WRIGHT and ELEANOR
WRIGHT (Book C pg 240), and the said ROBERT WRIGHT after the death of
the said JOHN WRIGHT, his father, died unmarried intestate and without issue
to survive him, and the said ELEANOR WRIGHT since also died intestate
leaving the said JOHN WRIGHT, PATIENCE now w/o JAMES EWING &
SUSANAH now w/o JOHN HOUSTON her issue by the said JOHN WRIGHT
decd to survive her ... . Wit: JAMES EWING, HENRY MILLER. Ackn 15 Jul
1774 before SAML JOHNSTON justice. (E:pg 523)

19 Sep 1771. Quit Claim. JAMES EWING of Hallam Township, York Co gent and PATIENCE his wife in consideration of two trs of land granted unto the said JAMES EWING and £50 quit claim unto JOHN WRIGHT of same place gent the residue of the several trs and lott of ground mentioned below ... whereas JOHN WRIGHT late of Hallam Township, York Co father of the afsd JOHN died owner of trs of land, one a 405 a. tr of land on the w side of Susquehanna River adj ABRAHAM FLURY, one other 100 a. tr of land in said township adj JAMES WRIGHT esqr, THOMAS MINSHALL esqr, HENRY DAVIS & land of the Proprietaries, one other 100 a. tr of land in Windsor Township, one other tr of land in Manchester Township being an undivided ½ pt/o 278 a. tr of land, and a lot of ground on Duke Street in the Town of York, No. 36, and the said JOHN WRIGHT the father made his will dated 3 Dec 1753 and did devise his real and personal estate to be divided into six shares [same as above] ... whereas the said JAMES WRIGHT surviving executor of the will of the said JOHN WRIGHT decd on 1 Sep 1768 did sell the 405 a. tr of land unto the said JOHN WRIGHT subject to the claim of the said JAMES EWING & PATIENCE his wife and SUSANNA WRIGHT (Book D pg 213), and the said JOHN WRIGHT the younger on 3 Sep 1768 did sell unto the said JAMES EWING a 100 a. tr of land pt/o the 405 a. tr of land adj ABRAHAM FLURY, the High Road from York to Wrights Ferry, JOHN WRIGHT & Grist Cr (Book C pg 531), and the said JAMES WRIGHT the possessor of the other ½ pt/o the 278 a. tr of land and RHODA his wife, the said JOHN WRIGHT and SUSANNA WRIGHT on 19 Sep 1771 did sell unto the said JAMES EWING a 26 a. tr of land pt/o the 278 a. tr of land adj WILLIAM WILLIS ... . Wit: THOS MINSHALL, JOHN EWING. Ackn 18 Sep 1777 before THOS MINSHALL justice. (E:pg 528)

28 Mar 1774. Deed. NICHOLAS WIREMAN of Huntington Township, York Co executor of the will of JAMES DAVISON late of Reading Township, York Co decd for £570 sold to SARAH, ELEANOR & OLIVIA DAVISON a 288 a. tr of land ... whereas the Proprietaries by two warrants dated 26 Mar 1747 and 18 Dec 1751 did grant unto the said JAMES DAVISON a 288 a. tr of land in Reading Township adj other land of JAMES DAVISON, JOHN DONNELLY, THOMAS CARSWEL, NICHOLAS MEYER, JAMES POAK & MICHAEL ACKERMAN, and the said JAMES DAVISON made his will, viz, I impower ALEXANDER BROWN and NICHOLAS WIREMAN my executors to sell my tr of land at public sale, and on 4 Jun last, was sold at publick vendue to SARAH DAVISON one of the legatees she being the highest bidder and in behalf of her self and her sisters ELEANOR & OLIVIA DAVISON for £570 ... . Wit: JAMES MORRISON, ISAAC DEARDORFF. Ackn 28 Mar 1774 before WILLIAM DELAP esqr justice. (E:pg 531)

27 Jun 1774. Deed of Mortgage. EBENEZER HORSMAN of Warrington Township, York Co yeoman for better securing the payment of £30 and also 5

shillings sold to PHILIP MINHART of same place a 118 a. tr of land in
Manahan Township adj JOHN LOVE, GABRIEL FICKEL, CASPER
WAGGONER & HENRY SEVER, surveyed to me by virtue of an application
dated 27 Apr 1774 ... whereas the said EBENEZER HORSMAN standeth
bound unto the said PHILIP MINHART for £60 conditioned for the payment of
£30 on 28 Jun 1775 ... provided that if the said EBENEZER HORSMAN shall
well and truly pay unto the said PHILIP MINHART £30 then this indenture to
be void ... . Wit: GABRIEL SMITH, JOHN SMITH Junr. Ackn 27 Jun 1774
before JOHN SMITH justice. (E:pg 533)

11 Jun 1774. Power of Attorney. HENRY KEPPELE Junr of the City of Phila
heir and legatee of MICHAEL GROSS late of Lancaster Borough decd and one
of the executors of the will of the said MICHAEL GROSS have appointed
ADAM HUBLEY Junr of the City of Phila my atty to ask, demand, sue for,
recover and receive of MICHAEL MILLER of York Co a debt of £320 being the
same sum of money secured to the said MICHAEL GROSS in his life time by
the said MICHAEL MILLER by a deed of mortgage recorded at York (Book D
pg 126) on 26 Jun 1769, and upon receipt of the payment to ackn satisfaction for
the said mortgage on record ... . Wit: WM ECKHART, LEONHARD [?].
Ackn 11 Jun 1774 before JOHN LAWRENCE justice. (E:pg 534)

F BOOK
1773-1775

23 Jun 1774. Deed of Release. JOHN WRIGHT of Hellam Township, York Co
gent and JOHN HOUSTON of York Town, York Co physician and SUSANAH
his wife for 5 shillings release unto JAMES WRIGHT of Hempfield Township,
Lancaster Co esqr a 164 a. 29 perches tr of land (pt/o a 278 a. tr of land) in
Manchester Township adj Codoras Cr, town land, FRANCIS & DANIEL
WORLEY & WILLIAM WILLIS ... whereas the Proprietaries by their patent
dated at Phila 7 Apr 1752 did grant unto JOHN WRIGHT (late of Hellam
Township decd), the afsd JAMES WRIGHT & WILLIAM WILLIS a 480 a. tr of
land in Manchester Township adj Codoras Cr, York Town land, NICHOLAS
BUT, FRANCIS WORLEY, JOHN SMITH, one OPIS land & CHARLES
JONES (Patent Book A vol. 16 pg 146), and after obtaining the patent it was
mutually agreed that the said JOHN WRIGHT the elder and JAMES WRIGHT
should have for their 2/3 share of the 480 a. tr a 278 a. tr of land, and the said
WILLIAM WILLIS should have the remainder ... the said JOHN WRIGHT the
elder is since dead but before his death made his will dated 3 Dec 1753 and did
devise his real and personal estate to be divided in six shares, to his wife one
share, to his two sons ROBERT & JOHN three shares (to include the plantation
on which he lived), and to his two daus each one share, and impowered his

executors to make sale of any other of his lands they should think proper, and appointed his wife ELEANOR WRIGHT and the afsd JAMES WRIGHT executors ... whereas the said WILLIAM WILLIS and BETTY his wife on 25 Feb 1767 did release all their right in the 278 a. of land unto the said JAMES WRIGHT and ELEANOR WRIGHT (Book C pg 240), and the said ROBERT WRIGHT after the death of his father the said JOHN WRIGHT died unmarried intestate and without issue to survive him, and the said ELEANOR WRIGHT since also died intestate leaving the afsd JOHN WRIGHT, PATIENCE now w/o JAMES EWING & the said SUSANAH w/o the afsd JOHN HOUSTON her issue by the said JOHN WRIGHT decd to survive her ... . Wit: JAMES EWING, HENRY MILLER. 23 Jun 1774 before WM LEAS justice. (F:pg 1)

24 Jun 1774. Deed of Release. JOHN WRIGHT the younger of Hellam Township, York Co gent for 5 shillings release unto JOHN HOUSTON of York Town, York Co gent and SUSANNA his wife two trs of land, 55 a. and 83 a. 29 perches ... whereas the Proprietaries [same as above] ... . Wit: JAMES EWING, HENRY MILLER. Ackn 24 Jun 1774 before WM LEAS justice. (F:pg 5)

14 Jun 1774. Deed of Mortgage. JOHN HAHN of Manheim Township, York Co yeoman for better securing the payment of £52.10 and also 5 shillings sold to CASPER REINICKER of York Co innholder 1 bay horse, 1 black horse, 1 plough, 1 harrow & 2 cows ... whereas the said JOHN HAHN stands bound unto the said CASPER REINICKER for £105 conditioned for the payment of £52.10 on or before 1 Jul next ensuing ... provided that if the said JOHN HAHN shall well and truly pay unto the said CASPER REINICKER £52.10 then this bill of sale to be void ... . Wit: JOS BOUDE, RACHEL BOUDE. Ackn -- Jun 1774 before RD MCALESTER justice. (F:pg 10)

14 Jun 1774. Deed of Mortgage. JOHN HAHN of Manheim Township, York Co yeoman and ELIZABETH his wife for better securing the payment of £66.10.6 and also 5 shillings sold to CASPER REINICKER of York Co innholder a 100 a. tr of land in Manheim Township adj PHILIP POTTEFELDT, JOHN DERWEIGHTER, NICHOLAS BEETINGER, VALENTINE ELTZROTH & GEORGE LEININGER ... whereas the said JOHN HAHN stands bound unto the said CASPER REINICKER for £133.1 conditioned for the payment of £66.10.6 on or before 1 Jul next ensuing ... provided that if the said JOHN HAHN shall well and truly pay unto the said CASPER REINICKER £66.10.6 then this indenture to be void ... . Wit: JOS BOUDE, RACHEL BOUDE. Ackn 22 Jun 1774 before RD MCALESTER justice. (F:pg 11)

24 Jun 1774. Quit Claim. Whereas JOHN WRIGHT the elder of Hellam Township, York Co lately died having first made his will dated 3 Dec 1753, part

thereof to wit, I order all my real and personal estate to be valued and divided in six shares, I leave to my wife ELEANOR one share, I leave to my two sons ROBERT & JOHN three shares which I order to be the plantation and tr of land whereon I now live, I leave to my two daus each one a share, and the said ROBERT WRIGHT also died intestate unmarried and without issue, and the said JOHN WRIGHT the younger on this date did release unto the said JOHN HOUSTON and SUSANNAH his wife (she being one of the daus of the said JOHN WRIGHT the elder decd) two trs of land [see F 5] in full satisfaction of their share of the real and personal estate of said JOHN WRIGHT decd and also of the said ELEANOR WRIGHT who since also died ... JOHN HOUSTON of York Town, York Co gent and SUSANNAH his wife in consideration of the lands granted to them quit claim unto JOHN WRIGHT the younger their right in the real and personal estate whereof the said JOHN WRIGHT the elder died owner and the real and personal estate of the said ELEANOR WRIGHT decd ... . Wit: JAMES EWING, HENRY MILLER. Ackn 24 Jun 1774 before WM LEAS justice. (F:pg 12)

16 Jul 1774. Deed. JOHN HOUSTON of York Town, York Co practitioner in physick and SUSANNAH his wife for £52.10 sold to MATHIAS DETTER of Manchester Township, York Co innkeeper a 5 a. tr of land in Manchester Township pt/o a larger tr adj JOHN HAUGNER, REINHART BUTT & SAMUEL UPDEGRAFF ... . Wit: JOHN CLARK Junr, WILLIAM SCOTT. Ackn 16 Jul 1774 before WILLIAM LEAS esqr justice. (F:pg 13)

9 Jul 1774. Deed. JOHN HOUSTON of York Town, York Co practitioner in physick and SUSANNAH his wife for £68.18 sold to SAMUEL JOHNSTON of York Town, York Co esqr a 6 a. 90 perches tr of land pt/o a larger tr adj JOSEPH DONALDSON, SAMUEL UPDEGRAFF & town land ... . Wit: WILLIAM SCOTT, DAVID CANDLER. Ackn 9 Jul 1774 before WILLIAM SCOTT esqr justice. (F:pg 15)

18 Jun 1774. Deed of Mortgage. MICHAEL MILLER of Huntington Township, York Co farmer for better securing the payment of £300 and also 5 shillings sold to JOHN HAY of York Town, York, Co carpenter a 52 a. tr of land in Huntington Township adj JOSHUA CANWORTHY, WILLIAM WYERMAN, JACOB BAIL & Bermudian Cr, as by a patent granted unto the said MICHAEL MILLER dated 16 May 1753 (Patent Book A vol. 17 pg 308 in Phila) ... whereas the said MICHAEL MILLER stands bound unto the said JOHN HAY for £600 conditioned for the payment of £300 on 18 Jun 1777 ... provided that if the said MICHAEL MILLER shall well and truly pay unto the said JOHN HAY £300 then this indenture to be void ... . Wit: MARY LES, HENRY TYSON. Ackn 18 Jun 1774 before WM LEAS justice. 30 Jul 1778

JOHN HAY discharged mortgage. Wit: ARCHD MCCLEAN recorder. (F:pg 17)

8 Jun 1771. Deed. ANTHONY SELL of Mountjoy Township, York Co yeoman and CATHARINA his wife for £1500 sold to HENRY HERGLEROADT of York Co yeoman a 200 a. tr of land in Heidleberg Township pt/o a tr of land called *Digges' Choice* adj Grues Cr & PETER MIDDLECALF, which JOHN DIGGES on 21 May 1751 sold unto the said ANTHONY SELL ... . Wit: JOS BOUDE, ROBT OWINGS. Ackn 8 Jun 1771 before HENRY SLAGLE justice. (F:pg 19)

16 Sep 1774. Deed. STOFFEL WILLET of Manheim Township, York Co farmer for £30 sold to THOMAS ARMOR of York Co a 50 a. tr of land which I grubbed, cleared, fenced, plowed and sowed about 14 years ago adj JOHN KOONTZ, PETER LAU & ANDREW HERSHY in Codorus Township ... . Wit: [?], GEO LEWIS LESLER. Ackn 16 Sep 1774 before RICHARD MCALESTER esqr justice. (F:pg 21)

6 Oct 1773 at Phila. Commission. SAMUEL EDIE of York Co esqr appointed sheriff of York Co by JOHN PENN. (F:pg 21)

6 Oct 1773 at Phila. To all judges, justices, magistrates and other officers, freemen and all other persons whatsoever within York Co ... whereas we have granted unto SAMUEL EDIE esqr the office of sheriff ... we require and command you that to the said SAMUEL EDIE you be aiding and assisting in all things that to the office of sheriff may in any wise belong ... . [*signed*] JOHN PENN. (F:pg 22)

15 Oct 1773. Bond. SAMUEL EDIE and ROBERT MCPHERSON esqr of Cumberland Township and DAVID MCCONAUGHY esqr of Menallen Township all in York Co are firmly bound unto our Sovereign Lord GEORGE the third for £2000 ... the condition of this obligation is such that if the said SAMUEL EDIE esqr shall well and truly serve and execute all the Kings writs and process to him directed then this obligation to be void ... . Wit: SAML JOHNSTON, JOHN CLARK Junr. (F:pg 22)

9 Apr 1774 at Phila. To JAMES HAMILTON, JOSEPH TURNER, WILLIAM LOGAN, RICHARD PETERS, LYNFORD LARDNER, BENJAMIN CHEW, THOMAS CADWALADER, RICHARD PENN, JAMES TILGHMAN, ANDREW ALLEN & EDWARD SHIPPEN Junr esqrs members of the Proprietary and Governors Council, and to ROBERT MCPHERSON, DAVID JAMESON, MARTIN EYCHELBERGER, ARCHIBALD MCGREW, JOHN POPE, SAMUEL JOHNSTON, SAMUEL EDIE, WILLIAM DELAP,

MATTHEW DILL, HENRY SLAGLE, WILLIAM SMITH, JOHN SMITH, CUNNINGHAM SAMPLE, RICHARD MCCALISTER, DAVID MCCONNAUGHY, WILLIAM RANKIN, JOSEPH UPDEGRAFF, WILLIAM SCOTT, JOSEPH DONALDSON, WILLIAM LEAS & WILLIAM BAILEY of York Co esqrs, reposing special trust and confidence in your loyalty, integrity and ability, we have assigned you jointly and separately our justices of the peace in York Co ... . [*signed*] JOHN PENN. (F:pg 23)

25 Sep 1771. Deed. JOHN LUKENS of the City of Phila, PA surveyor and SARAH his wife for £200 sold to their son CHARLES LUKENS of the Town of York, York Co surveyor a messuage and ½ lot of ground (being ½ pt/o Lot No. 104) on the n side of High Street in the Town of York, in breadth 32'6" and in length 230' bounded by lot formerly of JOHN GLEADY and now of PHILIP FISHBURN & other pt/o lot late of BENJAMIN SWOOPE and not in the tenure of GEORGE CHRISTIAN ZINN, which ½ lot of ground CONRAD BYERER & BARBARA his wife on 21 Nov 1768 (Book C pg 534) did grant unto the said JOHN LUKENS ... . Wit: ROBERT DILL, PETER THOMSON. Ackn 17 Aug 1774 before JOHN LAWRENCE esqr justice. (F:pg 25)

18 Aug 1774. Quit Claim. JOHAN RYNHARDT BUTT of Manchester Township, York Co yeoman and MARILIS his wife on 10 Oct 1765 did sell unto ZACHARIAH SHUGART two lots of ground, one which is on the Great Road leading from York Town to Monockasy now called King Street in Manchester Township, in breadth 140' and in length 230', bounded by Carlisle Alley, JOHAN RYNHARDT BUTT & MARTIN WHYGLE, and the other lot on the n side of Carlisle Alley, in breadth 140' and in length 230' bounded by JOHAN RYNHARDT BUTT & MARTIN WHYGLE, subject to the ground rent of 20 shillings for each lot unto the afsd JOHAN RYNHARDT BUTT every year forever ... and the said lots of ground by sundry conveyances were since vested in right of NICHOLAS REISINGER ... for £33.7 the said JOHAN RYNHARD BUTT & MARILIS his wife quit claim unto the said NICHOLAS REISINGER of same place yeoman the yearly ground rent of £20 shillings for each lot ... . Wit: JOHN MORRIS, ZACK SHUGOT (SHUGART). Ackn 18 Aug 1774 before MARTIN EYCHELBERGER justice. (F:pg 26)

7 May 1774. Deed. PHILIP ROTHROCK and CATHARINA his wife & PHILIP BENTZ and ELIZABETH his wife all of York Co for £130 sold to MICHAEL MILLER of Hellam Township, York Co yeoman all their right in a 300 a. tr of land ... whereas MICHAEL KOONTZ lately died intestate seized in a messuage and 300 a. tr of land in Hellam Township adj JOHN TRICKLER, HENRY STRICKLER, HENRY KANN, JACOB STENTZ & others, and left issue to survive him (to wit) PETER KOONTZ (KOONS) his eldest son & heir at law, PHILIP, JOHN, CATHARINE, MARY & SAMUEL, and the said

PETER KOONTZ eldest son on 1 May 1764 sold his right in the tr of land unto the said PHILIP ROTHROCK and PHILIP BENTZ (Book B pg 321) ... . Wit: SARAH MILLER, HENRY MILLER. Ackn 27 Jul 1774 before WM BAILEY justice. (F:pg 28)

19 Nov 1764. Deed. HENRY JACOBS of Paradise Township, York Co weaver and MARESEBELA (MARRSEBELA) his wife for £115 sold to SAMUEL JACOBS of Berwick Township, York Co yeoman a 115 ½ a. tr of land pt/o a 461 a. tr of land ... whereas the Proprietaries by their patent dated at Phila 18 Dec 1749 did grant to the said HENRY JACOBS a 377 a. tr of land adj said HENRY JACOBS other land and a 84 a. tr of land adj HENRY JACOBS other land & GEORGE DUNGAN, in the whole 461 a. (Patent Book 4 vol. 14 pg 343) ... . Wit: GEO EICHELBERGER, HENRY HARRIS. Ackn 19 Nov 1764 before MARTIN EYCKELBERGER justice. (F:pg 30)

5 Sep 1774. Deed of Mortgage. MARTIN BASH of Manallin Township, York Co miller for better securing the payment of £360 and also 5 shillings sold to NICHOLAS DELLOW (DELLO) of Lancaster Borough, and JOHN SCHALLENBERGER of Hempfield Township, Lancaster Co yeoman a messuage and 220 a. tr of land in Manheim Township which NICHOLAS BEETINGER on 15 Jan last past did grant unto the said MARTIN BASH ... whereas the said MARTIN BASH standeth bound unto the said NICHOLAS DELLOW & JOHN SCHALLENBERGER for £720 conditioned for the payment of £360 on 5 Sep 1775 ... provided that if the said MARTIN BASH shall well and truly pay unto the said NICHOLAS DELLOW & JOHN SCHALLENBERGER £360 then this indenture to be void ... . Wit: RD MCALISTER, ARCHD MCCLEAN. Ackn 5 Sep 1774 before RICHARD MCALISTER esqr justice. 28 Jun 1775 JOHN CLARK Junr by virtue of a Letter of Atty from NICHOLAS DELLOW and JOHN SCHALLENBERGER discharged mortgage. (F:pg 32)

5 Nov 1772. Deed of Gift. JACOB MILLER of Frederick Co, MD planter and CATHARINE his wife for natural love and affection and 5 shillings gave to our son JAMES MILLER of Manheim Township, York Co yeoman a 185 a. tr of land ... in pursuance of a warrant dated 3 Oct 1738 there was surveyed and laid out unto CONRAD PERKHAVER by ZACHARIAH BUTCHER a 270 a. tr of land in Manheim Township, and the said CONRAD PERKHAVER on 22 Jun 1741 did sell 135 a. or ½ pt/o the afsd tr of land to ADAM BEETINGER, and by a warrant dated 6 Oct 1753 there was granted to GEORGE BERKHAVER of York Co 50 a. of land adj JACOB [GRUP?] and the afsd ADAM BEETINGER by the afsd GEORGE BERKHIVER assigned to NICHOLAS BEETINGER, and the afsd ADAM BEETINGER and NICHOLAS BEETINGER on 4 Apr 1755 did sell the afsd two trs of land unto the said JACOB MILLER ... at the special

instance and request of the said JACOB MILLER the said two trs of land were
surveyed and laid out into one 185 a. tr in Manheim Township adj GEORGE
WISE, HENRY BEETINGER, JOHN JUDA & GEORGE WEISS ... . Wit:
RACHEL BOUDE, JOS BOUDE. Ackn 5 Nov 1772 before RD MCALISTER
justice. (F:pg 33)

25 Apr 1774. Deed of Mortgage. GEORGE RINGER of Manchester Township,
York Co yeoman and CHRISTINA his wife for better securing the payment of a
debt sold to JOHANNES KURTZ of same place yeoman a 131 ½ a. tr of land ...
whereas the Proprietaries by patent dated at Phila 12 May 1772 granted unto
MATHIAS SMYSER a 131 ½ a. tr of land in Manchester Township adj
JOSEPH COOK, MARY LOLLER, MICHAEL KINTER, JACOB
GUTTWALT & the heirs of JONAS SIPE (Patent Book AA vol. 13 pg 113),
and the said MATHIAS SMYSER and ANN ENGEL his wife on 27 May 1772
did convey unto the afsd JOHANNES KURTZ the 131 ½ a. tr of land, and the
said JOHANNES KURTZ and MARGARET ELIZABETH his wife sold the tr
of land unto the said GEORGE RINGER ... the said GEORGE RINGER
became bound unto the said JOHANNES KURTZ for several sums to be paid in
payments before 27 May 1784 ... provided that if the said GEORGE RINGER
shall well and truly pay unto the said JOHANNES KURTZ a debt of several
sums of money then this indenture to be void ... . Wit: PETER MUNDORFF,
GEO LEWIS LESLER. Ackn 13 Aug 1774 before WILLIAM SCOTT esqr
justice. 12 Dec 1778 JOHANNES KURTZ discharged mortgage. Wit:
ARCHD MCCLEAN recorder. (F:pg 36)

6 Sep 1774. Deed of Mortgage. HENRY HERGLERODE of Heidleberg
Township, York Co yeoman for better securing the payment of £1000 and also 5
shillings sold to ADAM SHERMAN of Germany Township, York Co yeoman a
200 a. tr of land in Heidelberg Township pt/o a tr of land called *Digges' Choice*
adj Griers Cr & PETER MIDDLECALF, which ANTHONY SELL and
CATHARINA his wife on 8 Jun 1771 sold unto the afsd HENRY
HERGLERODE (Book F pg 19) ... whereas the said HENRY HERGLERODE
standeth bound unto the said ADAM SHERMAN for £2000 conditioned for the
payment of £1000 on demand ... provided that if the said HENRY
HERGLERODE shall well and truly pay to the said ADAM SHERMAN £1000
then this indenture to be void ... . Wit: CHAS LUKENS, GEO LEWIS
LESLER. Ackn 6 Sep 1774 before WILLIAM BAILEY esqr justice. (F:pg 39)

5 Aug 1774. Deed of Mortgage. JAMES MARSHALL of Hamiltonban
Township, York Co yeoman for better securing the payment of £250 and also 5
shillings sold to EDWARD STILES of Oxford Township, Phila Co esqr a 253 a.
149 perches tr of land called *Mill Place* in Hamiltonban Township adj JAMES
RUSK, JOHN CRAWFORD, *Carrol's Delight*, WILLIAM BAIRD & RICHD

BAIRD, which by a patent dated 3 Aug instant was granted unto the said
JAMES MARSHALL (Patent Book AA vol. 14 pg 581 in Phila) ... whereas the
said JAMES MARSHALL standeth bound unto the said EDWARD STILES in
the penal sum of £500 conditioned for the payment of £250 on 5 Aug 1775 ...
provided that if the said JAMES MARSHALL shall well and truly pay unto the
said EDWARD STILES £250 then this indenture to be void ... . Wit: GEO
MAILEY, GEO ISHERWOOD. Ackn 6 Aug 1774 before THOMAS WILLING
esqr justice. (F:pg 40)

7 Mar 1774. Deed. MICHAEL HAHN of York Town, York Co and
ELIZABETH his wife & JOHN ROTHROCK of Manchester Township and
DOROTHEA his wife all of York Co for £200 sold to MICHAEL MILLER of
Hellam Township, York Co yeoman a 300 a. tr of land ... whereas MICHAEL
KOONTZ lately died intestate seized of a messuage and 300 a. tr of land in
Hellam Township adj JOHN TRIECHLER, HENRY STRICKLER, HENRY
RANN, JACOB STENTZ & others, and left ELIZABETH his widow and issue
to survive him, namely PETER his eldest son and heir at law, PHILIP, JOHN,
CATHARINA, SAMUEL and MARY since intermarried with ADAM
COOKAS, and the said JOHN (by the name of JOHN KUNTZ) one of the sons
of the said MICHAEL KUNTZ decd on 3 Jan 1771 did quit claim unto the said
MICHAEL HAHN & JOHN ROTHROCK all his estate right in the real and
personal estate of his said father (Book D pg 334), and the said CATHARINA
by the name of CATHARINA KOONTZ one of the daus of the said MICHAEL
KOONTZ decd on 18 Mar 1771 did quit claim unto the said MICHAEL HAHN
and JOHN ROTHROCK all her estate right in the real and personal estate of her
father (Book D pg 350) ... . Wit: [?], HENRY MILLER. Ackn 18 Aug 1774
before MARTIN EICHELBERGER justice. (F:pg 42)

18 Aug 1774. Deed of Mortgage. ISAAC GORTMAN of Manchester
Township, York Co weaver for better securing the payment of £30 and also 5
shillings sold to MARTIN DANNER of the Town of York, York Co yeoman
two lots of ground, one on the Great Road leading from York Town to
Monockasy (now called King Street) in Manchester Township, in breath 64' and
in length 230' bounded by FREDERICK BEMER, Carlisle Alley & JACOB
BOTT, the other lot the same breadth & length bounded by Carlisle Alley,
FREDERICK REMER, JOHAN RYNHARD BUTT & JACOB BUTT, being
the 8th lots from York Town land ... whereas the said ISAAC GORTMAN
standeth bound unto the said MARTIN DANNER for £60 conditioned for the
payment of £30 on 18 Aug 1777 ... provided that if the said ISAAC
GORTMAN shall well and truly pay unto the said MARTIN DANNER £30 then
this indenture to be void ... . Wit: JOHN MORRIS, BENJAMIN GORGAS,
[?]. Ackn 20 Aug 1774 before WILLIAM BAILEY esqr justice.   21 Mar 1781

MARTIN DANNER discharged mortgage. Wit: ARCHIBALD MCCLEAN
recorder. (F:pg 45)

12 Aug 1774. Deed of Mortgage. HENRY HERGLEROTE (HERKELROD) of
York Co yeoman for better securing the payment of £300 and also 5 shillings
sold to PATRICK MCSHERRY of York Co yeoman a 200 a. tr of land in
Heidleberg Township adj Guiers Cr & PETER MIDDLECALF ... whereas the
said HENRY HERGLEROTE standeth bound unto the said PATRICK
MCSHERRY for £600 conditioned for the payment of £300 on 1 Jul next
ensuing ... provided that if the said HENRY HERGLEROTE shall well and
truly pay unto the said PATRICK MCSHERRY £300 then this indenture to be
void ... . Wit: JACOB [?], DAVID GRIER. Ackn 12 Aug 1774 before
WILLIAM BAILEY esqr justice. (F:pg 47)

28 Apr 1774. Deed of Mortgage. BALTHUS HAMMER of Manallen
Township, York Co yeoman for better securing the payment of £65 and also 5
shillings sold to DERICK LOW of Hillsborrough Township and GEORGE
HALL of Bridge Water Township each of Sommerset Co, East NJ yeomen a 200
a. tr of land on the s br of Possum Cr in Menallen Township adj JOHN GRIST,
MICHAEL STAMBACH & THOMAS BOWEN, which originally was granted
& surveyed unto JOHN SIMMONS in pursuance of a warrant dated at Phila 20
Oct 1746 and by divers conveyances to the afsd BALTHUS HAMMER ...
whereas the said BALTHUS HAMMER standeth bound unto the said DERICK
LOW & GEORGE HALL for £130 conditioned for the payment of £65 on 3 Mar
next ensuing ... provided that if the said BALTHUS HAMMER shall well and
truly pay unto the said DERICK LOW & GEORGE HALL £65 then this
indenture to be void ... . Wit: JOHN MORRIS, [?]. Ackn 28 Apr 1774 before
JOSEPH UPDEGRAFF esqr justice. 14 Oct 1780 PETER CANINE atty for
DERICK LOW & GEORGE HALL discharged mortgage. Wit: ARCHD
MCCLEAN recorder. (F:pg 49)

30 Aug 1773. Deed. CATHERINA SPICKARD of the Town of York, York Co
and PHILIP SPICKARD of York Township, York Co adminrs of the estate of
HENRY SPICKARD late of Hellam Township, York Co decd for £175 sold to
MAGDALENA HECKARD of the Town of York, York Co widow Lot No. 37
on the n side of High Street in the Town of York bounded by Duke Street &
LUDWICK KRAFT, in breadth 65' and in length 230' ... whereas JOHN
WRIGHT entered his name for a lot of ground in the Town of York in Lancaster
Co (now York Co) No. 37, the ticket dated 10 Mar 1746, and ELENOR
WRIGHT & JAMES WRIGHT executors of the will of the said JOHN
WRIGHT since decd on 16 Mar 1761 did assign the Lot No. 37 unto HENRY
SPICKARD, and the afsd HENRY SPICKARD being seized of the lot of ground
lately died and the afsd CATHARINA SPICKARD late widow & relict of said

decd and the afsd PHILIP SPICKARD administered to the estate of said decd as
by Letter of Administration dated 24 Jul 1769, and in pursuance of an order of
the Orphans Court the lot of ground was exposed to publick sale to satisfy the
creditors of said decd ... . Wit: LUDWIG [KRAFT?], JOHN MORRIS. Ackn
30 Aug 1773 before JOHN ADLUM esqr justice. (F:pg 51)

14 Oct 1774. Deed of Mortgage. CONRAD WOLF of Manchester Township,
York Co farmer for better securing the payment of £200 and also 5 shillings sold
to ANTHONY WOLF of the Town of York, York Co yeoman a 158 a. tr of land
in Manchester & Dover Townships adj PHILIP WOLF, PETER BENTZ &
SIMON WITMEYER ... whereas the said CONRAD WOLF standeth bound
unto the said ANTHONY WOLF for £200 conditioned for the payment of £100
in payments before 1 Jun 1776 and the payment of £60 due and payable yearly
after the death of the said ANTHONY WOLF in four payments ... provided that
if the said CONRAD WOLF shall well and truly pay unto the said ANTHONY
WOLF the afsd debt then this indenture to be void ... . Wit: JOHN MORRIS,
JOHN HAY. Ackn 15 Oct 1774 before WILLIAM LEAS esqr justice. 2 Aug
1776 ANTHONY WOLFF discharged mortgage. Wit: SAML JOHNSTON
recorder. (F:pg 54)

[*Entered by mistake written in margin*] JOHAN RYNHARDT BUTT of
Manchester Township, York Co yeoman and MARILIS his wife ... whereas the
said JOHAN RYNHARD BUTT and MARILIS his wife on 10 Oct 1765 did sell
unto ZACHARIAH SHUGUST a tr of land on the Great Road leading from
York Town to Monackasy now called King Street in Manchester Township, in
breadth 140' and in length 230' bounded by Carlisle Alley, MARTIN WHYGLE
& JOHAN RYNHARD BUTT's other land, and the other on the n side of
Carlisle Alley in breadth 140' and in length 230' bounded by MARTIN
WHYGLE & other land of the said JOHAN RYNHARDT BUTT subject to the
payment of the ground rent of 20 shillings for each unto the said JOHAN
RYNHARDT BUTT ... . (F:pg 56)

5 Sep 1774. Deed of Mortgage. HENRY HERGLEROTE (HERGTEROLE)
(HERKEBROD) of York Co yeoman for better securing the payment of £204
and also 5 shillings sold to PATRICK MCSHERRY of York Co yeoman a 200
a. tr of land in Heidleberg Township adj Guiers Cr & PETER MIDDLECALF ...
whereas the said HENRY HERGLEROTE standeth bound unto the said
PATRICK MCSHERRY for £408 conditioned for the payment of £204 on 21
Jul next ensuing ... provided that if the said HENRY HERGLEROTE shall well
and truly pay unto the said PATRICK MCSHERRY £204 then this indenture to
be void ... . Wit: [?], DAVID GRIER. Ackn 5 Sep 1774 before WILLIAM
LEAS esqr justice. (F:pg 57)

25 May 1774. Deed of Mortgage. WILLIAM DAVIS of Heidelberg Township, York Co yeoman for better securing the payment of £1200 and also 5 shillings sold to CASPER REINICHER of Town of Hanover, York Co innkeeper four messuages and trs of land in Manheim and Heidelberg Townships, a 33 a. tr of land adj MICHAEL KARL, land patented under MD to JOHN DIGGES, JOHN GEORGE KOONTZ & NICHOLAS [KLCH?] and a 15 a. tr of land adj land patented under MD to the said JOHN DIGGES & MICHAEL KARL, and a 120 a. tr of land adj CASPER PERKIMER, and a 53 a. tr of land, being the same messuages and four trs of land which the said CASPER REINICKER and ANNA MARIA his wife by three indentures dated day before this date conveyed unto the said WILLIAM DAVIS (except out of the three first mentioned trs of land 24 a. which the said CASPER REINICKER and ANNA MARIA his wife conveyed to FREDERICK EICHELBERGER and also 13 a. conveyed by them to the use of the Protestant Congregation of Lutherans) ... whereas the said WILLIAM DAVIS stands bound unto the said CASPER REINICHER for £2400 conditioned for the payment of £1200 in payments before 12 Jun 1784 ... provided that if the said WILLIAM DAVIS shall well and truly pay unto the said CASPER REINICHER £1200 then this indenture to be void ... . Wit: JOS BOUDE, [?]. Ackn 25 May 1774 before HENRY SLAGLE justice. 28 Jan 1780 CASPER REINICHER discharged mortgage. Wit: ARCHD MCCLEAN recorder. (F:pg 59)

19 Oct 1774. Deed of Mortgage. JOHN MILLER of Shrewsberry Township, York Co yeoman for better securing the payment of £159 and also 5 shillings sold to SIGMUND MILLER of same place yeoman a 166 a. tr of land in Shrewsberry Township adj JOHN KELLAR, JACOB HIBLEY, JAMES MARSHALL, CHRISTIAN EBY & JACOB AULT ... whereas the said JOHN MILLER standeth bound unto the said SIGMUND MILLER for £318 conditioned for the payment of £159 in payments before 5 May 1785 ... provided that if the said JOHN MILLER shall well and truly pay unto the said SIGMUND MILLER £159 then this indenture to be void ... . Wit: JOHN MORRIS, HERMAN MILLER. Ackn 19 Oct 1774 before WILLIAM SCOTT esqr justice. (F:pg 63)

8 Aug 1772. Deed. PHILIP HOFF of Hallem Township, York Co yeoman and ROSINA his wife for £113.10 sold to DANIEL NEAFF of same place gent a 10 a. tr of land ... whereas the Proprietaries by their patent dated 12 Apr 1753 granted unto THOMAS MINSHALL a 253 ½ a. tr of land in the township afsd adj the dwelling plantation of THOMAS MINSHALL (Patent Book A vol. 19 pg 217), and the said THOMAS MINSHALL & MARY his wife on 13 Oct 1765 did convey unto his brother STEPHEN MINSHALL a 10 a. tr of land pt/o the 253 ½ a. tr adj JOHN FISSEL, HENRY STRICKLER & JOHN FURREY, and the said STEPHEN MINSHALL on 18 Dec 1766 sold ½ a. pt/o the 10 a. tr of

land to the said PHILIP HOFF on the s side of the Great Road leading from
York Town to Wrights Ferry adj HENRY STRICKLER, JOHN FURREY &
THOMAS MINSHALL esqr (Book C pg 487), and DAVID MCCONAUGHY
esqr late high sheriff of York Co by virtue of sundry writs issued out of the
Court of Common Pleas at suit of CASPER SINGER seized in execution the
residue of the 10 a. tr of land as the estate of the said STEPHEN MINSHALL
for a debt of £53.14.4 and 64 shillings 5 pence damages, and also on 18 Jul 1768
did expose the same to sale at public vendue and sold to the said PHILIP HOFF
for £56 he being the highest bidder, and the said DAVID MCCONAUGHY esqr
then sheriff in pursuance of the sale by his deed poll on 10 Aug 1768 conveyed
the tr of land unto the said PHILIP HOFF ... . Wit: [FRANCIS KUNZ?],
HENRY MILLER. Ackn 8 Aug 1772 before JOHN ADLUM esqr justice.
(F:pg 65)

6 Oct 1774 at Phila. Commission. CHARLES LUKENS of York Co esqr
appointed sheriff of York Co. [*signed*] JOHN PENN. (F:pg 68)

6 Oct 1774 at Phila. To: judges, justices, magistrates & other offers, freemen
and all other persons whatsoever within York Co, whereas by commission have
granted unto CHARLES LUKENS esqr the office of sheriff of York Co ... we
do require and command you that to the said CHARLES LUKENS you be
aiding and assisting in all things ... . [*signed*] JOHN PENN.(F:pg 68)

11 Oct 1774. Bond. CHARLES LUKENS and MICHAEL SWOOPE of York
Town and JAMES DELL of Monaughan Township all of York Co are firmly
bound unto our Sovereign Lord GEORGE the third for £2000 ... the condition
of this obligation is such that if the said CHARLES LUKENS shall well and
truly serve and execute all the Kings writs and process to him directed then this
obligation to be void ... . Wit: SAML JOHNSTON, R.N. CARNAN. (F:pg 69)

7 Nov 1774. Deed of Mortgage. NICHOLAS HOFEMAN of Dover Township,
York Co farmer for better securing the payment of £500 and also 5 shillings sold
to HENRY DAVIS of same place farmer a 318 a. tr of land in Dover Township
adj ANDREW GANTZER, PHILIP KIMMEL, CASPER LAMBERT, ADAM
SYPNER, MICHAEL WALLICK, JOSEPH BERGTOL & VALENTINE
FLOHR, which was granted by warrant dated 22 Dec 1753 unto JEREMIAH
DUNGAN ... whereas the said NICHOLAS HOFEMAN stands bound unto the
said HENRY DAVIS for £1000 conditioned for the payment of £500 in
payments before 1 May 1787... provided that if the said NICHOLAS
HOFEMAN shall well and truly pay unto the said HENRY DAVIS £500 then
this indenture to be void ... . Wit: JACOB DAŇTUL (DAŇTOL), [?]. Ackn 7
Nov 1774 before WILLIAM LEAS esqr justice. 19 Apr 1788 HENRY DAVIS
discharged mortgage. Wit: JACOB BARNITZ recorder. (F:pg 70)

13 Apr 1767. Deed. THOMAS KENNEDY of West Nantmill Township, Chester Co, PA for natural love and affection gave to his son JOHN KENNEDY of Huntington Township, York Co a messuage and 200 a. tr of land in Huntington Township adj WM SMITH, THOS BRAKEN & JOHN GRAHAM in the tenure of the said JOHN KENNEDY ... . Wit: JOHN CULBERTSON, ABIGAIL CULBERTSON. Ackn 24 Oct 1774 before JOHN POPE esqr justice. (F:pg 72)

9 Dec 1766. Deed. MATHIAS NESS of Shrewsberry Township, York Co yeoman for £50.10 sold to JACOB STEIN of same place yeoman a 50 a. tr of land pt/o a 173 ½ a. tr of land in Shrewsberry Township adj JOHN BERRY ... whereas in pursuance of an order dated 18 Mar 1746 from WILLIAM PARSONS late surveyor general there was surveyed 22 Jan 1754 for the use of the Proprietaries (in order to agree with MATHIAS NESS for the same) a 173 ½ a. tr of land in Shrewsberry Township, and the said MATHIAS NESS on 18 Mar 1746 did pay to EDMUND PHYSICK receiver for the Proprietaries 50 shillings in pt/o the purchase money for the tr of land but the terms of purchase do not appear to be agreed upon by the Proprietaries and the said MATHIAS, and the said MATHIAS NESS obtained a warrant dated at Phila 3 Dec 1764 to take up 50 a. of land to be surveyed to him adj his other land ... . Wit: CONROD [?], JACOB [?]. Ackn 3 Mar 1767 before JOHN ADLUM esqr justice. (F:pg 73)

11 Aug 1774. Deed of Mortgage. PETER RAWP of Warwick Township, Lancaster Co, PA yeoman for better securing the payment of £109 and also 5 shillings sold to DAVID ARCHIBALD of Windsor Township, York Co yeoman two trs of land in Windsor Township, a 65 a. 67 perches tr of land which in pursuance of the application No. 2370 dated 14 Jan 1767 was granted unto ALEXANDER ADAMS and a 117 a. 100 perches tr of land which in pursuance of application No. 2133 dated 11 Dec 1766 was laid unto JOSEPH LIGGET, the said trs lying contiguous with each other ... whereas the said PETER RAWP standeth bound unto the said DAVID ARCHIBALD for £218 conditioned for the payment of £109 in payments before 1 May 1782 ... provided that if the said PETER RAWP shall well and truly pay unto the said DAVID ARCHIBALD £109 then this indenture to be void ... . Wit: JOHN MORRIS, JOHN SHULTZ. Ackn 11 Aug 1774 before MARTIN EYCHELBERGER esqr justice. (F:pg 76)

1 Oct 1774. Deed of Mortgage. HENRY SCHRACK of Hopewell Township, York Co miller for better securing the payment of £150 and also 5 shillings sold to ELIZABETH GROSS of Lancaster Borough, Lancaster Co widow a 100 a. tr of land in Hopewell, Chanceford & Windsor Townships being pt/o the same land the said HENRY SCHRACK lately purch from HENRY AMEND now decd and on which is a grist mill and saw mill adj JACOB FISTER & JACOB

SMITH ... whereas the said HENRY SCHRACK standeth bound unto the said
ELIZABETH GROSS for £300 conditioned for the payment of £150 on 1 Oct
next ensuing ... provided that if the said HENRY SCHRACK shall well and
truly pay unto the said ELIZABETH GROSS £150 then this indenture to be void
... . Wit: JACOB ROTHROCK, JACOB [?]. Ackn 1 Oct 1774 before
WILLIAM LEAS esqr justice. 17 Apr 1779 PETER ZINGRY by virtue of a
letter of atty from ELIZABETH GROSS discharged mortgage. Wit: ARCHD
MCCLEAN recorder. (F:pg 77)

16 Nov 1774. Deed of Mortgage. MICHAEL LECHNER of Dover Township,
York Co yeoman for better securing the payment of £400 and also 5 shillings
sold to GEORGE LECHNER of same place yeoman two trs of land in Dover
Township, a 168 a. tr of land adj CASPER ROWLAND, VALENTINE FLOHR
& GEORGE ALBRIGHT, which LEONARD FLOHR on 6 Nov 1752 sold unto
the said GEORGE LECHNER (Book B pg 384) and a 115 a. tr of land adj
JOHN PRICE, ANDREW GANTZER & the afsd tr of land, which was granted
unto the said GEORGE LECHNER (by the name of GEORGE SCHLEGNER)
by warrant dated at Phila 24 Sep 1751 ... whereas the said MICHAEL
LECHNER standeth bound unto the said GEORGE LECHNER for £800
conditioned for the payment of £400 ... provided that if the said MICHAEL
LECHNER shall well and truly pay unto the said GEORGE LECHNER £400
then this indenture to be void ... . Wit: JACOB [?], GEO LEWIS LESLER.
Ackn 19 Nov 1774 before WILLIAM LEAS esqr justice. (F:pg 79)

18 Oct 1774. Deed of Mortgage. GEORGE WEISS of Manheim Township,
York Co yeoman and ESTHER his wife for better securing the payment of £663
and also 5 shillings sold to CASPER REINICKER of York Co innholder a 236
a. tr of land in Manheim Township adj FREDERICK GELWICKS,
VALENTINE OYLER, NICHOLAS FISHER & land late of JACOB MILLER,
whereon the said GEORGE WEISS now dwells ... whereas the said GEORGE
WEISS stands bound unto the said CASPER REINICKER for £1326
conditioned for the payment of £663 on or before 1 Nov next ensuing ...
provided that if the said GEORGE WEISS shall well and truly pay unto the said
CASPER REINICKER £663 then this indenture to be void ... . Wit: DAVID
HOUKE, JOS BOUDE. Ackn 19 Oct 1774 before RD MCALESTER justice.
(F:pg 81)

20 Sep 1774. Deed of Mortgage. BASTIAN ERIGH of Heidelberg Township,
York Co farmer for better securing the payment of £400 and also 5 shillings sold
to CONRAD KURTZ of York Township, York Co yeoman a 241 a, tr of land in
York Township adj FREDERICK PHLEGER, BASTIAN WHITEMAN,
MICHAEL BARDT, VALENTINE REIN & HERMAN YOUNKIN ... whereas
the said BASTIAN ERIGH standeth bound unto the said CONRAD KURTZ for

£800 conditioned for the payment of £400 in payments before 1 May 1787 ... provided that if the said BASTIAN ERIGH shall well and truly pay unto the said CONRAD KURTZ £400 then this indenture to be void ... . Wit: JOHN MORRIS, GEORGE CROFT. Ackn 20 Sep 1774 before WILLIAM LEAS esqr justice. (F:pg 83)

14 Mar 1774. Deed. THOMAS ROBERTS of Charlestown Township, Chester Co, PA yeoman for £30 sold to JOHN LEWIS of Berwick Township, York Co docter a 300 a. tr of land formerly the property of WILLIAM THOMAS HUGH & conveyed from him to FREDERICK CELLION on 19 May 1769 and conveyed from the said FREDERICK CELLION on 1 Apr 1771 unto the afsd THOMAS ROBERTS, in Warrington Township adj SAMUEL EDMUNDSON & WILLIAM KENEDY ... . Wit: JOHN HOOKER, ROBERT JOHNSTON CHESTER. Ackn 15 Mar 1774 before WILLIAM DELAP esqr justice. 31 Mar 1774 JOHN LOUIS assigns all his right in this deed unto HERMAN STIDGER. Wit: ROBERT JOHNSTON CHESTER, WILLIAM BOWMON. Ackn 13 Aug 1774 before HENRY SLAGLE justice. (F:pg 85)

24 Oct 1774. Deed of Mortgage. CONRAD BELTZHOOBER of Dover Township, York Co farmer for better securing the payment of £60 and also 5 shillings sold to JOHN OBERDEER of same place joiner a 77 a. tr of land in Dover Township adj PHILIP BENTZ, JOHN PENSEL & MARTIN FRY, which was surveyed in pursuance of an application granted to ISAAC SOLOMON No. 5579 dated 28 Aug 1769 ... whereas the afsd CONRAD BELTZHOOBER stands bound unto the said JOHN OBERDEER for £120 conditioned for the payment of £60 in payments before 27 Dec 1779 ... provided that if the said CONRAD BELTZHOOBER shall well and truly pay unto the said JOHN OBERDEER £60 then this indenture to be void ... . Wit: [?], [?]. Ackn 24 Oct 1774 before WILLIAM LEAS esqr justice. 2 Nov 1784 JOHN OBERDEER discharged mortgage. Wit: ARCHD MCCLEAN recorder. (F:pg 87)

4 Nov 1774. Deed. HENRY WALTER of York Town, York Co tinnman and MAGDALENA his wife for £100 sold to JACOB DURANG of same place barber a lott of ground on the e side of Beaver Street in the Town of York, No. 81, in breadth 57 ½' and in length 250' bounded by Lot No. 82 & Phila Street, which the Proprietaries by their patent dated 27 Sep 1753 granted unto JOSEPH WELSHANTZ, who with MAGDALENA his wife on 8 Aug 1758 conveyed the same unto JOHN BITTLE, who with SUSANNAH his wife on 3 Mar 1761 conveyed the same unto GEORGE STOLL, who with ANN his wife on 5 Mar 1764 conveyed the same unto the said HENRY WALTER ... . Wit: JOHN HAY, HENRY MILLER. Ackn 7 Nov 1774 before WILLIAM LEAS justice. (F:pg 89)

5 Nov 1774. Deed of Mortgage. JACOB DURANG of York Town, York Co barber and CATHARINE his wife for better securing the payment of £100 and also 5 shillings sold to HENRY WALTER of same place tinnman Lot No. 81 in the Town of York [*same as above*] ... whereas the said JACOB DURANG standeth bound unto the said HENRY WALTER for £200 conditioned for the payment of £100 in payments before 1 Apr 1779 ... provided that if the said JACOB DURANG shall well and truly pay unto the said HENRY WALTER £100 then this indenture to be void ... . Wit: JOHN HAY, HENRY MILLER. Ackn 7 Nov 1774 before WILLIAM LEAS esqr justice. 24 Dec 1776 HENRY WALTER discharged mortgage. Wit: SAML JOHNSTON recorder. (F:pg 91)

15 Oct 1774. Deed. PETER DICKS Junr of Paradise Township, York Co farmer and ELINOR his wife for £30 sold to PETER WOLF of Manchester Township, York Co tavern keeper a 2 a. tr of land pt/o a 152 a. tr adj Punch Run, the Great Road leading to York & said PETER WOLF ... whereas in pursuance of a warrant dated at Phila 1 Aug 1744 there was surveyed unto JOHN EMRICK BOT (by the name of EMRICK BOT) 152 a. of land in Paradise Township, and the said JOHN EMRICK BOT on 8 Dec 1755 sold unto CONRAD BOT (by the name of CONRAD BUTT) the afsd tr of land, and the said CONRAD BOT on 27 Jul 1756 sold unto PETER DICKS the afsd tr of land, and the said PETER DICKS assigned his right in the tr of land unto the said PETER DICKS Junr on 6 Oct 1758 ... . Wit: THOS ARMOR, [?]. Ackn 2 Nov 1774 before WILLIAM BAILEY esqr justice. (F:pg 93)

1 Nov 1774. Quit Claim. MARTIN EICHELBERGER of Manchester Township, York Co esqr and ZACHARIAH SHUGART of same place innkeeper for 5 shillings quit claim unto BARBARA SHERTLY of Dover Township, York Co widow and adminr of the estate of JOHN SHERTLY decd for the purposes of the will of said decd a tr of land in Dover Township adj PHILIP MOHR, GEORGE ILGERFRITZ & NICHOLAS HARMAN (and whereon the said BARBARA now dwells) ... . Wit: JOHN MORRIS, GEORGE ILGERFRITZ. Ackn 1 Nov 1774 before WILLIAM LEAS justice. (F:pg 95)

13 Oct 1774. Deed. ANTHONY WOLF of the Town of York, York Co yeoman and CATHERINA his wife for £100 sold to CONRAD WOLF of Manchester Township, York Co farmer a 158 a. tr of land pt/o a 300 a. tr of land adj PHILIP WOLF, SIMON WITMYER & PETER BENS ... whereas MARTIN RINE (alias RYAN) entered his name for 200 a. of land on the e side of Little Conawago Cr as by a certificate under the hands of GEORGE STEVENSON esqr dated 4 Feb 1752, and the said MARTIN RINE on 4 Jun 1758 made his will and did devise that two honest men shall have power to sell the plantation, and the said MARTIN RINE afterwards died and THOMAS

CRUMRINE & PHILIP MILLER were chosen and did administer the estate of the decd, and the said THOMAS CRUMRINE & PHILIP MILLER on 14 May 1771 did sell the 200 a. tr of land unto the said ANTHONY WOLF, and in pursuance of a warrant dated at Phila 30 Dec 1769 the afsd tr of land was surveyed and laid out unto the said ANTHONY WOLF as follows, in Manchester & Dover Townships containing 300 a., and the said ANTHONY WOLF and CATHERINA his wife on 1 Jun 1771 sold 160 a. pt/o the afsd tr of land unto PHILLIP WOLF ... and the said CONRAD WOLF paying unto the said ANTHONY WOLF & CATHERINA his wife yearly and every year during their natural lives on 1 Dec: 30 bushels of wheat, 20 bushels of rie, 10 bushels of buckwheat, 2 bushels of turnips, 2 bushels of potatoes, 10 pounds of hackled flax, 10 pounds of hackled hemp, 100 weight of pork, the 1/3 pt/o the fruit and cider, sufficient hay and second crop of hay for fothering, 1 cow, necessary hawling with wagon and teem, 15 bundles of straw and sufficient firewood ... . Wit: JOHN MORRIS, JOHN HAY. Ackn – Oct 1774 before WILLIAM LEAS esqr justice. (F:pg 96)

26 Jul 1773. Deed. DANIEL NEAFF of Hellam Township, York Co gent and ANN his wife for £100 sold to ABRAHAM FLOWREY of same place yeoman a 10 a. tr of land in Hellam Township ... whereas the Proprietaries by their patent dated 12 Apr 1753 did grant unto THOMAS MINSHALL a 250 ½ a. tr of land in the township afsd adj the dwelling plantation of the said THOMAS MINSHALL (Patent Book A vol. 19 pg 27), and THOMAS MINSHALL and MARY his wife on 30 Oct 1765 sold unto his brother STEPHEN MINSHALL a 10 a. tr of land pt/o the 250 ½ a. tr adj JOHN FISSEL, HENRY STRICKLER & JOHN FURREY, and the said STEPHEN MINSHALL on 18 Dec 1766 sold unto PHILIP HUFF a ½ a. tr of land pt/o the 10 a. of land on the s side of the Great Road leading from York Town to Wrights Ferry adj HENRY STRICKLER, JOHN FURREY & THOMAS MINSHALL (Book C pg 48), and DAVID MCCONAUGHY esqr late high sheriff of York Co by sundry writs out of the Court of Common Pleas seized in execution the residue of the afsd 10 a. tr of land as the estate of the said STEPHEN MINSHALL to satisfy a debt of £53.14.4 and 64 shillings 5 pence damages, and on 18 Jul 1768 exposed the same to sale by public vendue and sold unto PHILIP HUFF for £46 he being the highest bidder, and the said DAVID MCCONAUGHY conveyed to the said PHILIP HUFF on 10 Aug 1768, and the said PHILIP HUFF and ROSINA his wife on 8 Aug 1772 sold unto the said DANIEL NEAFF the 10 a. tr of land ... . Wit: GEO EICHELBERGER, [?]. Ackn 26 Jul 1773 before THOMAS MINSHALL justice. (F:pg 100)

1 Nov 1774. Deed of Mortgage. BENJAMIN CABLE of Manahon Township, York Co farmer for better securing the payment of £50 and also 5 shillings sold to HENRY LOHMAN of Warrington Township, York Co yeoman a 150 a. tr of

land in Manahon Township adj WILLIAM CUNNINGHAM, WILLIAM
RUSSEL & LEWIS WILLIAMS ... whereas the said BENJAMIN CABLE
standeth bound unto the said HENRY LOHMAN for £100 conditioned for the
payment of £50 on 1 Nov 1778 ... provided that if the said BENJAMIN CABLE
shall well and truly pay unto the said HENRY LOHMAN £50 then this
indenture to be void ... . Wit: GABRIEL SMITH, JOHN SMITH. Ackn 1 Nov
1774 before JOHN SMITH esqr justice. (F:pg 103)

19 Oct 1768. Deed. JOHN SCONNEL of Faun Township, York Co weaver (for
the further and better sure making) and for £60 sold to WILLIAM WILSON
(WILLSON) of Chanceford Township, York Co farmer a 123 a. tr of land ...
whereas in pursuance of a warrant dated at Phila 14 Dec 1751 there was
surveyed and laid out unto WILLIAM BUCHANAN a 123 a. tr of land in
Chanceford Township adj JOHN CAMPBLE, JIM CAMPBLE. CHARLES
OHARA & JOHN BUCHANAN, and the said WILLIAM BUCHANAN on 10
Apr 1753 sold the tr of land unto the afsd JOHN SCONNEL, and the said JOHN
SCONNEL on 20 Sep 1753 did certify that he assigned the instrument of writing
unto the afsd WILLIAM WILSON (without mentioning any consideration) ... .
Wit: GEORGE STAKE, GEO ROSS. Ackn 19 Oct 1768 before DAVID
JAMESON justice. (F:pg 105)

10 Aug 1768. Deed. DAVID MCCONAUGHY esqr high sheriff of York Co
for £56 sold to PHILIP HOFF a messuage and 10 a. tr of land ... whereas
CASPER SINGER recovered in the Court of Common Pleas against STEPHEN
MINSHALL (MINSHELL) late of Hellam Township, York Co tanner a debt of
£53.14.4 and 64 shillings 5 pence damages ... the sheriff seized in execution a
messuage and 10 a. tr of land in Hellam Township adj HENRY FURRY decd,
THOMAS MINSHALL esqr & PHILIP HOFF as the estate of the said
STEPHEN MINSHALL subject to former executions ... and sold the land to
PHILIP HOFF of Hellam Township yeoman for £56 he being the highest bidder
... . Wit: JAMES SMITH, DAVID GRIER. Ackn 1 Sep 1768 in open court.
SAML JOHNSTON prothy. (F:pg 107)

30 May 1774. Quit Claim. GEORGE BEAR yeoman & CHRISTINA his wife,
JOSEPH HURST yeoman and MARY his wife, MARTIN SHAFFER yeoman
and MARGARET his wife, ABRAHAM REIFF and BARBARA his wife all of
Earl Township, Lancaster Co, PA (the said CHRISTINA being late the widow &
relict of SAMUEL GROVE late of said township yeoman decd and the said
MARY, MARGARET & BARBARA being the only issue of the said SAMUEL
GROVE decd) for £650 by JOSEPH LONG to the said SAMUEL GROVE paid
and the further sum of 10 shillings quit claim unto the said JOSEPH LONG two
parcels of land ... whereas the Proprietaries by their patent dated 16 Jun 1750
did grant unto ADAM REDD & GEORGE REDD a 300 ¾ a. tr of land then in

Pensboro Township but now in Newbery Township, York Co (Patent Book A
vol. 14 pg 445), and the said ADAM REDD and MARIAM his wife and
GEORGE REDD on 2 Dec 1753 sold 200 a. pt/o the afsd tr of land unto the said
SAMUEL GROVE, and the Proprietaries by their patent dated 21 Oct 1760 did
grant unto the said SAMUEL GROVE a 55 a. 96 perches tr of land in Newbery
Township adj the afsd tr of land, WILLIAM HAYS, HENRY WILLIS &
WILLIAM POSMORE (Patent Book AA vol. 1 pg 155 in Phila), and the said
SAMUEL GROVE and CHRISTINA his wife on 9 Jun 1768 for £650 sold the
two trs of land to JOSEPH LONG of Repko Township, Lancaster Co yeoman,
and the indentures being eaten and damaged by vermine so that many of the
words being entirely out and unintelligible, at the instance and request of the
said JOSEPH LONG to make a further confirmation of the afsd two trs of land
... . Wit: CHRISTIAN SHIVER, ABRAHAM LONG. Proved 5 Dec 1774 by
CHRISTIAN SHUAR & ABRAHAM LONG before WILLIAM SCOTT justice.
(F:pg 109)

6 Dec 1764. Deed of Mortgage. CHRISTIAN OBERHOLTZER of Hempfield
Township, Lancaster Co, PA yeoman and MAGDALEN his wife for a debt of
£400 & £600 and saving, keeping harmless and indemnified and also 5 shillings
sold to JOHN HUBER, JACOB NEFF, DAVID BRUBACKER, BENEDICT
ESHELMAN, JOHN WITMER & CHRISTIAN SCHWAR all of Lancaster Co
farmers, two trs of land in Hellam Township, a 200 a. tr of land adj JACOB
STRICKLER, JOHN STRICKLER & DANIEL HARMAN and a 77 ¾ a. tr of
land adj BENEDICT FUNK, JOHN STRICKLER, MICHAEL PETERMAN &
GEORGE WANBAUGH, the same two trs of land which JOHN SHULTZ &
CATHARINE his wife on 12 Oct 1774 did grant unto the said CHRISTIAN
OBERHOLTZER ... whereas the said JOHN HUBER, JACOB NEFF, DAVID
BRUBACKER, BENEDICT ESHELMAN, JOHN WITMER & CHRISTIAN
SCHWAR together with the said CHRISTIAN OBERHOLTZER for the debt of
the said CHRISTIAN OBERHOLTZER stand bound unto MICHAEL
FORDINE OF Lancaster Borough. Lancaster Co in the penal sum of £800
conditioned for the payment of £400 on 8 Oct next ensuing ... and the said
JOHN HUBER, JACOB NEFF, DAVID BRUBACKER, BENEDICT
ESHELMAN, JOHN WITMER & CHRISTIAN SCHWAR together with the
said CHRISTIAN OBERHOLTZER for the debt of the said CHRISTIAN
OBERHOLTZER stand bound unto JOHN SHULTZ of York Co yeoman in the
penal sum of £1200 conditioned for the payment of £600 in payments ...
provided that if the said CHRISTIAN OBERHOLTZER shall well and truly pay
off and discharge the debts of £600 & £400 then this indenture to be void ... .
Wit: JOHN HAY, JOHN SHULTZ. Ackn 6 Dec 1774 before WILLIAM LEAS
justice. 17 Jan 1777 by letter of atty as well as right vested in myself DAVID
BRUBAKER discharged mortgage. Wit: SAML JOHNSTON recorder. (F:pg
112)

7 Nov 1774. Farm Lett. JAMES RANKEN of Newberry Township, York Co farmer in consideration of the rents and covenants hereinafter reserved, farm lett to JOHN RANKEN of York Township, York Co farmer a messuage & tr of land in York Township adj GEORGE BENTZ, NICHOLAS DEHL, Codorus Cr & the mill & land also let by the said JAMES RANKEN unto ROBERT HAMERSLY ... the said JOHN RANKEN from 1 Apr next ensuing during the term of 15 years paying from 1 Apr 1776 on 1 Apr next following £35 and every year unto the said JAMES RANKEN ... . Wit: WM RANKIN, ANN RANKIN. Ackn 16 Dec 1774 before WILLIAM RANKIN justice. (F:pg 116)

16 Dec 1774. Deed. SAMUEL MCELHEANY of Manheim Township, York Co yeoman for £70.5 sold to JOHN HEERETER of same place a 102 a. 29 perches tr of land in Manheim Township adj CONRAD GRO, HENRY GILMORE, JOHN SCAFTEL & HENRY LORE, which JAMES CLARK made application No. 1415 and obtained an order of survey dated 4 Oct 1766 and who with EVE his wife on 30 Apr 1770 conveyed unto me ... . Wit: GEORGE STAKE, THOS ARMOR. Ackn 16 Dec 1774 before WILLIAM SCOTT esqr justice. (F:pg 117)

3 Jan 1775. Deed of Mortgage. ULRICH LIGHTY of Manahan Township, York Co for £100 sold to ADAM FORSH of Paradise Township, York Co farmer a messuage and 145 a. tr of land in Manahan Township adj JOSEPH REED, HENRY WILSON & JOHN SAND, which the Proprietaries by their patent dated 28 Dec 1767 granted unto the said ADAM FORSH (Patent Book AA vol. 10 pg 214 in Phila) ... provided that if the said ULRICH LIGHTY shall well and truly pay unto the said ADAM FORSH £100 before 3 Jan 1780 then this indenture to be void ... . Wit: MATTHEW DILL, MARY DILL. Ackn 3 Jan 1775 before MATTHEW DILL justice. 28 Jun 1775 By virtue of a letter of atty from ADAM FORSH, JNO CLARK Junr discharged mortgage. (F:pg 118)

19 Sep 1774. Deed. THOMAS ARMOR of York Town, York Co surveyor for £10.15.6 sold to SAMUEL JOHNSTON of same place esqr a 142 ½ a. tr of land in Codorus Township adj JACOB HENRY, PHILIP EMIGH & land formerly of TOBIAS AMSPOKER the elder but now belonging to the said SAMUEL JOHNSTON, together with the warrant under which the land was surveyed 20 Sep 1762 to TOBIAS AMSPOKER ... . Wit: JOHN CLARK Junr, R.N. CARNAN. Ackn 19 Sep 1774 before WILLIAM BAILEY esqr justice. (F:pg 119)

9 Dec 1774. Deed of Mortgage. DANIEL CORFMAN of Shrewsberry Township, York Co yeoman for better securing the payment of £91 and also 5 shillings sold to BALTZER KOHLER of same place yeoman a tr of land in Shrewsberry Township adj the said BALTZER KOHLER & LAWRENCE

KLINEFELTER and whereon the said DANIEL CORFMAN now dwells ...
whereas the said DANIEL CORFMAN standeth bound unto the said BALTZER
KOHLER for £182 conditioned for the payment of £91 on 30 Aug 1776 ...
provided that if the said DANIEL CORFMAN shall well and truly pay unto the
said BALTZER KOHLER £91 then this indenture to be void ... . Wit: JOHN
MORRIS, GEORGE SCHLOSSER. Ackn 9 Dec 1774 before WILLIAM
BAILEY esqr justice. 9 Nov 1776 BALTZER KOHLER discharged mortgage.
Wit: SAML JOHNSTON recorder. (F:pg 120)

22 Feb 1769. Deed. JOHN HECKENDORN of York Town, York Co weaver
for £46.1 sold to GEORGE GEYER of same place yeoman a 214 a. tr of land ...
whereas VALENTINE ERTEL of Dover Township, York Co by an indenture of
mortgage dated 20 Jan 1763 did sell unto the said JOHN HECKENDORN (by
the name of JOHN HECKINTORN) a 214 a. tr of land in Dover Township adj
ADAM BOTT & FREDERICK ICHOLTZ, which was surveyed unto the said
VALENTINE ERTEL in pursuance of a warrant dated 5 Oct 1750, in said
indenture there is a condition contained for redemption of the said premises
upon payment of £37 on 20 Jan next ensuing date of indenture (Book B pg 24),
and the £37 or any part thereof was not paid and remains unpaid by means
whereof the said tr of land became forfeited unto the said JOHN
HECKENDORN ... . Wit: GEO EICHELBERGER, JACOB BILLMEYER
Junr. Ackn 22 Feb 1769 before MICHAEL SWOOPE esqr justice. (F:pg 122)

13 Oct 1774. Deed. JOHN HOUSTON of the Town of York, York Co
physician and SUSANNAH his wife for £140.2.6 sold to GEORGE ERNEST
SCHLOSSER of same place hossier a 14 ¾ a. tr of land pt/o a 55 a. tr of land adj
JAMES WRIGHT, JOHN HAUGNER, RINEHARD BUTT & MARTIN
EICHELBERGER ... whereas the Proprietaries by their patent dated at Phila 7
Apr 1752 did grant unto JOHN WRIGHT, JAMES WRIGHT & WILLIAM
WILLIS a 480 a. tr of land in Manchester Township (Patent Book A vol. 16 pg
140), and after obtaining the patent it was mutually agreed that the said JOHN
WRIGHT and JAMES WRIGHT should have 278 a. of land for their 2/3 shares
of the afsd tr of land, and that WILLIAM WILLIS should have the remainder,
and the said JOHN WRIGHT on 3 Dec 1753 made his will and did devise that
all my estate real and personal to be valued and divided in six shares, I leave to
my wife one share, to my two sons ROBERT & JOHN three shares which I
order to be the plantation on which I live, to my two daus each one share, and
did appoint ELEANOR WRIGHT and the said JAMES WRIGHT executors,
afterwards the said JOHN WRIGHT died leaving ELEANOR his widow and
issue the afsd ROBERT WRIGHT, JOHN WRIGHT, PATIENCE now w/o
JAMES EWING and SUSANNAH now w/o the afsd JOHN HOUSTON, and
the said WILLIAM WILLIS and BETTY his wife on 5 Feb 1764 in pursuance of
the afsd agreement did release all their right in the 278 a. tr of land unto the said

JAMES WRIGHT and ELEANOR WRIGHT (Book C pg 240), and the said ROBERT WRIGHT after the death of his father died also unmarried intestate and without issue, and the said ELEANOR WRIGHT since died also intestate leaving the afsd JOHN WRIGHT, PATIENCE & SUSANNAH to survive her, and the said JAMES EWING & PATIENCE his wife on 19 Sep 1771 did release unto the said JOHN WRIGHT all their right in the 278 a. tr of land (excepting 26 a.), and the said JAMES WRIGHT and RHODA his wife on 23 Jun ---- did release unto the said JOHN WRIGHT two trs of land pt/o the 278 a. tr of land (one 55 a. and the other 83 a. 29 perches), and the said JOHN WRIGHT on 24 Jun same year did release unto the afsd JOHN HOUSTON and SUSANNAH his wife the two trs of land of 55 a. and 83 a. 29 perches ... . Wit: JOHN MORRIS, JOHN HECKENDORN. Ackn 13 Oct 1774 before WILLIAM SCOTT justice. (F:pg 123)

29 Dec 1774. Deed. JACOB DOWDLE of York Town, York Co tanner and ANNA MARIA his wife for £500 sold to JOSEPH DONALDSON of same place merchant a lot of ground pt/o three lots of ground adj High Street, Water Street, CHARLES BARNET & said JACOB DOWDLE in the Town of York ... whereas the Proprietaries by their patent dated at Phila 21 Apr 1761 did grant unto the said JACOB DOWDLE a lot of ground on the s side of High Street in the Town of York, No. 137, in breadth 57 ½' and in length 214' bounded by Water Street, said JACOB DOWDLE (Lot No. 138) & Codorus Creek (Patent Book A vol. 18 pg 323) ... the Proprietaries by one other patent dated at Phila 21 Apr 1761 did grant unto the said JACOB DOWDLE a lot of ground (No. 138) in the Town of York on the w side of Water Street, in breadth 57'6" and in length 220' bounded by Codorus Cr & said JACOB DOWDLE (Lot Nos. 139 & 137) (Patent Book A vol. 18 pg 324) ... the Proprietaries by one other patent dated at Phila 21 Apr 1761 did grant unto the said JACOB DOWDLE a lot of ground in the Town of York (No. 139) in breadth 57 ½' and in length 225' bounded by Water Street, Codorus Cr & said JACOB DOWDLE (Lot No. 140 & 138) (Patent Book A vol. 18 pg 321) ... . Wit: GEORGE ERNST SCHLOSSER, WM LEAS. Ackn 29 Dec 1774 before WILLIAM LEAS esqr justice. (F:pg 126)

20 Sep 1774. Deed. JAMES WRIGHT of Hempfield Township, Lancaster Co, PA gent and RHODA his wife for £68 sold to JOSEPH DONALDSON of York Town, York Co merchant a 6 a. 22 perches tr of land adj York Town land, JOHN HOUSTON & THOMAS HARTLEY esqr, in Manchester Township pt/o a larger tr of land granted by patent to the said JAMES WRIGHT, JOHN WRIGHT in his lifetime and WILLIAM WILLIS and since by sundry conveyances vested in the said JAMES WRIGHT ... . Wit: MICK HAHN, JOS UPDEGRAFF. Ackn 20 Sep 1774 before WM LEAS esqr justice. (F:pg 129)

14 Nov 1774. Deed. WILLIAM MATTHEWS of York Town, York Co surveyor and HANNAH his wife for £119 sold to JOSEPH DONALDSON of same place merchant a 11 a. 142 perches tr of land adj Newberry Road, Doctor JOHN HOUSTON, THOMAS HARTLEY esqr & said JOSEPH DONALDSON, in Manchester Township, pt/o a larger tr of land which JAMES WRIGHT and RHODA his wife on 20 Sep last granted to the said WILLIAM MATTHEWS ... . Wit: THOS HARTLEY, WM LEAS. Ackn 14 Nov 1774 before WILLIAM LEAS esqr justice. (F:pg 131)

14 Dec 1774. Deed. JOHN HOUSTON of York Town, York Co physician and SUSANNAH his wife for £90 sold to JOSEPH DONALDSON of same place merchant a 8 a. 65 perches tr of land pt/o a 138 a. tr in Manchester Township adj York Town land, THOMAS HARTLEY esqr, SAMUEL UPDEGRAFF & SAMUEL JOHNSTON esqr, pt/o a 180 a. tr of land granted by patent dated 17 Apr 1752 unto JOHN WRIGHT, JAMES WRIGHT & WILLIAM WILLIS, the right of 138 a. part thereof being by virtue of sundry conveyances vested in the afsd JOHN HOUSTON ... . Wit: WM HARBONNE, WM LEAS. Ackn 14 Dec 1774 before WILLIAM LEAS esqr justice. (F:pg 132)

20 Sep 1774. Deed. JAMES WRIGHT OF Hempfield Township, Lancaster Co esqr and RHODA his wife for £150 sold to WILLIAM MATTHEWS of York Town, York Co surveyor two parcels of land in Manchester Township, a 8 ¼ a. tr of land adj Codoras Cr, JOSEPH UPDEGRAFF, Newberry Road & DAVID GRIER and a 14 a. tr of land adj Newberry Road, JOSEPH DONALDSON & JOHN HOUSTON ... . Wit: THOS MINSHALL, JOHN HOUSTON. Ackn 20 Sep 1774 before WILLIAM LEAS justice. (F:pg 134)

17 Jan 1775. Deed of Mortgage. JACOB WILLIAMS of Warrington Township, York Co house carpenter for better securing the payment of £84.1.1 and also 5 shillings sold to ANN THOMAS of Tyrone Township, Cumberland Co, PA spinster a 130 a. tr of land in Warrington Township adj JEHU THOMAS, JOSHUA DAVIS, TETER UPPAH, BENJAMIN WALKER & WILLIAM ROSS ... whereas the said JACOB WILLIAMS standeth bound unto the said ANN THOMAS for £168.2.2 conditioned for the payment of £84.1.1 on 17 Jan 1776 ... provided that if the said JACOB WILLIAMS shall well and truly pay unto the said ANN THOMAS £84.1.1 then this indenture to be void ... . Wit: WM MATTHEWS, WM PENROSE. Ackn 17 Jan 1775 before WILLIAM LEAS esqr justice. WM PENROSE by letter of atty from ANN THOMAS discharged mortgage. Wit: ARCHD MCCLEAN recorder. (F:pg 135)

5 Nov 1774. Deed of Mortgage. WILLIAM MILLER of Faun Township, York Co yeoman for better securing the payment of a debt and also 5 shillings sold to

THOMAS CORBYN of the City of London in that pt/o Great Britain called
England a 57 a. 66 perches tr of land in Faun Township called *Hazle Hill* adj
GEORGE SUTOR, Muddy Cr, GEORGE STEVENSON & BENONE
STERRET, which THOMAS CORBYN by his atty WILLIAM BROWN of the
City of Phila merchant on day before this date granted unto the said WILLIAM
MILLER ... whereas the said WILLIAM MILLER standeth bound unto the said
THOMAS CORBYN in several sums to be paid in payments before 5 Nov 1776
... provided that if the said WILLIAM MILLER shall well and truly pay unto
the said THOMAS CORBYN the afsd debt then this indenture to be void ... .
Wit: JOHN BASKEN, NATHAN JONES. Ackn 5 Nov 1774 before THOMAS
WILLING esqr justice. 10 Mar 1795 JOHN FORSYTH substitute atty for
THOMAS STEWARDSON who is atty for THOMAS CORBYN's executors
discharged mortgage. Wit: J. BARNITZ recorder. (F:pg 137)

21 Mar 1774. Deed. PETER LEONHART of Dover Township, York Co
cooper and MARGARET his wife for £200 sold to WILLIAM LEONHART of
same place farmer a 257 ¾ a. tr of land adj CHRISTOPHER LEONHART,
JACOB MYER, ADAM DEHL, GEORGE STOUGH & DANIEL MESSERLY
... whereas the Proprietaries by their warrant dated at Phila 4 Apr 1751 did
allow HENRY SHEITTRAN to take up 150 a. of land in Dover Township adj
JACOB LAMBERT, JACOB MYER, ADAM DEHL & DANIEL MESSERLY,
and the said HENRY SHEITTRAN on 13 Apr 1763 sold the afsd warrant and
land surveyed unto the said PETER LEONHART (Book B pg 63) ... . Wit:
DANIEL RAGEN, [?]. Ackn 21 Mar 1774 before JOS UPDEGRAFF justice.
(F:pg 138)

14 Nov 1774. Deed. JOHN HARRIS of Paxton Township, Lancaster Co
yeoman and MARY his wife for £850 sold to PHILIP SHREYNER
(SHREINER) of Manheim Township, York Co yeoman a 325 ½ a. tr of land in
Newberry Township adj MARGARET FINLEY, WILLIAM CHESNESS &
Susquehanna River and also a 43 ½ a. island in Susquehanna River near the afsd
tr of land called *Harris' Island* ... whereas the Proprietaries by their patent dated
at Phila 16 Mar 1737 granted unto JOHN HARRIS decd a 820 a. tr of land then
in Lancaster Co on the w side of Susquehanna now in Newberry Township,
York Co, and by another patent dated 20 Oct 1743 did grant unto the afsd JOHN
HARRIS decd a 200 a. tr of land adj the afsd tr including an island in the
Susquehanna River, and the said JOHN HARRIS decd and by his will dated 22
Nov 1746 dying seized of the afsd trs of land and island did after having devised
to his sons JOHN HARRIS & WILLIAM HARRIS 420 a. pt/o the said trs or
1020 a. on the upper part next to DANIEL PREST to include the improvement,
the will directs, "I leave to ESTHER my wife in lieu of her dower 600 a. of land
including an island being the residue of my 1020 a. tr provided she continues my
widow during her natural life and on her death or marriage I allow the 600 a. of

land to come to JOHN HARRIS, WILLIAM HARRIS, SAMUEL HARRIS & DAVID HARRIS sons of said JOHN HARRIS decd and ESTHER w/o Dr. WILLIAM PLUNKET a dau of said JOHN HARRIS decd and to ESTHER FINLEY late ESTHER PATTERSON and to MARGARET FINLEY heirs of ELIZABETH FINLEY another dau of said JOHN HARRIS decd"... whereas JOHN HARRIS one of the parties to this indenture hath purch the share of WILLIAM HARRIS & MARGARET his wife on 19 Sep 1761, the share of SAMUEL HARRIS and ELIZABETH his wife on 19 Sep 1761, and the share of WILLIAM PATTERSON and ESTHER his wife on 11 Sep 1770 ... and by virtue of a writ of partition JOHN HARRIS' shares purch afsd has been surveyed and laid off the tr of land to the said JOHN HARRIS ... . Wit: WILLIAM RANKIN, SOLOMON PATTEN. Ackn 14 Nov 1774 before WILLIAM RANKIN justice. (F:pg 140)

8 Nov 1774. Deed of Mortgage. GEORGE KOOGH of the Town of Hanover, York Co and MARGARET his wife for better securing the payment of a debt and also 5 shillings sold to PETER WYNEBRENNER of Dover Township, York Co yeoman a 140 a. tr of land in Dover Township adj ADAM DEHL, CHILIAN LONG, GEORGE STOUGH, JOSEPH KLEPFER, PETER BARDMESS & JEREMIAH BEAR, which the said GEORGE KOOGH on day before this date purch from the said PETER WYNEBRENNER ... whereas the said GEORGE KOOGH standeth bound unto the said PETER WYNEBRENNER in several sums to be paid in payments before 7 Nov 1780 ... provided that if the said GEORGE KOOGH shall well and truly pay unto the said PETER WYNEBRENNER the afsd debt then this indenture to be void ... . Wit: JACOB [?], [?]. Ackn 9 Nov 1774 before RD MCALISTER justice. (F:pg 142)

14 Oct 1774. Deed of Mortgage. JOHN THOMPSON of Chanceford Township, York Co miller for better securing the payment of £600 and also 5 shillings sold to MARY NICOL executrix of the estate of WILLIAM NICOL decd of same place a 95 a. 34 perches tr of land in Chanceford, Fawn & Hopewell Townships adj WILLIAM WILSON, the Manifolds, ROBERT DUNLAP, JOHN PANE & others, which was surveyed to WILLIAM NICOL decd in pursuance of a warrant ... whereas the said JOHN THOMPSON standeth bound unto the said MARY NICOL for £1200 conditioned for the payment of £600 in payments, £100 on 1 Dec next ensuing and £100 on 1 Dec 1775 and £100 1 Dec every year till paid ... provided that if the said JOHN THOMPSON shall well and truly pay unto the said MARY NICOL £600 then this indenture to be void ... . Wit: JOSEPH READ, JESSE BEALES. Ackn 14 Oct 1774 before WILLIAM SMITH justice. (F:pg 144)

14 Jun 1762. Articles of Agreement. HENRY MYER of Little Conewaga, York Co yeoman for £659 has agreed to sell unto JOHN MYER of Conejohela, York Co, his 95 a. tr of land in PA and 182 a. in MD on Plum Cr adj CONRAD BOTT & THOMAS ADAMS, and to make the said JOHN MYER a legal deed on or before 15 Oct next and to deliver peaceable possession to the said JOHN MYER before 24 Jun instant, and the said JOHN MYER covenants to pay the afsd consideration money, to wit, £109 in ready money & £150 on 15 Oct next & £100 yearly from that time till the whole is paid, and for the true performance hereof the said parties bind themselves to each other in the sum of £1318 ... . Wit: PETER SHUGERT, JAS SMITH. Proved 24 Dec 1774 by JAMES SMITH & PETER SHUGERT before WILLIAM SCOTT esqr justice. (F:pg 145)

1 Nov 1774. Deed of Mortgage. GEORGE EALY of Warrington Township, York Co farmer for better securing the payment of £200 and also 5 shillings sold to HENRY LOHMAN of same place yeoman a 200 a. tr of land in Warrington Township adj MICHAEL BOWER & SAMUEL COX ... whereas the said GEORGE EALY standeth bound unto the said HENRY LOHMAN for £400 conditioned for the payment of £200 on 1 May 1776 ... provided that if the said GEORGE EALY shall well and truly pay unto the said HENRY LOHMAN £200 then this indenture to be void ... . Wit: GEORGE MCMILLAN, JOHN SMITH. Ackn 1 Nov 1774 before JOHN SMITH esqr justice. 26 Apr 1791 FREDERICK REIDER executor of the will of HENRY LOHMAN discharged mortgage. Wit: J. BARNITZ recorder. (F:pg 146)

19 Feb 1765. Deed. ARCHIBALD BAIRD (BEARD) of Hamiltons Ban Township, York Co for £200 (and also that RICHARD BAIRD doth promise to pay on demand yearly and every year during his natural life such a support of all things necessary as the said ARCHD BAIRD shall need on penalty of making void the present bargain) sold to said RICHARD BAIRD of same place a 121 a. tr of land on each side of Middle Cr in Hamiltons Bane Township called the *Mill Place* together with 80 a. of *Carrolls Delight* adj the said *Mill Place* and is pt/o said place according to a line run by SAMUEL WITHROW and a line settled with my son WILLIAM for the other part of it and also my right to a meadow field on the old place as it is set forth in a bond from my son WILLIAM BAIRD dated 22 Apr 1761 together with 50 a. on the n br of Middle Cr ... . Wit: DAVID WALLACE, DAVID BAIRD. Proved 10 Oct 1767 by DAVID BAIRD before ROBT MCPHERSON justice. (F:pg 148)

22 Dec 1774. Deed. RICHARD BAIRD of Petters Township, Cumberland Co, PA yeoman for £150 sold to HUGH DINWODY and SAMUEL MOOR of Hamiltons Bann Township, York Co a 318 a. tr of land (except the timber in Pine Swamp for 10 years) ... whereas there was granted by the Proprietaries to

ARCHIBALD BAIRD a warrant for 50 a. of land in Hamiltons Bann Township in the forks of Middle Cr called the *Boly Place* dated about 1762 by virtue of which there was surveyed and laid out to the said RICHARD BAIRD by ARCHIBALD MCCLEAN dep surveyor 318 a., and the said ARCHIBALD BAIRD did convey the same to the said RICHARD BAIRD his son ... . Wit: ALEX JOHNS, DEBORAH LATTA (LATA). Ackn 22 Dec 1774 before THOMAS LATTA justice. Whereas the said RICHARD BAIRD did obtain an application for a small piece of land adj the afsd 318 a. tr and he makes over all his right into said piece of land ... . Wit: ALEXA JOHNS, DEBORAH LATTA. Ackn 22 Dec 1774 before THOMAS LATTA justice. (F:pg 149)

2 May 1774. Deed. CHRISTIAN GRAFF of Newberry Township, York Co farmer and ABRAHAM SHELLEY of Ropko Township, Lancaster Co and CATHRINA his wife for £150 sold to DANIEL SHELLEY of Derry Township, Lancaster Co yeoman all their share (being ¾) in a 315 a. tr of land ... whereas in pursuance of a warrant dated at Phila 27 Dec 1753 there was surveyed and laid out unto ALBRECHT GRAFF a 315 a. tr of land adj his other land bought of ELIZABETH COLLINS & Susquehannah River in Newberry Township, and the said ALBRECHT GRAFF died intestate leaving BARBARA his widow, said CHRISTIAN GRAFF his only son and two daus ELIZABETH w/o the afsd DANIEL SHELLEY and KATHERINE w/o the afsd ABRAHAM SHELLEY ... . Wit: JACOB [MYER?], TIMOTHY KIRK, ELLIS LEWIS. Ackn 2 May 1774 before WILLIAM RANKIN esqr justice. (F:pg 150)

6 Feb 1775. Deed of Mortgage. DAVID EVANS of Dover Township, York Co yeoman for better securing the payment of £42 and also 5 shillings sold to ADAM DIHL of same place yeoman a 130 a. tr of land in Dover Township adj PHILIP WOLF, PHILIP GAUFF, PETER BRUMBACH, LUDWICK SPIECE & the heirs of JACOB UPP decd, whereon the said DAVID EVANS now dwells ... whereas the said DAVID EVANS standeth bound unto the said ADAM DIHL for £84 conditioned for the payment of £42 on 24 Jan next ... provided that if the said DAVID EVANS shall well and truly pay unto the said ADAM DIHL £42 then this indenture to be void ... . Wit: JOHN MORRIS, [?]. Ackn 6 Feb 1775 before WILLIAM SCOTT esqr justice. 8 Feb 1776 ADAM DIHL discharged mortgage. Wit: SAML JOHNSTON. (F:pg 152)

17 Jan 1775. Deed of Mortgage. JOHN POTTER of Berwick Township, York Co yeoman for better securing the payment of £154.16 and also 5 shillings sold to PHILIP BENTZ of the Town of York, York Co yeoman a 202 a. 35 perches tr of land called *Potters Field* in Berwick Township adj Little Conewagoe Cr, Widow TAYLER, HENRY MUCK, MATHIAS BAKER & JOSEPH POALK ... whereas the said JOHN POTTER stands bound unto the said PHILIP BENTZ for £309.12 conditioned for the payment of £154.16 on 17 Nov next ... provided

that if the said JOHN POTTER shall well and truly pay unto the said PHILIP
BENTZ £154.16 then this indenture to be void ... . Wit: GEORGE CRAFT,
GEORGE MOUL. Ackn 18 Jan 1775 before WILLIAM SCOTT justice. 4 Jun
1777 PHILIP BENTZ discharged mortgage. Wit: ARCHD MCCLEAN
recorder. (F:pg 153)

23 Jan 1775. Deed of Mortgage. OLIVER RAMSEY of Dover Township, York
Co yeoman for better securing the payment of £100 and also 5 shillings sold to
ABRAHAM NAFE of same place yeoman a 110 a. tr of land in Dover Township
adj the heirs of JACOB MILLER decd, ADAM GRIM, JACOB SMITH,
HENRY SCHENK, CHARLES SEIPE & MICHAEL LEIDEIGH ... whereas
the said OLIVER RAMSEY standeth bound unto the said ABRAHAM NAFE
for £200 conditioned for the payment of £100 yearly and every year on 20 Sep
next ensuing until 20 Sep 1780 ... provided that if the said OLIVER RAMSEY
shall well and truly pay unto the said ABRAHAM NAFE £100 then this
indenture to be void ... . Wit: JOHN MORRIS, GEORGE SCHLOSSER.
Ackn 23 Jan 1775 before WILLIAM SCOTT esqr justice. (F:pg 155)

30 Jan 1775. Deed of Mortgage. VALENTINE CRANTZ of Manchester
Township, York Co yeoman for better securing the payment of £250 and also 5
shillings sold to ROBERT STRETTELL JONES of the City of Phila esqr a
messuage and 233 ½ a. tr of land in Manchester Township adj MARTIN
ECKELBERGER, JOHN STUART, JACOB SCHMEISSER, the road leading to
York, JOSEPH GRAYBILL, MICHAEL EBERT & PHILIP ROTHROCK, pt/o
a larger tr of land which SAMUEL EDIE esqr high sheriff of York Co on 1 Jun
1774 sold unto the said VALENTINE CRANTZ ... whereas the said
VALENTINE CRANTZ together with FREDERICK MEHL of Germantown,
Phila Co skindresser stand bound to the said ROBERT STRETTELL JONES for
£500 conditioned for the payment of £250 on 30 Jan next ensuing ... provided
that if the said VALENTINE CRANTZ shall well and truly pay unto the said
ROBERT STRETTELL JONES £250 then this indenture to be void ... . Wit:
PETER MILLER, ABRM SHOEMAKER. Ackn 31 Jan 1775 before THOS
WILLING esqr justice. (F:pg 156)

10 Feb 1775. Deed of Mortgage. SAMUEL HORNISH of Cocollico Township,
Lancaster Co farmer for better securing the payment of £300 and also 5 shillings
sold to NICHOLAS DELLOW of Lancaster Borough, Lancaster Co a tr of land
in Manheim Township which CHRISTIAN LEFFELL seated and improved
upon and afterwards made his will and devised the same to his son PETER then
a minor, and the said CHRISTIAN LEFFELL afterwards died possessed of the
improvement leaving MARIA BARBARA his widow, the said PETER his eldest
son and sundry other minor children, and NICHOLAS BEETINGER after the
decease of the said CHRISTIAN, on 18 Jun 1759 obtained a warrant for 150 a.

to be surveyed to him in trust for the heirs of CHRISTIAN LEFFELL decd adj
CHRISTIAN KERR in Manheim Township, and the said PETER LEFFELL
eldest son and heir at law of the said CHRISTIAN LEFFELL having first
obtained an order from the Orphans Court held 14 Sep 1761 that he should hold
and enjoy the said land, and the said PETER LEFFELL afterwards on 12 Jun
1762 sold all his right unto the said NICHOLAS BEETINGER, and the said
NICHOLAS BEETINGER on 15 Jan 1774 sold the tr of land unto MARTIN
BASH, and the said MARTIN BASH on 10 Feb 1775 sold the tr of land unto the
said SAMUEL HORNISH ... whereas the said SAMUEL HORNISH stands
bound unto the said NICHOLAS DELLOW for £600 conditioned for the
payment of £300 in payments before 1 May 1781 ... provided that if the said
SAMUEL HORNISH shall well and truly pay unto the said NICHOLAS
DELLOW £300 then this indenture to be void ... . Wit: JOHN
HECKENDORN, JOHN SHALLENBERGER. Ackn 10 Feb 1775 before
WILLIAM LEAS justice. 24 Aug 1790 CATHARINE DELLOW (DELLO) w/o
NICHOLAS DELLOW (who has absconded himself) discharged mortgage.
Wit: J. BARNITZ recorder. (F:pg 158)

5 Nov 1773. Deed. CHARLES DIHL of Codorus Township, York Co yeoman
and CHRISTINA his wife for £60 sold to ANDREAS SCHWARTZ of York Co
yeoman a 50 a. parcel of land in Shrewsberry Township adj the said ANDREAS
SCHWARTZ's other land, said CHARLES DIHL, NICHOLAS HENRY &
NICHOLAS SCHUSTER, pt/o a 170 a. tr of land which the Proprietaries by
their patent dated 12 Jun 1761 granted unto FREDERICK FISSEL, who with his
wife MARY on 9 Jun 1768 conveyed the 170 a. to the said CHARLES DIHL ...
. Wit: SARAH MILLER, HENRY MILLER. Ackn 5 Nov 1773 before
MARTIN EYCHELBERGER justice. (F:pg 160)

20 Feb 1775. Deed of Mortgage. JACOB SPONSALER of Germany
Township, York Co yeoman for better securing the payment of £110 and also 5
shillings sold to GEORGE SPONSALER of same place yeoman 1 black stallion,
1 grey mare, a yearling bay colt, 8 sheep, 3 cows, a bed, bedstead & bedding. 2
chests, 2 iron potts, 3 pewter basons, 6 pewter plates, 1 heckle, 5 hogs, 2 waggon
loads of hay, 1 plough & harrow, 1 iron stove, 6 a. of wheat and 6 a. of rye in the
ground ... whereas the said JACOB SPONSALER stands bound unto the said
GEORGE SPONSALER for £220 conditioned for the payment of £110 on 20
Feb next ensuing ... provided that if the said JACOB SPONSALER shall well
and truly pay unto the said GEORGE SPONSALER £110 then this bill of sale to
be void ... . Wit: JOS BOUDE, ISAAC DROGGET. Ackn 20 Feb 1775 before
RD MCALISTER justice. (F:pg 163)

4 Mar 1775. Deed. PHILIP ZEIGLER of Manchester Township, York Co
yeoman and MARGARET his wife for £10 sold to HENRY WELSH of the

Town of Hanover, York Co house carpenter Lot No. 69 in the Town of Hanover subject to the yearly rents to RICHARD MCCALISTER and other reservations and services ... whereas RICHARD MCCALISTER esqr by his indenture of lease dated 31 May 1763 did grant unto the said PHILIP ZEIGLER a lott of ground in the Town of Hanover, No. 69, in breadth 57'6" and in length 230' bounded by Baltimore Street, Lot No. 68 & Lot No. 70, pt/o a larger tr of land called *Digges' Choice* which the said RICHARD MCCALISTER holds in right of JOHN DIGGES decd (Book A vol. 2 pg 12) ... . Wit: [?], [MICHAEL ?]. Ackn 4 Mar 1775 before WM BAILEY justice. (F:pg 164)

7 Feb 1775. Deed. ULRICH FEITZ (FEETZ) of Baltimore Co, MD yeoman and EVA ELIZABETH his wife and ANNA CATHARINA ROOP widow and relict of CHRISTIAN ROOP of York Co yeoman decd for £22 sold to MICHAEL KUNKLE and JACOB KAUFELDT of York Co yeomen a 100 a. tr of land ... whereas the said CHRISTIAN ROOP in his lifetime by sundry conveyances became owner and seized of a 100 a. tr of land in Shrewsberry Township adj JOSEPH MCFARLEN, MICHAEL KLINEFELTER, JOHN FLOWER, DAVID LONG & DANIEL BAILEY, being ½ pt/o a larger tr of land granted by an application to JOHN HILL, and the said CHRISTIAN ROOP being so seized since died without having made a will leaving issue to survive him, to wit, the said EVA ELIZABETH his only dau now w/o the said ULRICH FEITZ, and the tr of land descended to the said EVA ELIZABETH ... . Wit: ADAM WENTZ, MARTIN LANGERT. Ackn 17 Feb 1775 BY ULRICH FEITZ & EVA ELIZABETH his wife before RICHARD MCALISTER esqr justice. Proved 7 Feb 1775 by ADAM WENTZ & MARTIN LANGERT for CATHARINA ROOPE before RICHARD MCALISTER justice. (F:pg 165)

21 Jan 1725. Deed of Release. Whereas a tr of land confirmed unto me YODER MAISNER by the within patent is not my property nor in my possession, I having about 2 years past sold and conveyed the same unto NICHOLAS CAUFFELDT ... know ye, that I YODER MAISNER for £51.7.9 repaid unto me by the Proprietaries hereby release unto them all my right to the tr of land ... . Wit: ARCHD MCCLEAN. Ackn 24 Jan 1775 before RD MCALISTER justice. (F:pg 167)

12 Dec 1774. Quit Claim. Whereas the Proprietaries by their warrant dated at Phila 6 Jun 1770 did grant unto MICHAEL GRUE (now of VA but formerly of Manheim Township, York Co) to take up 60 a. of land adj LODOWICK DERWACTER & others in Manheim Township, provided the same was not already surveyed or appropriated, and it was found upon trial by the dep surveyor that the said land granted by the warrant had been formerly surveyed and patented unto [*blank*] SCHRRACK and is now the property of GEORGE ROSS esqr and Company ... know ye, that MICHAEL GRUE for £4.10 repaid

unto me by the Proprietaries (being the sum which I had paid unto them) quit
claim unto the said Proprietaries the tr of land and warrant ... . Wit: HENRY
SLAGLE, ARCHD MCCLEAN. Ackn 12 Dec 1774 before HENRY SLAGLE
justice. (F:pg 168)

8 Jun 1774. Deed. JACOB CAIGE of Heidelberg Township and RUDOLPH
(alias RICHARD) CAIGE of Windsor Township both of York Co yeomen for
£1100 paid by JOHN WRIGHT late of Hellam Township, York Co decd,
JAMES WRIGHT & WILLIAM WILLIS sold to the said JAMES WRIGHT of
Hempfield Township, Lancaster Co, PA and WILLIAM WILLIS of Manchester
Township, York Co (and in trust for the heirs of the said JOHN WRIGHT decd)
a 600 a. tr of land ... whereas SAMUEL BLUNSTON by virtue of power
granted by the Proprietaries to give licence to such persons as should apply for
settlements on the w side of Susquehannah River did by a grant dated 4 Mar
1734 allow HANS CAIGE to settle and improve on 600 a. of land on the w side
of Cadorus Cr adj York Town land at the place first settled by THOMAS
LINVILL, and the said HANS CAIGE being seized in the 600 a. of land died
having first made his will dated 8 May 1748 and did bequeath the afsd tr of land
unto the afsd JACOB CAIGE & RUDOLPH CAIGE his sons ... . Wit:
BALTZER SPANGLER, DAVID CANDLER. Ackn 8&11 Jun 1774 before
WILLIAM LEAS justice.   (F:pg 169)

9 Mar 1775. Deed of Release. JOHN HOUSTON of the Town of York, York
Co physician for 5 shillings grant and release unto GEORGE SCHLOSSER,
PETER LIND, MATHIAS DETTER & SAMUEL UPDEGRAFF of same place
yeomen full and free ingress, egress & regress of a 12' alley in Manchester
Township between the said GEORGE SCHLOSSER, PETER LIND, MATHIAS
DETTER & SAMUEL UPDEGRAFF & others, in common with those persons
who have land contiguous to the said alley ... . Wit: JOHN MORRIS, JAMES
ROBB. Ackn – Mar 1775 before WILLIAM SCOTT justice. (F:pg 170)

16 Nov 1774. Deed. PHILIP BECKAR of Manchester Township, York Co
yeoman and EVE his wife for £360 sold to MARTIN HOK of Cocalico
Township, Lancaster Co yeoman a 127 a. tr of land in Manchester Township
pt/o a 122 ¾ a. tr of land which in pursuance of a warrant dated 14 Mar 1767
was surveyed and laid out unto PHILIP HOSE, the same land which WHYRICK
RUDISILL originally improved, who with ANNA BARBARA his wife on 14
Mar 1752 sold unto the said PHILIP HOSE, who on 22 Jan 1768 sold unto the
said PHILIP BECKAR pt/o the tr of land adj the road leading from York Town
to Carlisle, ADAM FACKLER, MARTIN RUPERT, MARTIN WHEIGLE ... .
Wit: JOHN MORRIS, [?]. Ackn 16 Nov 1774 before WILLIAM SCOTT
justice. (F:pg 171)

3 Mar 1775. Deed of Mortgage. JACOB MUSCHEROSCHER of Manheim Township, York Co yeoman for better securing the payment of £21 and also 5 shillings sold to GEORGE EICHELBERGER of York Town, York Co merchant a tr of land in Manheim Township adj SAMUEL GARBER, JOHN APPLE & CHARLES YOUNG, being the same land which was entered in the name of ISAIAH STEPHENS dated 17 Oct 1766 and on [*blank*] granted to LEVY STEPHENS who procured a survey and found to contain 90 a., and the said LEVY STEPHENS on 17 May 1774 sold the tr of land to GEORGE EICHELBERGER, and the said GEORGE EICHELBERGER sold the 90 a. of land to the afsd JACOB MUSCHEROSCHER ... whereas the said JACOB MUSCHEROSCHER standeth bound unto the said GEORGE EICHELBERGER for £42 conditioned for the payment of £21 ... provided that if the said JACOB MUSCHEROSCHER shall well and truly pay unto the said GEORGE EICHELBERGER £21 then this indenture to be void ... . Wit: [FREDERICK VANBUREN?], DAVID CANDLER. Ackn 2 Mar 1775 before WILLIAM LEAS esqr justice. (F:pg 174)

17 Feb 1775. Deed of Mortgage. ADAM MICHAEL of Dover Township, York Co yeoman and ANNA MARIA his wife for better securing the payment of £163 and also 5 shillings sold to CASPER REINICKER of York Co innholder two trs of land in Dover Township, a 95 1/3 a. tr of land adj CASPER ROWLAND, PETER STREAR, JACOB MYER, PETER OBB, JOHN PITZEL & MICHAEL CONN, which in pursuance of a warrant was surveyed to ADAM BORTMUS of York Co who on 29 Oct 1773 conveyed the same unto the said ADAM MICHAEL, and a 6 a. tr of land adj the afsd tr & PETER STREHR, pt/o a larger tr of land originally granted by warrant dated at Phila 26 Mar 1745 unto HENRY ZOUCK who conveyed the same to the said PETER STREHR who on 1 Feb instant granted the 6 a. of land to the afsd ADAM MICHAEL ... whereas the said ADAM MICHAEL stands bound unto the said CASPER REINICKER for £326 conditioned for the payment of £163 on 2 Jan next ... provided that if the said ADAM MICHAEL shall well and truly pay unto the said CASPER REINICKER £163 then this indenture to be void ... . Wit: JOS BOUDE, ARCHD MCCLEAN. Ackn 17 Feb 1775 before HENRY SLAGLE justice. 28 Nov 1776 CASPER REINICKER discharged mortgage. Wit: ARCHD MCCLEAN recorder. (F:pg 175)

15 Mar 1775. Deed of Mortgage. FREDERICK MYER of Hellam Township, York Co farmer for better securing the payment of £240 and also 5 shillings sold to PETER MUCKLER of Codorus Township, York Co farmer a 206 a. 38 perches tr of land in Codorus Township surveyed by virtue of two warrants unto the said PETER MUCKLER in two trs but lying contiguous and now comprehended as one tr adj JACOB SHEARER & ADAM SLEPPY ... whereas the said FREDERICK MYER stands bound unto the said PETER MUCKLER

for £480 conditioned for the payment of £240 in payments before 1 Apr 1782 ... provided that if the said FREDERICK MYER shall well and truly pay unto the said PETER MUCKLER £240 then this indenture to be void ... . Wit: [?], WM LEAS. Ackn 15 Mar 1775 before WILLIAM LEAS justice. 22 Jul 1782 PETER MUCKLER discharged mortgage. Wit: ARCHD MCCLEAN recorder. (F:pg 177)

1 Apr 1775. Deed. ISABELLA TENGLER late ISABELLA FUNCK of York Town, York Co widow £60 sold to JONAS RUDISILLY of Manchester Township, York Co farmer a 188 a. tr of land ... whereas JOHN FUNCK about 1749 died owner and seized of a 188 a. tr of land (then in pt/o Lancaster Co) now in Manchester Township, York Co adj NICHOLAS WILT, JOHN SHARP, land lately of LUDWIG WEISANG & others, leaving the said ISABELLA his widow and issue to survive him, having first made his will dated 17 Feb 1748/9 pt/o which in the words "my wife SIBILLA FONK shall have my plantation whereon I live now and all the cattle to keep as her own till she marries another husband then shall it be made up with her children as she thinks fitt" (proved in Lancaster) ... after the intermarriage of the said ISABELLA with her second husband a settlement was made with the children of said decd and they received satisfaction for their right to said land as by receipts in the hands of the guardians ... . Wit: JACOB [SIMS?], HENRY MILLER. Ackn 1 Apr 1775 before WILLIAM LEAS justice. (F:pg 179)

1 Apr 1775. Deed. HENRY JONES of Straban Township, York Co yeoman and ANN his wife for £357.15 sold to NICHOLAS VANHORN late of Cicel Co, MD a 150 a. tr of land pt/o a 450 a. tr of land adj NATHANIEL MCCOSS, STEPHEN GIFFEN, DAVID DENWODY, land late of Colonel HANCE HAMILTON & the said HENRY JONES ... whereas the Proprietaries by their patent dated at Phila 13 Apr 1772 did grant unto SAMUEL BELL a 450 a. tr of land called *Belmont* in Straban Township in the *Manner of Maske* adj DAVID DENWODY, land late of Colonel HANCE HAMILTON, JOHN SEMPLE, NATHANIEL MCCOSS & STEPHEN GIFFEN (Patent Book AA vol. 12 pg 85), and the said SAMUEL BELL & MARTHA his wife sold to the said HENRY JONES the 450 a. tr of land on 15 Apr 1774 (Book E pg 487) ... . Wit: ADAM VANCE, ROBT MCPHERSON. Ackn 1 Apr 1775 before ROBERT MCPHERSON esqr justice. (F:pg 181)

24 Mar 1775. Deed. PHILIP SCHNELL of York Township, York Co yeoman and JUDITH his wife for £550 sold to JACOB LINGENFELTER of Cadorus Township, York Co yeoman a 219 a. tr of land in Berwick Township adj JACOB KIMMERLIN, JOHN GRIM, ABRAHAM HOUSEWORTH, FREDERICK WOOLF, EDWARD MCGLOCKLIN & ADAM SOWER, which in pursuance of a warrant dated 22 Jul 1762 was surveyed and laid out unto

PETER DELLO, and the said PETER DELLO died seized in the tr of land leaving issue NICHOLAS DELLO, MICHAEL DELLO, JOHN DELLO, PETER DELLO, MARY w/o GOTLIP BREAGENER & MARGARET w/o CASPER FINCK, and on 20 Jan 1768 the said NICHOLAS DELLO, JOHN DELLO, PETER DELLO, GOTLIP BREAGENER & MARY his wife, CASPER FINCK & MARGARET his wife did release unto the said MICHAEL DELLO the 219 a. tr of land, and the said MICHAEL DELLO (by the name of MICHAEL DELLOW) on 27 Apr 1768 sold unto the said PHILIP SCHNELL the 219 a. tr of land … . Wit: JOHN MORRIS, [?]. Ackn 3 Apr 1775 before WILLIAM LEAS justice. (F:pg 184)

4 Apr 1775. Deed of Mortgage. JOHN GRAYBLE of Manchester Township, York Co yeoman for better securing the payment of £279 and also 5 shillings sold to BALTZER KNERTZER of Newberry Township, York Co yeoman a 170 a. tr of land in Manchester Township adj JOHN HUMNGHAUSER, JACOB GUTWALT, JACOB GINSEL, the heirs of BARNET GEMLING, MICHAEL QUICKLE & Little Conawago Cr, whereon the said JOHN GRAYBLE now dwells … whereas the said JOHN GRAYBLE standeth bound unto the said BALTZER KNERTZER for £558 conditioned for the payment of £279 in payments before 16 Mar 1779 … provided that if the said JOHN GRAYBLE shall well and truly pay unto the said BALTZER KNERTZER £279 then this indenture to be void … . Wit: JOHN MORRIS, JACOB GAERTNOR. Ackn 4 Apr 1775 before WILLIAM SCOTT esqr justice. 10 Jun 1789 BALTZER KNERTZER discharged mortgage. Wit: J. BARNITZ recorder. (F:pg 187)

9 May 1768. Deed. JOHN FRANCKEBERGER of Berwick Township, York Co yeoman and BARBARA his wife in consideration of the payment of the yearly rent and performance of the covenants and agreements herein after mentioned and also 5 shillings sold to PHILIP ALDLAND of Paradise Township, York Co a lot of ground, No. 76, on the se side of King Street in the Town of Berlin, in breadth 65' and in depth 220' bounded by Lot No. 77 & Lot. No. 75 … whereas the Proprietaries by their patent dated 26 Dec 1764 did grant unto the said JOHN FRANCKEBERGER a 186 a. tr of land in Berwick Township (Patent Book AA vol. 6 pg 87), and the said JOHN FRANCKEBERGER hath laid out a town on the afsd tr of land which he called Berlin and is desirous that the same shall forever be called by that name … paying unto the said JOHN FRANCKEBERGER the yearly rent of 1 silver milled Spanish piece of eight or so much money of PA as will purch such 1 silver milled Spanish piece of eight, on 1 Mar in each and every year forever … . Wit: [?], ABRAHAM MILEY. Ackn 9 May 1768 before JOHN SMITH justice. (F:pg 189)

5 Apr 1775. Deed of Mortgage. JACOB CRONEBAUGH of Dover Township,
York Co yeoman for better securing the payment of a debt and also 5 shillings
sold to GEORGE PHILIP ZIEGLER Junr of Manchester Township, York Co
yeoman a 242 a. tr of land ... whereas the Proprietaries by their patent dated at
Phila 3 Mar last past granted unto the afsd JACOB CRONEBAUGH a 242 a. tr
of land called *Peterton* which in pursuance of a warrant dated 11 Jun 1763 was
surveyed for PETER PRUMBACK (or CRONEBAUGH) in Dover Township
adj PHILIP KAUFF, PETER PENCE, LUDWICK SPIECE, JACOB
WEIMERT, HENRY LEINBACH, FELIX LINEBACH, PHILIP JACOB
JULIUS & JOSEPH COUGHNOUR, and the said PETER CRONEBAUGH by
his will dated 22 Jan 1774 did devise the same to JACOB CRONEBAUGH
(Patent Book AA vol. 15 pg 134) ... whereas the said JACOB CRONEBAUGH
became bound unto the said GEORGE PHILIP ZIEGLER in several sums
conditioned for several payments before 24 Jan 1784 ... provided that if the said
JACOB CRONEBAUGH shall well and truly pay unto the said GEORGE
PHILIP ZIEGLER Junr the afsd debt then this indenture to be void ... . Wit:
[?], GEO LEWIS LESLER. Ackn 5 Apr 1775 before WILLIAM LEAS esqr
justice. 5 Jan 1795 GEORGE PHILIP ZIEGLER discharged mortgage. (F:pg
192)

13 Jan 1764. Deed. HENRY PETER (HENERY PETTERS) of York
Township, York Co yeoman and CATRINA his wife for natural love and
affection and also 5 shillings sold to PETER PETER of same place son of said
HENRY PETER a 170 a. tr of land in York Township on which the said
HENRY PETER now dwells adj land late of CONRAD HOLTZBAUM now in
the tenure of PHILIP CROLL, MECHOR HENNEBERGER, JOHN PETER,
JOHN MARKS & the residue of HENRY PETER's tr now in the occupation of
JACOB PETER ... . Wit: GEORGE EICHELBERGER, JAMES SMITH.
Ackn 27 Mar 1772 before WILLIAM SMITH justice. (F:pg 195)

4 Jun 1771. Deed. JACOB GODSCHALK (GODSHALK) of the City of Phila,
PA clockmaker for £35 sold to JOHN HOOVER of Hempfield Township,
Lancaster Co yeoman a tr of land in Manheim Township adj land late of
ANDREW HERSHY now of said HOOVER, HENRY WEST & PETER ERB,
which I entered an application 23 Jan 1767 No. 2551 ... . Wit: JOHN KEBLE,
DAVID KENNEDY. Ackn 4 Jun 1771 before WILLIAM ALLEN esqr justice.
(F:pg 197)

27 Feb 1775. Deed. JOHN HOOVER (HUBER) for 20 shillings sold to
JACOB BURKHARD of Warwick Township, Lancaster Co all my right in a tr
of land together with the within deed ... . Wit: GEORGE SHAFFNER, CAS
SHAFFNER. Ackn 11 Apr 1775 before WILLIAM LEAS justice. (F:pg 198)

27 Feb 1775. Deed. JOHN HUBER of Hempfield Township, Lancaster Co, PA miller and ANN his wife for £2000 sold to JACOB BURKHARD of Warwick Township co afsd yeoman two trs of land in Manheim Township, 213 a. a tr of land adj CHRISTIAN HIRSHY & CHARLES YOUNG, pt/o a 600 a. tr of land which was granted by the Proprietary of MD by patent dated 13 May 1734 unto ANDREW HERSHY late of Lancaster Co decd (Liber ETN1 fol. 78 in MD), and the said ANDREW HIRSHY being so seized died first making his will (after giving some few specific legacies) did devise all the rest of his estate to be divided amongst his children, and the children of the afsd ANDREW HIRSHY did come to a partition of the larger tr of land on which division the afsd 213 a. tr of land fell to the share of the said JOHN HUBER in right of his wife ANNA one of the daus of the said decd, and the rest of the children by their deeds of release dated 8 Oct 1761 & 4 Jan 1763 did grant all their right to the tr of land to the said JOHN HUBER, and a 140 ½ a. tr of land adj THOMAS WILSON, JACOB BOLLINGER, ANDREW HIRSHY & MARK FURNEY, which the Proprietaries by their patent dated 17 Aug 1772 did grant unto the said JOHN HUBER (Patent Book AA vol. 13 pg 193 in PA) ... . Wit: GEORGE SHAFFNER, CAS SHAFFNER. Ackn 11 Apr 1775 before WILLIAM LEAS justice. (F:pg 198)

11 Apr 1775. Assignment. NICKOLAUS DELLOW (NICOLAS DELLO) for a valuable consideration assign unto JOHN LEMAN of Hempfield Township, Lancaster Co the within mortgage and all the money thereon due and payable and all my right in the tr of land therein mentioned ... . Wit: SIMON SHNEIDER, CAS SHAFFNER. Ackn 13 Apr 1775 before WILLIAM SCOTT justice. 27 Oct 1778 by virtue of a letter of atty from JOHN LEMAN, [?] MOFF discharged mortgage. Wit: ARCHD MCCLEAN recorder. (F:pg 202)

5 Nov 1774. Deed of Mortgage. JOHN MYER of Codorus Township, York Co farmer for better securing the payment of £600 and also 5 shillings sold to WILLIAM MKELHENNY of Reading Township, York Co taylor a 200 a. tr of land in Reading Township adj MICHAEL BASSERMAN, HENRY NELL, NICHOLAS BUSHEE & DAVID EARHART, granted by warrant unto DANIEL HARE dated 28 Oct 1748 for 100 a. and one other warrant granted unto the said WILLIAM MKELHENNY dated 26 Mar 1754 for 50 a. ... whereas the said JOHN MYER stands bound unto the said WILLIAM MKELHENNY for £1200 conditioned for the payment of £600 in payments before 1 May 1788 ... provided that if the said JOHN MYER shall well and truly pay unto the said WILLIAM MKELHENNY £600 then this indenture to be void ... . Wit: JOHN HECKENDORN, [?]. Ackn 5 Nov 1774 before WILLIAM LEAS esqr justice. 25 Aug 1791 WILLIAM MKELHENNY discharged mortgage. Wit: J. BARNITZ recorder. (F:pg 203)

19 Apr 1775. Deed. JOHN HOSS of Baltimore Co, MD yeoman and MARY his wife for £350 sold to JOHN BOAZ of York Co yeoman a 151 a. 60 perches tr of land in Manheim Township called *Charleton* adj JACOB BIXLER, JOHN BIXLER, MICHAEL HOWER & GEORGE ROSS and Company, which was granted by patent dated at Phila 24 Jul 1767 unto JACOB KEESLER (Patent Book AA vol. 10 pg 35), and which was granted by the said JACOB KEESLER and ESTHER his wife on 16 Nov 1770 unto the said JOHN HOSS (Book D pg 348) ... . Wit: JOHN CLARK Junr, R.N. CARNAN. Ackn 19 Apr 1775 before WILLIAM SCOTT justice. (F:pg 205)

23 Feb 1762. Deed. JACOB HEAK of Manchester Township, York Co yeoman for £126 sold to GEORGE STEVENSON of York Town, York Co esqr a tr of land whereon I lately dwelt on a br of Codorus Cr in Codorus Township which was surveyed to TOBIAS AMSPOKER in pursuance of a warrant dated at Phila 9 Mar 1753 ... . Wit: JNO BOYD, JAC MOORE. Ackn 23 Feb 1762 before HANCE HAMILTON esqr justice. (F:pg 208)

17 Apr 1775. Deed. JOHN RALSTON of Hopewell Township, York Co yeoman and MARY his wife for £311 sold to JOHN SCHNELL of same place farmer a 250 ½ a. tr of land in Hopewell Township adj ROBERT GASTON & JAMES SWENY, which DAVID MCCONAUGHEY esqr then high sheriff of York Co on 3 Apr 1768 sold unto ANDREW FINLEY, and the said ANDREW FINLEY on 1 Apr 1770 sold the tr of land unto FRANCIS CUNNINGHAM, and in pursuance of an application, No. 3888, dated at Phila 2 Jun 1767 a 250 ½ a. tr of land was surveyed and laid out unto the said FRANCIS CUNNINGHAM in Hopewell Township adj ANDREW FINLEY, JAMES CRAWFORD, DANIEL MCFARLAND & WILLIAM BOGLE, and the said FRANCIS CUNNINGHAM on 18 Aug 1770 sold the 250 ½ a. tr of land unto the afsd JOHN RALSTON ... . Wit: CHAS LUKENS, JOHN MORRIS. Ackn 17 Apr 1775 before WILLIAM SCOTT justice. (F:pg 209)

20 Jul 1774. Deed. WILLIAM MCCANDLESS of Hartford Co, MD and ESTHER his wife for £500 sold to JAMES MCCANDLESS of Fann Township, York Co a 382 a. 25 perches tr of land ... whereas in pursuance of several warrants granted to ALEXANDER MCCANDLESS in his life time, there was surveyed and laid off for the said ALEXANDER MCCANDLESS a large tr of land in Fann Township, and the said ALEXANDER MCCANDLESS died seized of the tr of land, leaving his son JAMES the sole executor of his will and at the request of the said JAMES MCCANDLESS there was a warrant dated at Phila 5 Mar 1768 and accordingly there was surveyed and laid out a 382 a. 25 perches tr of land called *Youngmans Choice*, and agreeable to the will of the said ALEXANDER MCCANDLESS the 382 a. 25 perches tr of land became the property of WILLIAM MCCANDLESS being a legatee therein mentioned

together with £12.10 purchase money with the same ... . Wit: WILLIAM
SMITH, DAVID KENNEDY. Ackn 20 Jul 1774 before WILLIAM SMITH
justice. (F:pg 212)

7 Apr 1774. Deed. CHRISTIAN BECHTEL of Manheim Township, York Co
yeoman for £50 sold to JOHN SCHENCK of same place yeoman a 68 ¾ a. tr of
wood land in Manheim Township adj the said CHRISTIAN BECHTEL &
GEORGE ROSS and Company, pt/o a larger tr of land which was granted unto
me by warrant dated 27 Oct 1767 and surveyed for my use on 10 Feb 1768 ... .
Wit: ARCHD MCCLEAN, [?]. Ackn 6 Dec 1774 before RD MCALISTER
justice. (F:pg 215)

1 May 1773. Deed. ABRAHAM GICKLER of Manheim Township, York Co
yeoman for £300 sold to CHRISTIAN BECHTEL of same place yeoman a 184
a. tr of land in Manheim Township adj other land of the said CHRISTIAN
BECHTEL, CONRAD MAUL & JAMES MEREDITH, which was granted unto
PETER GICKLER father of the said ABRAHAM GICKLER by a warrant dated
31 May 1762, and by the said PETER GICKLER on 19 Mar 1765 sold unto the
said ABRAHAM GICKLER, surveyed 25 Nov 1766 ... . Wit: [?], ARCHD
MCCLEAN. Ackn 18 Feb 1774 before RD MCALISTER justice. (F:pg 217)

7 Apr 1774. Deed. JOHN SCHENCK of Manheim Township, York Co yeoman
and MARY his wife for £50 sold to CHRISTIAN BECHTEL of same place
yeoman a 7 a. tr of land pt/o a 150 a. tr of land adj other land of said
CHRISTIAN BECHTEL, other land of JOHN SCHENCK, ADAM
EICHELBERGER (formerly of JOHN EMICH) & Codorus Cr ... whereas on 1
Apr 1767 MARTIN BECHTEL of York Co and VERONICA his wife sold to
the said JOHN SCHENCK a tr of land (pt/o a 150 a. tr called *Batchelors Choice*)
now in Manheim Township adj PETER WELTE, FRANCIS NULL, said
CHRISTIAN BECHTEL, JOHN EMIGH, FREDERICK EICHELBERGER &
HENRY BOWMAN ... . Wit: ARCHD MCCLEAN, [?]. Ackn 6 Dec 1774
before RD MCALISTER justice. (F:pg 219)

26 Apr 1775. Deed. PETER SPRINGER of Earl Township, Lancaster Co, PA
yeoman eldest son and heir at law of GEORGE SPRINGER decd for £120 sold
to FREDERICK FITZ of Windsor Township, York Co yeoman a 123 a. 131
perches tr of land ... whereas HENRY KELLER in his life time seated himself
and improved upon a 50 a. parcel of land then in York Township but now in
Windsor Township adj DAVID HUNTER, CONRAD FRY, ADAM HINELY &
CONRAD BEVER and died possessed, not having obtained any warrant or grant
for the same, and the relict of the said decd sold the same to GEORGE HENRY
KENIGH who sold the same to CHRISTOPHER LUTZ, who sold the same to
JUSTUS TRABERT and ADAM HINEDELY who assigned the same to the said

GEORGE SPRINGER in his life time, who by his will appointed SAMUEL LANDUS and CHRISTOPHER LANDUS executors and impowered them to make sale of the same for the purposes in the will mentioned, and the said GEORGE SPRINGER afterwards died owner and seized of the said messuage and tr of land, and SAMUEL KELLER eldest son and heir at law of HENRY KELLER afsd late of York Co yeoman decd, on 18 Feb 1763 did grant the messuage and tr of land unto SAMUEL LANDUS and CHRISTIAN LANDUS the executors of said GEORGE SPRINGER decd for the better enabling them to perform the trust reposed in them, and in pursuance of a warrant dated 22 Jan 1767 there was surveyed and laid out for SAMUEL LANDUS and CHRISTIAN LANDUS in trust for the heirs of GEORGE SPRINGER decd the afsd 123 a. 131 perches tr of land in Windsor Township adj CHRISTOPHER HINEDEL, JAMES HAMMOND, WENDEL REISINGER & GEORGE STEVENSON, and PETER SPRINGER hath since the death of his said father applied to the Orphans Court and by his petition setting forth that his said father GEORGE SPRINGER had died intestate seized of the said 130 a. tr of land in Windsor Township adj JACOB LUTZ, CHRISTOPHER HINDEL & DEVAULT GUET, and the said intestate had left a widow CHRISTINA and issue to survive him, namely PETER SPRINGER his eldest son, BARBARA, ELIZABETH & ANNA SPRINGER and prayed the Court to divide the land, whereupon the Court found the land would not divide without spoiling the whole and was valued at £70, and the Court did allot the land to the said PETER SPRINGER, he giving security to pay the other children their share ... . Wit: ADAM CREVER, GEO LEWIS LESLER. Ackn 26 Apr 1775 before MARTIN EYCHELBERGER justice. (F:pg 222)

27 Feb 1775. Deed of Mortgage. JOHN HAMMER (HEMMER) of Tyrone Township, York Co yeoman and MARGARET his wife for better securing the payment of £55 and also 5 shillings sold to JAMES HAMMOND of same place farmer a 303 a. tr of land in Tyrone Township adj THOMAS WILLIAMS & JOHN THOMAS, surveyed and laid out in virtue of a warrant dated at Phila 1 Sep 1749 ... whereas the said JOHN HAMMER standeth bound unto the said JAMES HAMMOND for £120 conditioned for the payment of £55 ... provided that if the said JOHN HAMMER shall well and truly pay unto the said JAMES HAMMOND £55 then this indenture to be void ... . Wit: MARGARET HOLEMS, JANE POPE. Ackn 20 Feb 1775 before JNO POPE justice. (F:pg 225)

7 Apr 1775. Deed. FREDERICK TRYER of the Town of Petersburg, York Co yeoman and CHRISTINA his wife for £35 sold to ABRAHAM SELL of York Co yeoman Lot Nos. 77 & 78 in the Town of Petersburg ... whereas PETER LITTLE late of York Co and URSULA his wife on 8 Jun 1772 for £6 did sell unto the said FREDERICK TRYER lotts of ground in the Town of Petersburg,

Nos. 77 & 78, each in front 66' and in length 264', bounded by King Street leading to York Town and to Frederick Town, MD ... . Wit: JOS BOUDE, RACHEL BOUDE. Ackn 7 Apr 1775 before RD MCALISTER justice. (F:pg 227)

6 Mar 1775. Deed of Mortgage. BOLTZER MOUDY of Manahan Township, York Co carpender for better securing the payment of £67.4.9 and also 5 shillings sold to GEORGE HEIKES of Huntington Township, York Co taylor two trs of land in Manahan Township adj MICHAEL MAMBER, CHASPER GROOB, WILLIAM GODFRY & CALUB BAILS, in the two trs 95 a. 41 perches and also the grain now growing in the ground, a bay mare & two cows ... whereas the said BOLTZER MOUDY standeth bound unto the said GEORGE HEIKES for £134.9.6 conditioned for the payment of £67.4.9 on 27 Nov 1777 ... provided that if the said BOLTZER MOUDY shall well and truly pay unto the said GEORGE HEIKES £67.4.9 then this indenture to be void ... . Wit: [?], JOHN SMITH. Ackn 6 Mar 1775 before JOHN SMITH esqr justice. 17 Apr 1784 GEORGE HEIKES discharged mortgage. Wit: ARCHD MCCLEAN recorder. (F:pg 229)

8 Oct 1774. Deed. ISAAC ROBINSON of the tr called *Carrols Delight* in Cumberland Township, York Co yeoman for £50 sold to MOSES MCCLEAN of same township surveyor a 55 a. tr of land in Cumberland Township bounded by a line called GALLAHAN's line of *Carrols Tract,* the heirs of ROBERT MCNUTT, WILLIAM BOYD & land of said ISAAC ROBINSON held under a MD right, pt/o the same tr of land which was purch from CHARLES CARROL esqr but afterwards discovered not to be contained within his lines and then was granted unto me by a warrant dated 22 Apr 1765 ... . Wit: HUGH DENWODY, WM MCCLEAN. Ackn 22 Apr 1775 before WILLIAM MCCLEAN esqr justice. (F:pg 231)

27 Apr 1775. Deed. ADAM HOFFMANN of York Township, York Co yeoman & CHRISTINA his wife for £350 sold to LAWRENCE REITER of Lebanon Township, Lancaster Co yeoman two trs of land in Windsor Township, a 156 a. 29 perches tr of land adj PETER REISINGER, PHILIP MILLHOFF, GEORGE WAMBACH & JACOB SHANE, which in pursuance of a warrant dated at Phila 20 Feb 1767 was surveyed and laid out unto JOHN KLEIN, and a 28 a. 109 perches tr of land adj the afsd tr, GEORGE WAMBACH, PETER WAMBACH & PHILIP MILLHOFF, which on 12 May 1770 was surveyed to JOHN KLEIN, and the said JOHN KLEIN on 1 Dec 1773 did grant the afsd two trs of land unto the said ADAM HOFFMAN ... . Wit: [?], GEO LEWIS LESLER. Ackn 27 Apr 1775 before WILLIAM RANKIN justice. (F:pg 232)

29 Apr 1775. Deed. HUGH NELSON of Hopewell Township, York Co
blacksmith and AGNESS his wife for £110 sold to PETER BREY-FOGEL of
Rockland Township, Berks Co a 101 a. 144 perches tr of land in Hopewell
Township adj WILLIAM WHITTON, which was surveyed in pursuance of the
application of JOHN MONTGOMERY, No. 2128, for 100 a. dated 11 Dec
1766, and the said JOHN MONTGOMERY on 13 Jul 1767 sold to JOHN
GEMMILL who assigned the same to JAMES JOHNSTON, and the said
JAMES JOHNSTON on 5 Oct 1771 sold the said application & survey together
with his improvement to the afsd HUGH NELSON ... . Wit: WM KERSEY,
GATER WEVERLING. Ackn 29 Apr 1775 before WILLIAM SCOTT esqr
justice. (F:pg 235)

5 Oct 1744 at Phila. The Proprietaries in pursuance of a warrant dated 3 Oct
1738 there was surveyed and laid out on 9 Jun 1741 unto ADAM FARNEY of
Lancaster Co a tr of land on a br of Little Conewago on the w side of
Sasquehannah River 223 a., now at the instance and request of the said ADAM
FARNEY we would be pleased to grant him a confirmation of the same ... for
£34.11.3 to our use paid by the said ADAM FARNEY we have granted unto the
said ADAM FARNEY 223 a. of land (Patent Book A vol. 11 pg 402 in Phila) ...
. [signed] GEORGE THOMAS esqr lieutenant governor of PA for the
Proprietaries. 12 Sep 1750 ADAM FARNEY of Heckelberg Township, York
Co assigns over his right of the within deed unto MARK FARNEY of said
township. Wit: [?], [?]. Ackn before PATT WATTSON justice. (F:pg 237)

2 May 1775. Deed. JOSEPH SMITH of York Town, York Co brewer and
BARBARA his wife for £1432 sold to PETER SCHLIMMER of Windsor
Township, York Co yeoman a lott of ground with the dwelling house, brew
house & malt house (and the brewing utensils) on the w side of Beaver Street in
York Town, No. 109, in breadth 57'6" and in length 250' bounded by Lot No.
110, whereon the said JOSEPH SMITH now lives ... . Wit: PHILIP [?],
HENRY MILLER. Ackn 4 May 1775 before WILLIAM BAILEY justice.
(F:pg 240)

3 May 1775. Deed of Mortgage. PETER SCHLIMMER of Windsor Township,
York Co yeoman and MAGDALENA his wife for better securing the payment
of £1300 and also 5 shillings sold to JOSEPH SMITH of York Town, York Co
yeoman Lot No. 109 in the Town of York [same as above] ... whereas the said
PETER SCHLIMMER standeth bound unto the said JOSEPH SMITH for £2600
conditioned for the payment of £1300 in payments before 1 May 1788 ...
provided that if the said PETER SCHLIMMER shall well and truly pay unto the
said JOSEPH SMITH £1300 then this indenture to be void ... . Wit: [?],
HENRY MILLER. Ackn 4 May 1775 before WILLIAM BAILEY justice.
(F:pg 242)

27 Apr 1775. Deed. ANDONEY NEW of Manhaim Township, York Co
yeoman for £400 sold to LEONHART GERCKENHEISER of same place
yeoman a 195 a. 32 perches tr of land called *Rock Hill* in Manhaim Township
adj WOLLRICH HUBER & STEPHEN PETERY, which was surveyed for the
afsd ANDONEY NEW 28 May 1768 by order of survey No. 4782 dated 2 Mar
1768 ... . Wit: HENRY DANNER, ELISABETH DANNER. Ackn 6 May
1775 before RD MCALISTER justice. (F:pg 244)

8 May 1775. Deed. JACOB WELTZHOOFER and BALTZER FITZ adminrs
of the estate of JOHN COMFORT late of York Co yeoman decd who died
intestate for £1005 sold to DANIEL RUDY of Manheim Township, Lancaster
Co yeoman a 186 a. 140 perches tr of land ... whereas the Proprietaries by their
patent dated at Phila 17 Sep 1768 did grant unto the said JOHN COMFORT
decd a 340 a. tr of land called *Comfort* adj MICHAEL FREEZ, GEORGE
SHALLER, ROBERT SMITH, CHRISTIAN NEWCOMER, Widow FEREE,
CHRISTIAN STONER & HENRY SMITH (Patent Book AA vol. 11 pg 12),
and the said JOHN COMFORT in his life time sold pt/o the afsd tr of land and
being so seized in a 186 a. 140 perches tr of land adj ROBERT SMITH,
CHRISTIAN NEWCOMER, JACOB BECK, BALTZER FITZ, HENRY
SMITH, MICHAEL FREEZ & GEORGE SHALLER, died intestate without
leaving a sufficient personal estate to pay his debts, and at an Orphans Court
held 26 Mar 1774 the said JACOB WELTZHOOFER and BALTZER FITZ
exhibited their petition to sell the tr of land for defraying the said intestate's
debts, and it was ordered that the said adminrs should make sale of the tr of land
at public vendue, and on 6 Mar last past they sold the tr of land to the said
DANIEL RUDY he being the highest bidder for £1005 ... . Wit: [?], HENRY
MILLER. Ackn 8 May 1775 before MARTIN EYCHELBERGER justice. (F:pg
247)

18 Feb 1775. Deed. DANIEL RUDY of Manheim Township, Lancaster Co, PA
yeoman for £250 sold to GEORGE RUDY of Cumberland Township, York Co a
267 a. tr of land in Paradise Township adj VALENTIN BERKHUMER,
MATHIAS BRINLEY, FREDRICK STOBER, TEETRICH SALTZGEBER,
HENRY WHEELER, JACOB HAURY & RICHARD PETERS, which by virtue
of a warrant dated 14 Jun 1763 was surveyed unto HANCE HAMILTON esqr
who on 23 May 1768 granted all his right to the tr of land unto the said DANIEL
RUDY ... . Wit: [?], CAS SHAFFNER. Ackn 8 May 1775 before MARTIN
EYCHELBERGER justice. (F:pg 250)

4 May 1775. Deed of Mortgage. ISAAC DRUGGET (DROGGET) of the
Town of Hanover, York Co tobacconist for better securing the payment of
£85.15.9 and also 5 shillings sold to ANDREAS SILING and ADAM
WINTERODE of Germany Township, York Co and GEORGE REINICKER of

Heidleberg 1 house clock, 2 black cows, 2 table, 3 chests, 3 beds, 1 kitchen dresser, 1 corner cupboard, 3000 weight of leaf tobacco, a compleat set of tobacconists tools, sundry pewter basons, plates & spoons, 4 cedar washing tubs, 3 cedar buckets, a large iron kettle, three iron potts, 2 iron pans, 3 bedsteads, 1 tin watering pott, 3 hogs, 4 chairs, 1 German Bible & sundry other German books, sundry household goods, the time of an indented servant man named MICHAEL CAMPBELL who has about 2 ½ years to serve, sundry men and women ... whereas the said ISAAC DROGGET stands bound unto the said ANDREAS SILING, ADAM WINTERODE & GEORGE REINICKER for £171.11.6 conditioned for the payment of £85.15.9 on or before 1 Jun next ensuing ... provided that if the said ISAAC DRUGGET shall well and truly pay unto the said ANDREAS SILING, ADAM WINTERODE & GEORGE REINICKER £85.15.9 then this bill of sale to be void ... . Wit: JOS BOUDE, GEO SEIVERT. Ackn 5 May 1775 before RD MCALESTER justice. (F:pg 252)

11 Apr 1775. Deed. JOHN PIFER of Shrewsberry Township, York Co farmer & MARGARET his wife for £110 sold to MELCHER PIFER of same place farmer a 136 a. tr of land ... whereas in pursuance of a warrant granted unto the said JOHN PIFER 7 Dec 1773 there was surveyed and laid off unto the said JOHN PIFER a 136 a. 14 perches tr of land in Shrewsberry Township adj NICHOLAS SHUSTER, RUDOLPH YONT, PETER NASHWANGER, JOHN DAGON & CONRAD KURFMAN ... . Wit: MARY LEAS, PANL METZGER. Ackn 11 Apr 1775 before WM LEAS justice. (F:pg 254)

10 Nov 1764. Quit Claim. PETER SPRINGLE of Manchester Township yeoman and HANNAH his wife, JOHN STRICKLER of Hallam Township yeoman and ELIZABETH his wife, LUDWIG TRIVER of Codorus Township yeoman and BARBARA his wife, MICHAEL SPRINGLE (SPRINKLE) of Manchester Township yeoman and ELIZABETH his wife, LUDWIG KEEFER of Codorus Township yeoman and MARGARET his wife, CHRISTIANA KEEFER of Codorus Township widow, ADAM TROREBAUGH of Shrewsbury Township yeoman & KATRINA his wife & HENRY SPRINGLE (SPRINKLE) of Paradise Township yeoman and MARY his wife, all of York Co for £96 quit claim unto GEORGE SPRINGLE of Manchester Township, York Co yeoman a 200 a. tr of land ... whereas in pursuance of a warrant dated at Phila 22 Nov 1746 there was surveyed and laid out on 13 Apr 1747 unto MICHAEL SPRINGLE a 200 a. tr of land in Manchester Township formerly pt/o Lancaster Co now York Co adj MICHAEL SPRINGLE, land late of FELIX MILLER decd & PHILIP LOW, and the said MICHAEL SPRINGLE afterward died leaving issue, the afsd PETER SPRINGLE his eldest son, ELIZABETH now w/o JOHN STRICKLER, BARBARA now w/o LUDWIG TRIVER, MICHAEL SPRINGLE, MARGARET w/o LUDWIG KEEFER, CHRISTIANA KEEFER,

KATRINA now w/o ADAM TROREBAUGH, HENRY SPRINGLE &
GEORGE SPRINGLE ... . Wit: GEO STEVENSON, JOHN BOYD, GEORGE
HOLTZINGER. Ackn 10 Nov 1764 before MICHAEL SWOOPE justice. (F:pg
256)

29 Apr 1775. Deed. JACOB KELLER of York Co yeoman and ESTHER his
wife late ESTHER SPRINGLE (one of the daus of MICHAEL SPRINGLE late
of Manchester Township, York Co yeoman decd) for £40 sold to GEORGE
SPRINGLE of Manchester Township, York Co yeoman (one of the sons of said
decd) all their estate right in a 200 a. tr of land [same as above] ... . Wit: [?],
HENRY MILLER. Ackn 29 Apr 1775 before WILLIAM LEAS justice. (F:pg
259)

13 Feb 1775. Deed of Mortgage. GEORGE WAMPFLER of York Town, York
Co weaver for better securing the payment of £96.3.8 and also 5 shillings sold to
MARY ELIZABETH KIENTZ & ADAM LEITNER of same place a lot of
ground on the n side of Phila Street in the Town of York, No. 157, bounded by
Lot No. 158 & Lot No. 156, in breadth 65' ... whereas the said GEORGE
WAMPFLER standeth bound unto the said MARY ELIZABETH KIENTZ &
ADAM LEITNER for £192.7.4 conditioned for the payment of £96.3.8 ...
provided that if the said GEORGE WAMPFLER shall well and truly pay unto
the said MARY ELIZABETH KIENTZ & ADAM LEITNER £96.3.8 then this
indenture to be void ... . Wit: FREDERICK YOUCE, GEO LEWIS LESLER.
Ackn 13 May 1775 before WILLIAM SCOTT esqr justice. 25 Feb 1778
ADAM LEITNER and for the heirs of MARY ELIZABETH KIENTZ now decd
discharged mortgage. Wit: ARCHD MCCLEAN recorder. (F:pg 261)

16 Feb 1775. Deed. WILLIAM BITTNER (BITNER) of Comerland Co, PA
joyner for £3.10 sold to ANTHONY (ANTHONEY) KNISLY of Warrington
Township, York Co farmer a 50 a. tr of land in Warrington Township adj the
said ANTHONY KNISLY's other land, FELIX PANCEL, SAMUEL COOPER,
JACOB BEALS, JOHN BAGHMAN & DITRICH KISER granted unto the said
WILLIAM BITTNER by warrant as appeared by a receipt from the hand of
PETER MILLER dated 19 Mar 1765 for 50 a. of land ... . Wit: GABRIEL
SMITH, JOHN SMITH. Ackn 16 Feb 1775 before JOHN SMITH justice. (F:pg
262)

18 May 1775. Deed of Mortgage. ANTHONY KNEISSLEY of Warrington
Township, York Co yeoman for better securing the payment of £50 and also 5
shillings sold to HENRY SEHLY of Berwick Township, York Co inn keeper a
263 a. 112 perches tr of land in Warrington Township adj CHARLES BOYER,
FELIX PENCLEY, LEVY STEPHENS & JACOB BEALS, which in pursuance
of a warrant was granted unto WILLIAM BITTNER 30 Apr 1765, and the said

WILLIAM BITTNER on 16 Feb last past sold the tr of land unto the said
ANTHONY KNEISSLEY [see above] ... whereas the said ANTHONY
KNEISSLEY standeth bound unto the said HENRY SEHLY for £100
conditioned for the payment of £50 on or before 18 May next ensuing ...
provided that if the said ANTHONY KNEISSLEY shall well and truly pay unto
the said HENRY SEHLY £50 then this indenture to be void ... . Wit: SARAH
MILLER, GEO LEWIS LESLER. Ackn 18 May 1775 before WILLIAM
SCOTT esqr justice. 15 Jun 1795 HENRY SEHLY discharged mortgage. Wit:
J. BARNITZ recorder. (F:pg 263)

12 Apr 1775. Deed of Mortgage. MARTEN GLATEY (MARDEN GLADEY)
of Warrington Township, York Co shumackar for better securing the payment of
£70 and also 5 shillings sold to HANRE LOWMAN of same place taylor a 125
a. tr of land in Warrington Township adj JAMES EWING, WILLIAM
GRIFFITH & JOHN THOMAS ... whereas the said MARTEN GLATEY
standeth bound unto the said HANRE LOHMAN for £140 conditioned for the
payment of £70 on 12 Apr 1779 ... provided that if the said MARTEN
GLATEY shall well and truly pay unto the said HANRE LOWMAN £70 then
this indenture to be void ... . Wit: MARTEN GLATE, FRADERICK RIDAR.
Ackn 22 May 1775 before WILLIAM BAILEY justice. (F:pg 266)

2 Apr 1773. Bond. ROBERT GORDON of Baltimore Co, MD yeoman bound
to make over to WALTER ROBISON of York Co farmer 42 a. of land in Fawn
Township which he obtained a mortgage or bill of sale for from JAMES
THOMPSON who purch the same from JAMES CROMY and by an obligation
given to me by ROBERT GORDON to WALTER ROBISON dated 11 Jul 1770,
by these presence make over to WALTER ROBISON the 42 a. of land n of the
temporary line and s of the new provincial line being pt/o a survey made for
JAMES CROMY by virtue of a warrant dated 1748, for the true performance of
the same do bind myself to defend the 42 a. of land to WALTER ROBINSON
... . Wit: SAMUEL POAK, GRISEL POAK. Ackn 26 Apr 1773 before
CUNINGHAM SEMPLE justice. (F:pg 267)

7 Dec 1772. Deed. ROBERT GORDON of Baltimore Co, MD for £4.2 sold to
WALTER ROBISON of York Co farmer a 40 a. tr of land which was granted to
me by the Land Office in Phila dated --- 1770 to be surveyed to me adj
THOMAS COOPER & others in Fawn Township ... . Wit: GRISEL POAK,
SARAH GORDON. Ackn 26 Apr 1773 before CUNINGHAM SEMPLE
justice. (F:pg 268)

15 Sep 1773. Deed. NICHOLAS BETTINGER of Berwick Township, York
Co yeoman and CHRISTIANA his wife for £300 sold to FRANCIS MARSHAL
of same place farmer ½ pt/o a 166 a. tr of land ... whereas the Proprietaries by

their patent dated at Phila 12 May 1765 did grant unto ABRAHAM
HOUSWORTH a 166 a. tr of land in Berwick Township adj Pigion Hills,
PETER DELOW & HENRY KENKHART (Patent Book AA vol. 6 pg 230), and
GEORGE EICHELBERGER esqr high sheriff of York Co on 2 May 1771 did
convey unto the said NICHOLAS BETTINGER the said tr of land (Book E pg
364) ... . Wit: RD MCALISTER, [?]. Ackn 5 May 1775 before HENRY
SLAGLE esqr justice. (F:pg 269)

22 May 1775. Deed. GEORGE MICHAEL STOBER of Paradise Township,
York Co yeoman and CHRISTINA his wife for £300 sold to JACOB STOBER
of same place yeoman a 260 ½ a. tr of land in Paradise Township adj
RUDOLPH KLEINPETER, JACOB HAMAN, CASPER SPENGLER & Pigeon
Hills, which in pursuance of a warrant dated at Phila 21 Oct 1751 was granted
unto FREDERICK STOBER, and the said FREDERICK STOBER on 15 May
1766 conveyed the 260 ½ a. tr of land to the said GEORGE MICHAEL
STOBER (Book D pg 194) ... . Wit: [?], GEO LEWIS LESLER. Ackn 22
May 1775 before MARTIN EYCHELBERGER justice. (F:pg 271)

26 May 1775. Deed of Mortgage. ROBERT JOHNSTON CHESTER of
Berwick Township, York Co inn holder for better securing the payment of £30
and also 5 shillings sold to ANDREW FREDRIX Senr of Paradise Township,
York Co yeoman a 6 ¾ a. tr of land pt/o a larger tr of land (the whole tr being
held by patent granted to JOHN FRANKEBERGER and the part conveyed by
the said JOHN FRANKEBERGER & BARBARA his wife unto JACOB
MILLER, and the said JACOB MILLER conveyed the said part unto the afsd
ROBERT JOHNSTON CHESTER as by the deed lodged in the custody of the
said ANDREW FREDRIX Senr) on Cannewago Cr in Berwick Township adj
lots in the Town of Berlin ... whereas the said ROBERT JOHNSTON
CHESTER standeth bound unto the said ANDREW FREDRIX Senr for £60
conditioned for the payment of £30 ... provided that if the said ROBERT
JOHNSTON CHESTER shall well and truly pay unto the said ANDREW
FREDRIX Senr £30 then this indenture to be void ... . Wit: GEO
EICHELBERGER, GEO LEWIS LESLER. Ackn 29 May 1775 before WM
BAILEY justice. 16 Oct 1777 ANDREW FREDRIX discharged mortgage.
Wit: ARCHD MCCLEAN recorder. (F:pg 274)

2 May 1775. Deed of Mortgage. RICHARD BLATCHFORD of Warrington
Township, York Co weaver for better securing the payment of £170 and also 10
shillings sold to RICHARD EGGLESTON of Manahan Township, York Co
cordwinder a 182 a. tr of land in Manahan Township adj GEO MCMILLAN,
BAXTER's land, BRICE BLAIR, WM PORTER, HUGH OHAIL,
CHRISTOPHER QUIGLEY ... whereas the said RICHARD BLATCHFORD
stands bound unto the said RICHARD EGGLESTON for £340 conditioned for

the payment of £170 in payments before 27 Nov 1787 ... provided that if the said RICHARD BLATCHFORD shall well and truly pay unto the said RICHARD EGGLESTON £170 then this indenture to be void ... . Wit: JAMES FEGAN, JOHN MCMILLAN. Ackn 2 May 1775 before JOHN SMITH esqr justice. (F:pg 276)

29 May 1775. Deed. JOSHUA HUTTON of Newberry Township, York Co yeoman and RACHEL his wife for £440 sold to WILLIAM MATTHEWS of York Co surveyor a 101 a. 98 perches tr of land pt/o a 300 a. tr of land that was granted unto JOSEPH HUTTON by patent dated 4 Nov 1762, which the said JOSEPH HUTTON by his will dated 26 Aug 1771 gave unto his son the afsd JOSHUA HUTTON, in Newberry Township adj TIMOTHY KIRK, the pt/o the tr the afsd JOSEPH HUTTON gave unto his son JOSEPH HUTTON, WILLIAM GARRETSON, other land of the said JOSHUA HUTTON & WILLIAM LEWIS ... . Wit: JOHN RANKIN, TIMOTHY KIRK. Ackn 29 May 1775 before WILLIAM RANKIN esqr justice. (F:pg 278)

29 May 1775. Deed. JOSHUA HUTTON of Newberry Township, York Co yeoman for £10 sold to WILLIAM MATTHEWS of York Co surveyor a 14 a. 146 perches tr of land (pt/o a 29 a. 132 perches tr of land which was surveyed unto my father JOSEPH HUTTON late of Newberry Township decd in pursuance of a warrant for 25 a. dated 18 Oct 1753) in Newberry Township adj said WILLIAM MATTHEWS & JOHN GARRETSON ... . Wit: JOHN RANKIN, TIMOTHY KIRK. Ackn 29 May 1775 before WILLIAM RANKIN esqr justice. (F:pg 280)

24 Apr 1775. Deed of Mortgage. PHILLIP CRONE of Dover Township, York Co carpenter for better securing the payment of £225 and also 5 shillings sold to MORDICAI WILLIAMS of Newberry Township, York Co taylor a 162 a. tr of land in Dover Township adj PHILLIP HENRY MOORE, land late of VALENTINE ERTLE, MELCHIOR BENEDICK, JACOB CARPENTER & CONRAD HEAK ... whereas the said PHILLIP CRONE standeth bound unto the said MORDICAI WILLIAMS for £550 conditioned for the payment of £225 in payments before 1 Nov 1785 ... provided that if the said PHILLIP CRONE shall well and truly pay unto the said MORDICAI WILLIAMS £225 then this indenture to be void ... . Wit: WM MATTHEWS, JOHN BANE. Ackn 24 Apr 1775 before WILLIAM RANKIN esqr justice. (F:pg 281)

5 Jan 1775. Deed. JAMES MORRISON of Reading Township, York Co yeoman and SARAH his wife for 5 shillings sold to WILLIAM WAKELY & JOHN CHAMBERLEAN of same place yeoman a 134 a. tr of land in the township afsd adj JEREMIAH CHAMBERLAIN, HENRY GROSS, HENRY HULL & SAMUEL BEATY, being the same place on which we now dwell ...

upon special trust and confidence that the said WILLIAM WAKELY & JOHN CHAMBERLEAN do as soon as convenient make sale of said plantation and tr of land and out of the money arising from such sale pay all the debts due by the said JAMES MORRISON and the residue of said money unto the said JAMES MORRISON ... . Wit: [?], [?]. Ackn 5 Jan 1775 before JOHN SMITH justice. (F:pg 283)

2 Jun 1775. Deed. WILLIAM WAKELY (WEAKLY) and JOHN CHAMBERLAIN (CHAMBERLEAN) of Reading Township, York Co yeoman for £225 sold to JONAS LIGHTLY of same place yeoman a 124 a. tr of land [same as above] ... . Wit: CHRISTIAN STAKE, THOS HARTLEY. Ackn 2 Jun 1775 before WILLIAM LEAS justice. (F:pg 284)

29 Apr 1775. Deed. EVAN MINSHALL of Manahan Township, York Co house carpenter for £225 sold to GEORGE MILLER of Warrington Township, York Co farmer a 150 a. tr of land in Manahan Township ... whereas in pursuance of a warrant dated 4 Apr 1751 granted unto JOHN GILES there was surveyed a 150 a. tr of land in Manahan Township adj SAMUEL NELSON, ROBERT ROSEBOUROUGH, RICHARD PETERS esqr, WILLIAM NELSON & ALEXANDER WILSON, and the said JOHN GILES on 29 May 1765 sold the tr of land to ISAAC LEREW, and the said ISAAC LEREW & AGNESS his wife on 30 Jun 1772 conveyed the tr of land unto the said EVAN MINSHALL ... . MATW DILL, [?]. Ackn 29 Apr 1775 before JOHN SMITH justice. (F:pg 285)

12 Apr 1775. Deed. PETER SCHWARTZ of York Town, York Co clockmaker for better securing the payment of £40.5.9 and also 5 shillings sold to CHARLES BARNITZ & GEORGE LEWIS LESLER of same place a lot of ground on Queen Street in the Town of York, No. 14, adj Lot No. 15, in front 65' and back 230', which JACOB SCHWARTZ on 17 Jun 1772 conveyed unto the afsd PETER SCHWARTZ (Book E pg 369) ... whereas the said PETER SCHWARTZ standeth bound unto the said CHARLES BARNITZ & GEORGE LEWIS LESLER for £80.11.6 conditioned for the payment of £40.5.9 on or before 25 May next ensuing ...provided that if the said PETER SCHWARTZ shall well and truly pay unto the said CHARLES BARNITZ & GEORGE LEWIS LESLER £40.5.9 then this indenture to be void ... . Wit: PHILLIP [?], ADAM CREVER. Ackn 12 Apr 1775 before WM BAILEY justice. 16 Oct 1777 CHARLES BARNITZ & GEORGE LEWIS LESLER discharged mortgage. Wit: ARCHD MCCLEAN recorder. (F:pg 287)

9 Jun 1775. Deed. BALTHAZAR KOHLAR of Shrewsberry Township, York Co farmer for £15.5 sold to JOHN KOHLAR (KOHLER) of same place blacksmith a tr of land in Shrewsberry Township adj DANIEL KARFFMAN,

land of said BALTHAZAR KOHLAR (of which this is part) & said JOHN
KOHLER, being pt/o a 222 a. tr of land surveyed unto HUMPHRY
MONTGOMER in pursuance of a warrant dated 19 May 1752 in Shrewsberry
Township adj DAVID SHAFFER & JOHN FREELAND, the right of the said tr
of land by divers assignments and conveyances is vested in the said
BALTHAZAR KOHLAR, and also a warrant and tr of land granted to the said
BALTHARZAR KOHLAR 27 Aug 1772 adj his other land , JOHN FREELING
& PHILIP LOW ... . Wit: DANIEL KURFFMAN, WM KERSEY. Ackn 9
Jun 1775 before WILLIAM LEAS esqr justice. (F:pg 288)

9 Jun 1775. Deed. THOMAS SHEPHERD (eldest son and heir at law of
WILLIAM SHEPHERD late of York Co yeoman decd) for £396 sold to JOHN
MICKLE the younger and JAMES MOORE both of York Co yeomen a 131 a. tr
of land ... whereas the Proprietaries by their patent dated 4 Jan 1742 granted
unto the said WILLIAM SHEPHERD a 131 a. tr of land on Possum Cr w of
Susquehanna River then within Lancaster Co but now York Co adj JOHN COX,
WILLIAM GRIER & JOSEPH HUGHES (Patent Book A vol. 13 pg 111), and
the said WILLIAM SHEPHERD afterwards died intestate owner of the tr of land
leaving issue to survive him, namely the said THOMAS his eldest son,
SOLOMON, WILLIAM & MARY, and the said THOMAS on 29 Apr last by
his petition to the Orphans Court to make partition of the tr of land, the Court
found the land would not admit of a division without spoiling the whole, and
valued the land at £333, and it was ordered by the Court that the said THOMAS
SHEPHERD should hold and enjoy the tr of land he paying the other children
their share of the valuation ... . Wit: JAS SMITH, FRANCIS KUNTZ. Wit to
receipt: THOMAS STOCKTON, WILLIAM DELAP. Ackn 9 Jun 1775 before
WILLIAM DELAP justice. (F:pg 290)

5 May 1775. Quit Claim. BETTY HUTTON widow & relict of JOSEPH
HUTTON late of Newberry Township, York Co decd for £50 quit claim unto
JOSHUA HUTTON all estate right, interest, claim & demand whatsoever as she
had to the house and other privileges that the said JOSHUA HUTTON by the
will of his father was required to grant and do for the afsd BETTY HUTTON
and all the estate right of her in that pt/o the land willed to the said JOSHUA
HUTTON ... whereas the said JOSEPH HUTTON by his will dated 26 Aug
1771 did give unto his wife the afsd BETTY HUTTON the new end of the
dwelling house with the privilege of the fire place in the other end of the house
and having one horse, one cow & six sheep kept for her by his son JOSHUA
HUTTON (unto whom he bequeathed that pt/o the land that the mansion house
stood upon) during her natural life or widowhood ... . Wit: JOHN RANKIN,
SAMUEL PEDEN. Ackn 5 May 1775 before WM RANKIN esqr justice. (F:pg
301)

24 Apr 1775. Deed. JACOB FIKES of Huntington Township, York Co farmer and SUSANNA his wife for £450 sold to JOHN ALBERT of same place a 150 a. tr of land ... whereas VALINTIN FIKES obtained a 7 shillings warrant from the Proprietaries at Phila dated [*blank*] and by virtue of the warrant there was surveyed a 150 a. tr of land on the s side of Susquehanna River then in Lancaster Co but now in Huntington Township, York Co adj the said VALINTIN FIKES, FREDRICK MYERS, MICHAEL MILLER now NICHOLAS MYER & by a conditional line made by JOHN POWEL & JOHN FEALDS now ABRAHAM FIKES, and the said VALINTIN FIKES on 5 Apr 1743 sold the land and warrant unto THOMAS POWELL, and the said THOMAS POWELL by his assignment made over all his right of the tr of land unto JOHN POWEL on 14 Mar 1750, and the said JOHN POWELL on 31 Oct 1759 made over all his right in the tr of land unto the afsd JACOB FIKES ... . Wit: ISAAC HOLL, GABRIL SMITH. Ackn 24 Apr 1775 before JOHN SMITH justice. (F:pg 302)

23 Apr 1774. Deed. JAMES COOPER of Oxford Township, Chester Co, PA for £20 sold to THOMAS CURRY, JAMES WALLACE, GAUN ALLISON, ANDREW FULTON, ALEXANDER MOOR all farmers of Hopewell Township, JOHN MCCLURG, JOHN MCNEARY, GEORGE CAMPBELL farmers of Chanceford Township, York Co, JOHN MCCAY & WILLIAM STEWART farmers of Windsor Township, York Co a 2 a. tr of land where the Old Scotch Presbyterian Meeting House stands being surveyed to said JAMES COOPER with his other land surrounding it by virtue of a warrant in Chanceford Township taken out in 1767 ... . Wit: ROBERT BLAIN, SAMUEL SMITH. It is also agreed the afsd purchasers shall have a right and liberty to a spring called the Chestnut Spring. Ackn 23 Apr 1774 before WILLIAM SMITH justice. (F:pg 303)

17 Jun 1775. Deed of Mortgage. JOHN BUSHANG (BUSHONG) of York Township, York Co blacksmith for £100 sold to PETER DINKLE of York Town, York Co sadler a messuage & 200 a. tr of land in York & Shrewsbury Townships adj MICHAEL THROARBACH, PHILIP KROM & others, it being the same whereof WILLIAM SPRINCKLE the elder lately died owner and seized and which WILLIAM SPRINCKLE, HENRY SPRINCKLE & the said JOHN BUSHANG executors of the will of the said decd on 7 Apr 1774 sold unto PHILIP RIM ... provided that if the said JOHN BUSHANG shall well and truly pay unto the said PETER DINKLE £100 on or before 7 Jun 1777 then this indenture to be void ... . Wit: ANDREAS BILLMEYER, WILLIAM SCOTT. Ackn 17 Jun 1775 before WILLIAM SCOTT justice. 17 Nov 1777 PETER DINKLE discharged mortgage. Wit: ARCHD MCCLEAN recorder. (F:pg 304)

29 May 1775. Deed. ALEXR DOWNING & AGNES his wife of Chanceford Township, York Co yeoman for £290 sold to the Reverend JAS CLERKSON of same place a 124 a. 73 perches tr of land ... whereas a 124 a. 73 perches tr of land in the afsd township late pt/o Lancaster Co was surveyed 11 Apr 1757 for THOMAS MORGAN by virtue of two warrants, the one for 50 a. dated 15 Mar 1743 and the other for 50 a. dated 19 Dec 1746, in all 124 a. 73 perches as surveyed by WILLIAM MATHEWS dep surveyer 28 Feb 1775 at the request of the said ALEXR DOWNING, and the said ALEXR DOWNING hath purch the land from NATHANIEL MORGAN heir to the afsd THOS MORGAN ... . Wit: ANDREW FULTON, ALEXR MOORE. Wit to receipt: GAWIN ALLISON. Ackn 13 Jun 1775 before WILLIAM SMITH justice. (F:pg 305)

29 May 1775. Deed. ALEXANDER DOWNING & AGNES his wife of Chanceford Township, York Co yeoman for £90 sold to the Reverend JAS CLERKSON of same place a 41 a. 17 perches tr of land ... whereas a 41 a. 17 perches tr of land in the afsd township surveyed 23 Dec 1774 for ALEXR DOWNING by virtue of a 50 a. warrant dated at Phila 15 Dec 1774 ... . Wit: ANDREW FULTON, ALEXR MOORE. Wit to receipt: GAWIN ALLISON. Ackn 13 Jun 1775 before WILLIAM SMITH justice. (F:pg 307)

13 Jun 1775. THOMAS CURRY, JAMES WALLACE, GAVIN ALLISON, ANDREW FULTON, ALEXANDER MOOR all of Hopewell Township farmers, JOHN MCCLURG, JOHN MCNEARY, GEORGE CAMPBLE of Chanceford Township farmers, JOHN MCCAY & WILLIAM STEWART of Windsor Township farmers ... whereas in a deed poll dated 23 Apr last made between JAMES COOPER of Oxford Township, Chester Co, PA and the afsd trustees of the other part, the said JAMES COOPER did sell unto the afsd trustees 2 a. tr of land where the Old Scotch Presbyterian Meeting House stands & also the liberty of a spring near the same, and there is to be erected a large building or place of public worship called the Scotch Presbyterian Church under the pastoral care & inspection of the Reverend JAMES CLARKSON professing to adhere to the whole doctrine worship discipline & government of the Church of Scotland same as exhibited in her Publick Standards ... in the several acts of assembly passed between the years 1644 & 1649 ... the building to be erected in trust for the use & service of the afsd congregation ... said ground may be applied for a place to bury their dead and a school house for said congregation ... . Wit: ALEXR DOWNING, THOMAS MACKEY. Ackn 13 Jun 1775 before WILLIAM SMITH justice. (F:pg 308)

1 May 1775. Deed. JOHN DIGGES son and heir at law and one of the devisees of EDWARD DIGGES late of St. Marys Co, MD decd who was also a son and heir at law of JOHN DIGGES late of Prince Georges Co, MD decd and HENRY NEALE of St. Marys Co afsd for £99.9.10 sold to SAMUEL PIXLER of

Heidleberg Township, York Co yeoman a 62 a. tr of land in Heidleberg
Township (pt/o *Digges' Choice*) adj Little Cadorus ... whereas there was
patented unto the afsd JOHN DIGGES decd a 10,501 a. tr of land called *Digges'
Choice* to lay in Baltimore Co, MD but is since found to be in York Co, and the
said JOHN DIGGES being so seized departed this life leaving behind him the
afsd EDWARD DIGGES, WILLIAM DIGGES & HENRY DIGGES, which
said EDWARD DIGGES also departed this life leaving behind him the afsd
JOHN DIGGES party hereto and daus ELIZABETH DIGGES now w/o
WILFRED NEALE & ELEANOR DIGGES, and the said WILLIAM DIGGES
& HENRY DIGGES, WILFRED NEALE & ELIZABETH his wife and
ELEANOR DIGGES on 6 Apr last past did sell unto the said HENRY NEALE
all their right in the afsd tr of land in trust for the intent and purpose that the said
HENRY NEALE may be seized of an estate in the said lands and may convey
such pts/o the land agreed to be conveyed by the said JOHN DIGGES in his
lifetime or by the said WILLIAM DIGGES or HENRY DIGGES to such persons
as have contracted for the same ... . Wit: RD MCALISTER, MICHAEL
DANNER. Ackn 1 May 1775 before RD MCALISTER justice. (F:pg 310)

17 Jun 1775. Deed. JACOB MOYER of Heidleberg Township, York Co
yeoman and MAGDELENA his wife for £900 sold to JOHN WISLAR of York
Co yeoman a 117 a. tr of land ... whereas the Proprietaries of MD by their patent
dated [*blank*] granted unto JOHN DIGGES late of MD a large tr of land in
Baltimore Co, MD but since found to be in York Co called *Digges' Choice*, and
the said JOHN DIGGES on 17 Nov 1759 sold unto the afsd JACOB MOYER a
117 a. tr of land now in Heidleberg Township pt/o the afsd *Digges' Choice* adj
STEPHEN ULLERY (Liber B.J.N. No. 4 fol. 56,57&58 in MD) ... . Wit: JOS
BOUDE, BENJAMIN SWAIN, [?]. Ackn 17 Jun 1775 before RD
MCALISTER justice. (F:pg 311)

9 May 1775. Deed. JOHN GOBEL (GABEL) of Shrewsberry Township, York
Co farmer and GERTHRAUT his wife for £28 sold to FELIX HILDEBRAND
of [*blank*] Township, York Co farmer a 62 a. 6 perches tr of land in Shrewsberry
Township, which in pursuance of the application No. 5320 dated at Phila 13 Jan
1769 was surveyed and laid out unto the said JOHN GOBEL adj GEORGE
MYERS & the heirs of PHILIP SIMMONS decd ... . Wit: DAVID
CANDLER, GEORGE EGE. Ackn 9 May 1775 before MARTIN
EYCHELBERGER justice. (F:pg 313)

1 May 1775. Deed. JOHN DIGGES son and heir at law of one of the devisees
of EDWARD DIGGES late of St. Marys Co, MD decd who was also a son and
heir at law of JOHN DIGGES late of Prince Georges Co, MD, and HENRY
NEAL of St. Marys Co, MD for £180 sold to CHRISTIAN BARE of Heidleberg
Township, York Co yeoman a 126 ¼ a, tr of land in Heidleberg Township pt/o

Digges' Choice adj RICHARD MCCALISTER esqr, PETER SHULTZ & the heirs of JOHN DIGGES ... whereas there was patented unto the afsd JOHN DIGGES decd a 10,501 a. tr of land called *Digges' Choice* (patent lay in Baltimore Co, MD) but is since found to be in York Co, and the said JOHN DIGGES being so seized departed this life leaving the afsd EDWARD DIGGES, WILLIAM DIGGES & HENRY DIGGES, which said EDWARD DIGGES also departed this life leaving the afsd JOHN DIGGES party hereto and daus ELIZABETH now w/o WILFRED NEALE and ELEANOR DIGGES, and the said WILLIAM DIGGES, HENRY DIGGES, WILFRED NEALE and ELIZABETH his wife and ELEANOR DIGGES on 6 Apr last past sold unto the said HENRY NEALE all their right in the afsd tr of land called *Digges' Choice*, in trust for the intent and purpose that the said HENRY NEALE may be seized of an estate in the land and may convey to such parts of the land agreed to be conveyed by the said JOHN DIGGES in his lifetime, and by the said EDWARD DIGGES in his lifetime, or by the said WILLIAM DIGGES or HENRY DIGGES ... . Wit: RD MCALISTER, MICHAEL DANNER. Ackn 1 May 1775 before RD MCALISTER justice. (F:pg 314)

2 Mar 1775. Deed of Mortgage. JACOB SCHEFFER of York Town, York Co cordwainer and ELIZABETH his wife for better securing the payment of a debt and also 5 shillings sold to JACOB DAUTEL of same place tanner Lot No. 65 in York Town ... whereas SAMUEL EDIE esqr high sheriff on 8 Jun 1774 did sell (as the estate of GEORGE STEVENSON) a lot of ground in York Town on the w side of George Street and on the s side of Phila Street, No. 65, in front 57'6" and in length 250', unto THOMAS HARTLEY (HARTLY) esqr, and the said THOMAS HARTLEY on 18 Aug last past sold the afsd lot of ground unto the said JACOB DAUTEL, and the said JACOB DAUTEL this date sold the Lot No. 65 unto the afsd JACOB SCHEFFER ... and the said JACOB SCHEFFER became bound unto the said JACOB DAUTEL in several sums conditioned for the payment of the several sums before 1 Apr 1781 ... provided that if the said JACOB SCHEFFER shall well and truly pay unto the said JACOB DAUTEL the afsd debt then this indenture to be void ... . Wit: GEORGE CRAFT, GEO LEWIS LESLER. Ackn 2 Mar 1775 before WILLIAM LEAS justice. 8 May 1782 ANNA MARIA DAUTEL widow and adminr of the estate of JACOB DAUTEL discharged mortgage. Wit: ARCHD MCCLEAN recorder. (F:pg 316)

31 Oct 1774. Deed. HENRY ROBINSON of Chanceford Township, York Co farmer for £170 sold to JOHN MATSON of same place farmer a 89 a. tr of land ... whereas in pursuance of a warrant dated 14 Dec 1751 there was surveyed and laid out to WILLIAM BUCHANAN a 89 a. tr of land in Chanceford Township adj CHARLES OHARRA, and the said WILLIAM BUCHANAN on 15 Mar 1757 did convey to DAVID HUNTER the afsd tr of land, and the said DAVID

HUNTER on 1 Aug 1766 sold unto the afsd HENRY ROBINSON the afsd tr of land ... . Wit: WM ROWAN, JAS HILL. Ackn 4 May 1775 before WM SCOTT justice. (F:pg 319)

11 Apr 1775. Deed of Mortgage. MICHAEL KINTER of Manchester Township, York Co yeoman and CHRISTINA his wife for better securing the payment of £63.6.4 and also 5 shillings sold to JOHN FURREY of same place yeoman a 150 a. tr of land in Manchester Township adj ANDREAS KLINE, JACOB GOTWALT, SIMON MELLHORN & others, whereon the said MICHAEL KINTER now lives ... whereas the said MICHAEL KINTER standeth bound unto the said JOHN FURREY for £126.12.8 conditioned for the payment of £63.6.4 on 1 Apr 1777 ... provided that if the said MICHAEL KINTER shall well and truly pay unto the said JOHN FURREY £63.6.4 then this indenture to be void ... . Wit: SARAH MILLER, HENRY MILLER. Ackn 11 Apr 1775 before WM SCOTT justice. 7 Apr 1780 JOHN FURREY discharged mortgage. Wit: ARCHD MCCLEAN recorder. (F:pg 320)

17 Nov 1772. Deed. JAMES SMITH of York Town for £200 sold to ARTHUR SMITH of Newberry Township, York Co yeoman a tr of land adj ISAAC PIKE, JOHN RICE, other land of the said JAMES SMITH & land late of JOHN FARMER (warrant dated 5 Jun 1762) ... . Wit: DAVID MCMECHEN, JAMES SMITH. Ackn 17 Nov 1772 before JOHN ADLUM justice. 18 Apr 1775 ARTHUR SMITH for £219 sold to JACOB DRUORBOUGH the within mentioned plantation. Wit: ROBERT DENNIS, JOSEPH WELSH. Ackn 18 Apr 1775 before WM RANKIN justice. (F:pg 322)

18 Jun 1775. Deed. ARTHUR SMITH and CHRISTIN his wife of Newberry Township, York Co for £219 sold to JACOB DRUARBOUGH of same place farmer a 150 tr of land adj ISAAC PIKE, JOHN RISE, JAMES SMITH, JAMES RANKIN & land late of JOHN FARMER (warrant dated at Phila 2 Jun 1762) for my taking up 150 a. of land ... . Wit: ROBERT DENNIS, ROBERT MILLER. Ackn 18 Apr 1775 before WM RANKIN justice. (F:pg 323)

2 May 1775. Deed. RICHARD EGGLETON cordwinder of Manahan Township, York Co for £200 sold to RICHARD BLATCHFORD (PLACHFORD) of Warrington Township, York Co weaver a messuage and 182 a. tr of land whereon the said RICHARD EGGLESTON now lives adj GEORGE MCMILLAN, BAXTER's land, BRICE BLAIR, WILLIAM PORTER, HUGH OHAIL & CHRISTOPHER QUIGLEY ... . Wit: JAMES FEGAN, JOHN MCMILLAN. Ackn 2 May 1775 before JOHN SMITH justice. (F:pg 324)

22 Nov 1774. Deed. EPHRAIM JOHNSON of Baltimore Co, MD yeoman & RACHEL his wife for £35 sold to THOMAS WILSON of Fawn Township,

York Co yeoman a 21 a. 135 perches tr of land in Fawn Township called
Hopsons Choice adj ISAAC ANDERSON & BENJAMIN JOHNSON, which
was granted unto the said EPHRAIM JOHNSON by patent dated at Phila 12
May now last past (Patent Book AA vol. 14 pg 327) ... . Wit: JOHN GILL,
RICHARD WEBB. Wit to receipt: ISABEL MITCHELL. Ackn 1 Dec 1774
before WILLIAM SMITH justice. (F:pg 326)

22 Nov 1774. Deed. EPHRAIM JOHNSON of Baltimore Co, MD yeoman and
RACHEL his wife and JACOB JOHNSON of Fawn Township, York Co
yeoman for £340 sold to THOMAS WILSON of Fawn Township, York Co
yeoman a 183 a. 16 perches tr of land in Fawn Township pt/o a 434 a. 47
perches of land called *Plumb Green* granted unto the afsd EPHRAIM
JOHNSON and JACOB JOHNSON by patent dated at Phila 28 Jul last past
(Patent Book AA vol. 14 pg 565) adj JAMES WEBB, GEORGE PAIN,
THOMAS STEWART & ISAAC ANDERSON ... . Wit: JOHN GILL,
RICHARD WEBB. Wit to receipt: ISABEL MITCHELL. Ackn 1 Dec 1774.
(F:pg 327)

16 May 1775. Deed. RICHARD MCCALISTER of Heidleberg Township,
York Co yeoman for £3 sold to JOSHUA OWINGS of same place a piece of
ground in the Town of Hanover in township afsd, No. 70, in breadth 57'6" and
in length 230' bounded by Baltimore Street & Lot No. 69, pt/o a larger tr of land
called *Digges' Choice* which the said RICHARD MCCALISTER holds in right
of JOHN DIGGES decd ... paying to the said RICHARD MCCALISTER on 1
May the yearly rent of 8 shillings ... . Wit: JAS CALHOUN, GEO SEIVERT.
Ackn 24 May 1775 before HENRY SLAGLE justice. (F:pg 329)

19 May 1752 at Phila. Receipt. EDMUND PHYSICK (for the Proprietaries)
received from JOHN BUSH 50 shillings in part for 50 a. to be surveyed him
near ROBERT HOOPER & JOHN ALBRIGHT on a br of Fishing Cr in Hellam
Township. (F:pg 331)

13 Mar 1758. For £2.17.6 paid by GEORGE STEVENSON of York I hereby
assign over all my estate right & interest to the within receipt & land thereby
granted to the said GEORGE STEVENSON and I promise to make a lawful
conveyance to the said GEORGE STEVENSON when required. [*signed* ?].
Wit: [?], PHIL SPEWBART. (F:pg 331)

10 Jun 1775. Before WILLIAM SCOTT esqr justice of York Co personally
came JOHN BUSCH in the above instrument of writing named JOHN BUSH
who ackn he executed the same ... . (F:pg 331)

18 Feb 1775. Deed. ANN NOBLIT of York Township, York Co widow and executrix of ABRAHAM NOBLIT esqr for £77 sold to THOMAS ARMOR my full undivided 1/3 pt/o each of three trs of land as they were granted unto the said JOSEPH KEYS, JAMES RANKIN & WILLIAM RANKIN, in the whole 385 a. ... whereas JOSEPH KEYS on 17 Jul 1762 did convey all his dwelling plantation in Newberry Township adj Susquehannah River, WILLIAM WILLSON & others, surveyed in pursuance of a warrant dated at Phila 18 Nov 1752, unto the said ABRAHAM NOBLIT, the instrument of writing in the hands of GEORGE STEVENSON, and the said ABRAHAM NOBLIT made his will, "I give to ANN NOBLIT, my wife, all the residue of my estate, real and personal, houses & lands to have use and enjoy forever" will dated 1 Nov 1764, and the said ANN NOBLIT by her agreement dated 28 Sep 1765 did convey 1/3 pt/o the afsd tr of land and also 1/3 pt/o other lands unto the said THOMAS ARMOR ... and JAMES RANKIN on 20 Oct last did convey unto the said ANN NOBLIT 100 a. of land adj WILLIAM BAXTER & others in Newberry Township, one of the trs mentioned in said agreement, and the said WILLIAM RANKIN esqr on 17 Feb instant did convey unto the said ANN NOBLIT another 100 a. of land mentioned in said agreement ... . Wit: WM LEAS, MARY HAMERSLY. Ackn 18 Feb 1775 before WILLIAM RANKIN esqr justice. (F:pg 331)

14 Jul 1775. Deed of Mortgage. ULRICK HOSTETTLER of Germany Township, York Co yeoman for better securing the payment of £27.17.6 and also 5 shillings sold to MICHAEL DOTTERER of same place yeoman 2000 sheaffs of wheat, 1000 sheaffs of rye, 1 black mare, 2 yearling heifers, 1 old wagon, 1 plough & irons which goods and chattels are now on the plantation of ANNA MARIA HOSTETER the mother of the said ULRICK HOSTETTLER in township afsd ... whereas the said ULRICK HOSTETTLER stands bound unto the said MICHAEL DOTTERER for £55.15 conditioned for the payment of £27.17.6 on or before 14 Jan next ensuing ... provided that if the said ULRICK HOSTETTLER shall well and truly pay unto the said MICHAEL DOTTERER £27.17.6 then this indenture to be void ... . Wit: JOS BOUDE, RACHEL BOUDE. Ackn 14 Jul 1775 before RD MCALISTER justice. 11 Aug 1779 MICHAEL DOTTERER Senr adminr of the estate of MICHAEL DOTTERER Junr discharged mortgage. Wit: ARCHD MCCLEAN recorder. (F:pg 333)

7 Apr 1775. Deed. GEORGE MILLER and CATHARINE his wife and JOHN SCHNELL and ANNA his wife all of Reading Township, York Co for £300 sold to JOHN SMITH esqr of Warrington Township, York Co two trs of land lying contiguous in Reading Township adj FRANCIS HODGE, PHILIP SHRIBER, THOMAS CRUSWEL, JOSEPH BROWN & WILLIAM MCKELHEMY, 200 a. of land ... whereas JACOB YOUNGBLOOD lodged money with THOMAS COOKSON esqr to procure him a warrant for 100 a. of

land including his improvement in Reading Township on 20 Apr 1747, and the
said JACOB YOUNGBLOOD afterwards did sell all his right in the said
improvement unto JOHN FREY on 2 Mar 1749, and the said JOHN FREY
afterward obtained a warrant in his own name for another 100 a. to be surveyed
to him adj his other land in Reading Township over Susquehannah then in
Lancaster Co but now in York Co, warrant dated at Phila 26 Jun 1749, and the
said JOHN FREY did sell both trs of land unto the afsd CATHARINE and
ANNA then CATHARINE FREY and ANNA FREY daus of the said JOHN
FREY on 7 Nov 1771 ... . Wit: [?], HENRY SLAGLE, [?]. Ackn 7 Apr 1775
before HENRY SLAGLE justice. (F:pg 333)

22 May 1775. Deed. ADAM HOFF of Cadorus Township, York Co yeoman
and JULIANA his wife for £460 sold to ANDREAS HOFF of same place farmer
a tr of land in Cadorus Township which in pursuance of the application No. 4487
dated at Phila 15 Oct 1767 and in pursuance of a warrant dated at Phila 31 Mar
1768 was surveyed and laid out unto the said ADAM HOFF a 233 a. 64 perches
tr of land adj JACOB STOMBAGH, JACOB BOLLINGER, ANDREW
HUSHLY, FRANCIS HOFF & JACOB LESHEY, the said ADAM HOFF
always excepting 70 a. of land now in possession of FRANCIS HOFF ... . Wit:
JOHN MORRIS, JACOB GAERTNER. Ackn 23 May 1775 before WM
BAILEY justice. (F:pg 335)

18 Jul 1774. Articles of Agreement. JOHN COOPER doth agree that
NICHOLAS COOPER shall have free & uninterrupted liberty of the water with
the liberty of the race as it is now carried from my mill head of water when the
said mill is not grinding to water his meadow or other uses & liberty for him to
build when they are required piles of wood or stone to carry the said water from
my side of the mill cr to his side in troughs forever ... . Wit: JOHN BOYD,
WM ROWAN. (F:pg 337)

18 Jun 1774. Deed. SAMUEL EDIE esqr high sheriff of York Co for £1564
sold to JAMES RANKIN a 377 a. 130 perches tr of land ... whereas JAMES
BENEZET lately in the Supreme Court of PA held at Phila recovered against
GEORGE STEVENSON a debt of £1772 and £9.14.6 damages ... the sheriff
seized in execution as the estate of the said GEORGE STEVENSON a 300 a. tr
of land in York Township on both sides of Little Codorus Cr and on the e side of
Great Codorus Cr adj GEORGE BENTZ & land late of said GEORGE
STEVENSON, together with a grist mill, merchant mill and shelling mill which
by a resurvey made in pursuance of a warrant dated at Phila 26 Jun last past
found to contain 377 a. 130 perches adj PETER DEHL, PHILIP GRAYBILL &
Codorus Cr,   and exposed to public vendue and the same was sold to JAMES
RANKIN for £1564 he being the highest bidder ... . Wit: JOHN CLARK Junr,

JOSEPH STOCTON. Ackn in open Court. EDWARD SHIPPEN proth. (F:pg 337)

6 Jun 1775. Quit Claim. JOHN HARMAN of Manchester Township, York Co farmer and ELIZABETH his wife (late ELIZABETH COOPER widow & relict of CORNELIUS COOPER late of Hellam Township, York Co yeoman decd) for £12 quit claim unto HENRY COOPER of Hellam Township all manner of dowers and right and title of dowers whatsoever which they (in right of said ELIZABETH as widow and relict of said decd) have in a 200 a. tr of land in Hellam Township adj the Forge ... . Wit: [?], HENRY MILLER. Ackn 6 Jun 1775 before MARTIN EYCHELBERGER justice. (F:pg 339)

6 Jun 1775. Deed. HENRY HENSHEY of Cocolico Township, Lancaster Co blacksmith and BARBARA his wife for £250 sold to HENRY BEICHER of Codorus Township, York Co farmer a 115 a. 57 perches tr of land in Codorus Township adj JOHN REAVER, JACOB BOLLINGER, MICHAEL DANNER & VINCENT COOPER, which was surveyed for CHRISTIAN PEIDLER by virtue of a warrant dated 23 Jul 1743, and the said CHRISTIAN PEIDLER sold unto JOHN MOYER by the name of HANNIS MYER, and the said JOHN MOYER & BARBARA his wife sold unto the said HENRY HENSHEY 27 Feb last past ... . Wit: JOHN HECKENDORN, WM LEAS. Ackn 6 Jun 1775 before WM LEAS justice. (F:pg 340)

6 Jun 1775. Deed. HENRY HENSHEY of Cocolico Township, Lancaster Co blacksmith and BARBARA his wife for £600 sold to HENRY BEICHER of Codorus Township, York Co farmer a 133 a. tr of land in Codorus Township adj JOHN REAVER, said HENRY HENSHEY, MICHAEL DANNER & JACOB RUDESELL, which the Proprietaries by their patent dated 25 Jul 1767 did grant unto JOHN MOYER (Patent Book AA vol. 10 pg 42), and by the said JOHN MOYER and BARBARA his wife sold unto the said HENRY HENSHEY 27 Feb last past ... . Wit: JOHN HECKENDORN WM LEAS. Ackn 6 Jun 1775 before WM LEAS justice. (F:pg 341)

27 Feb 1775. Deed. JOHN MOYER of Cadoras Township, York Co yeoman and BARBARA his wife for £600 sold to HENRY HENSHEY of Cocolico Township, Lancaster Co blacksmith a tr of land in Codorus Township [same as above] ... . Wit: JOHN HECKENDORN, WM LEAS. Ackn 27 Feb 1775 before WM LEAS justice. (F:pg 343)

5 Nov 1774. Deed. JOHN REBER of Cadorus Township, York Co yeoman for £1.10 sold to JOHN MEYER Senr of same place farmer fully free and absolute liberty & privilege to a run or small cr on the e side of my dwelling house and running through the meadow ground of my plantation, also free and absolute

liberty of conveying a sufficiency of water out of said cr through my land to land of the said JOHN MYER by a ditch or channel 2' wide and 1' deep and 17 perches long ... provided the said JOHN MYER do not cause injury or damage whatsoever to the meadow ground or lo land of the said JOHN REBER by stopping the said cr so high as to overflow the banks ... . Wit: JOHN MORRIS, THOMAS IRONS. Ackn 5 Nov 1774 before WM SCOTT justice. (F:pg 345)

6 Feb 1775. Deed of Release. JOHN MYER in the foregoing instrument of writing for £2 sold unto HENRY HENSHEY of Cocolico Township, Lancaster Co blacksmith all the water privilege mentioned in the aforegoing instrument of writing absolute right to make use of such water in the same manner I had heretofore ... . Wit: JOHN HECKENDORN, WM LEAS. Ackn 6 Feb 1775 before WM LEAS justice. (F:pg 346)

6 Jun 1775. Deed of Release. HENRY HENSHEY in the above instrument of writing for £2 sold to HENRY BEICHER of Codorus Township, York Co all the water privilege mentioned in the foregoing instrument of writing with absolute right to make use of such water as by the said JOHN REBER granted to the said JOHN MOYER and by him to me in the same manner as I had heretofore ... . Wit: JOHN HECKENDORN, WM LEAS. Ackn 6 Jun 1775 before WM LEAS justice. (F:pg 347)

22 May 1775. Deed. THOMAS WHITE of Berwick Township, York Co yeoman and MARY his wife (which said MARY is one of the daus of BARNABAS CURRY late of York Co yeoman decd) for £450 sold to PETER HOWSHILL of same township yeoman a 136 a. tr of land adj JACOB SARBAUGH, HENRY MOLER & others in Berwick Township ... whereas in an Orphans Court held 29 Mar 1758 upon the petition of the said THOMAS WHITE and MARY his wife (the real estate of the said BARNABAS CURRY decd having been found not partible [*partionable*] amongst the widow and children of the said intestate and the other children of said intestate having all refused to take the same at the valuation) it was ordered by said Court that the said THOMAS WHITE and MARY his wife (upon paying £400 or giving good security for the same) should hold the 136 a. tr of land whereof the said intestate died owner and seized in Berwick Township, and the said THOMAS WHITE and MARY his wife having fully paid and satisfied the widow and other children of said intestate their share of £400, the tr of land became fully vested in the said THOMAS WHITE and MARY his wife ... . Wit: JAMES SMITH, WM SCOTT. Ackn 22 May 1775 before WM SCOTT justice. (F:pg 348)

3 Aug 1775. Deed of Mortgage. BENJAMIN ERSBELL cooper of Hopewell Township, York Co for £52.9.10 sold to ANDREW THOMSON (THOMPSON) of same place 1 brown cow, 1 read cow with white face, 1 read steer with white

face, 1 brown heffer, two red calves, 1 walnut chest, 1 croscut saw, 1 joynter, 1
cooper adge, 2 drawing knives, 1 set of plowirons, 1 cedar chest, 1 bookcase, 2
iron potts, 2 iron pot racks, 9000 barral staves, 4 putter plates, 1 coopers ax, 1
table, 1 chack reel, 7 hogs, 1 ½ a. of flax, ½ a. of potetas, 3 cedar pails, 1 iron
squair, 1 handsaw, maulrings & wedges, 1 stack of hay and all other goods,
household stuff and implements of household and trade ... the condition of this
bill of sale is such that if the said BENJAMIN ERSBELL shall well and truly
pay unto the said ANDREW THOMSON £52.9.10 this bill of sale to be void ...
. Wit: JOHN TRAVIS, SAMUEL MCGOWAN. Ackn 4 Aug 1775 before
WILLIAM SMITH justice. (F:pg 350)

18 Jun 1774. Deed. WILLIAM MATTHEWS of York Town, York Co
surveyor and HANNAH his wife for £100 sold to JAMES WEBB of Fawn
Township, York Co yeoman a 133 a. tr of land ... whereas the Proprietaries by
their patent dated at Phila 31 Mar last past did grant unto the said WILLIAM
MATTHEWS a 133 a. tr of land called *Small Gain* in Fawn Township adj
GEORGE PAIN, the Province Line, BENJAMIN JOHNSTON's heirs &
HENRY COWGILL Junr (Patent Book AA vol. 14 pg 218) ... . Wit:
PRISCILLA PHILLIPS, WM LEAS. Ackn 18 Jun 1774 before WM LEAS
justice. (F:pg 351)

27 Feb 1775. Deed. JOHN MOYER of Codorus Township, York Co yeoman
and BARBARA his wife for £250 sold to HENRY HENSHEY of Lancaster Co
blacksmith a 115 a. 57 perches tr of land in Codorus Township adj JOHN
REVER, JACOB BOLINGER, MICHAEL DANNER, VINCENT COOPER &
said JOHN MOYER's other land, which was surveyed for CHRISTIAN
PEIDLER by virtue of a warrant dated 23 Jul 1743, and the said CHRISTIAN
PEIDLER sold unto the said JOHN MOYER by the name of HANNES MYER
... . Wit: JOHN HECKENDORN, WM LEAS. Ackn 27 Feb 1775 before WM
LEAS justice. (F:pg 353)

24 Jul 1775. Deed of Release. SAMUEL BIXLER of Heidleberg Township,
York Co yeoman and ELISABETH his wife for consideration of the premises
and 5 shillings release unto JOHN MILLER of same place millwright and miller
a messuage and garden and water corn and grist mill and 6 ¼ a. of land in
Heidleberg Township pt/o a 62 a. tr of land adj SAMUEL BIXLER & the road
leading to York ... whereas by patent there was granted unto JOHN DIGGES
(the elder decd) a 10,501 a. tr of land called *Digges' Choice* in Baltimore Co,
MD but is found to be in York Co, and the said JOHN DIGGES did in his life
time sell unto JOHN BIXLER now also decd (who was the father of the said
SAMUEL BIXLER) a 62 a. tr of land pt/o the said *Digges' Choice*, and the said
JOHN DIGGES afterwards died intestate without having actually conveyed the
62 a. tr of land unto the said JOHN BIXLER and did leave issue to survive him,

EDWARD DIGGES his oldest son and heir at law and younger children
WILLIAM DIGGES & HENRY DIGGES, which said EDWARD DIGGES also
sometime after the death of his father the said JOHN DIGGES the elder departed
this life leaving issue to survive him JOHN DIGGES (the younger only son and
heir at law) and daus ELISABETH DIGGES now w/o WILFRED NEALE &
ELEANOR DIGGES, and the said JOHN BIXLER decd did in his life time sell
unto the said JOHN MILLER and did agree to convey a messuage and garden
and a water corn and grist mill and 6 ¼ a. tr of land pt/o the 62 a. afsd but was
not in his lifetime possessed of such title as would enable him fully to convey
the same, and the said JOHN BIXLER being so seized of the residue of said 62
a. and also other lands made his will dated 31 Aug 1763 and did order "it is my
will that my wife shall have my plantation except the mill for her usage for 4
years after my decease and then my son SAMUEL is to have my plantation
whereon I now dwell except the mill and 6 a. of land that belonged to the mill I
have sold to my son in law JOHN MILLER for £320, the £20 he is to keep for
his wife's heirs pt/o which I bequeath unto my steep dau MERCY which is now
the said JOHN MILLER's wife and the £300 he is to pay in payments" ...
whereas the afsd WILLIAM DIGGES, HENRY DIGGES, WILFRED NEALE
& ELISABETH his wife and ELEANOR DIGGES by their deed dated 6 Apr
last past did release and confirm unto HENRY NEAL all their right in the tr of
land called *Digges' Choice*, in trust for the purpose he may be seized of an estate
and may convey and make good titles to such pts/o the lands as have been
agreed to be conveyed by the said JOHN DIGGES the elder in his lifetime and
by the said EDWARD DIGGES in his life time or by the said WILLIAM
DIGGES or HENRY DIGGES (recorded in MD), and by an indenture of release
dated 1 May now last past the said JOHN DIGGES (the younger) heir at law of
his father the said EDWARD DIGGES decd and also of his grandfather the said
JOHN DIGGES (the elder) decd and the said HENRY NEALE released unto the
said SAMUEL BIXLER by the name of SAMUEL PIXLER a tr of land in
Heidleberg Township pt/o the afsd *Digges' Choice* and also the 62 a. tr afsd adj
Little Codorus (Book F pg 310), and the said 6 a. is wholly included within the
62 a. tr of land ... . Wit: JOHN GALENTINE, ARCHD MCCLEAN. Ackn 1
Aug 1775 before RD MCALISTER justice. (F:pg 355)

23 Feb 1775. Deed of Mortgage. JACOB PLAUZER of Manchester Township,
York Co for better securing the payment of £52 and also 5 shillings sold to
PETER BEITLER of Hellam Township, York Co yeoman a 198 a. tr of land in
York Township adj GEORGE STEPHENSON, PHILIP GRAYBLE, JACOB
SWOOPE, Codorus Cr & the Proprietaries ... whereas the said JACOB
PLAUZER standeth bound unto the said PETER BEITLER for £104 conditioned
for the payment of £52 on 1 Jun next ensuing ... provided that if the said
JACOB PLAUZER shall well and truly pay unto the said PETER BEITLER £52
then this indenture to be void ... . Wit: JOHN MORRIS, GEORGE

SCHLOSSER. Ackn 23 Feb 1775 before WILLIAM LEAS esqr justice. (F:pg 359)

22 Mar 1774. Deed of Release. GEORGE NAGLE and MARY ELISABETH his wife of Windsor Township, York Co for £25 released unto CHRISTINA HELSEL of same place widow their share in a tr of land which is coming to them in right of the said MARY ELISABETH dau of STOPHEL HELSEL decd ... whereas the said STOPHEL HELSEL lately died owner and seized of an improvement and 230 a. tr of land in Windsor Township adj LAURENCE HERSHNER, NICHOLAS YOUNG, FEIL BENNOR & others and left the said CHRISTINA HELSEL his widow and JOHN, PHILIP, JACOB, NICHOLAS, STOPHEL, CATHARINE, GEORGE, CATHARINE [sic], ELISABETH & the said MARY ELISABETH his issue to survive him, and also left some personal estate ... . Wit: [?], HENRY MILLER, WILLIAM SCOTT. Ackn 19 Aug 1775 before WM SCOTT justice. (F:pg 361)

14 Jun 1775. Deed of Mortgage. HENRY BEICHER of Manheim Township, York Co farmer for better securing the payment of £450 and also 5 shillings sold to HENRY HENSHEY of Cocolico Township, Lancaster Co tanner a 133 a. tr of land in Manheim Township adj JOHN REAVER, other land of said HENRY BEICHER, MICHAEL DANNER & JACOB RUDESELL, which the Proprietaries by their patent dated at Phila 25 Jul 1767 did grant unto JOHN MOYER (Patent Book AA vol. 10 pg 42) ... whereas the said HENRY BEICHER standeth bound unto the said HENRY HENSHEY for £900 conditioned for the payment of £450 in payments before 1 May 1786 ... provided that if the said HENRY BEICHER shall well and truly pay unto the said HENRY HENSHEY £450 then this indenture to be void ... . Wit: JOHN HECKENDORN, WM LEAS. Ackn 30 Jun 1775 before WILLIAM LEAS esqr justice. 29 Apr 1785 HENRY HENSHEY discharged mortgage. (F:pg 362)

10 Feb 1775. Deed. MARTIN BASH of Menallan Township, York Co miller for £500 sold to SAMUEL HORNISH of Cocolico Township, Lancaster Co farmer a tr of land in Manheim Township ... whereas CHRISTIAN LEFFELL in his lifetime seated and improved upon a tr of land in Manheim Township then in Lancaster Co but now in York Co and afterwards made his will and devised to his son PETER (then a minor), viz, "it is my will that my eldest son PETER shall have the right to my improvement and he shall pay to his brothers and sisters as much till they are all even share and share alike" and afterwards died leaving MARIA BARBARA his widow, the said PETER his eldest son and sundry other minor children, and NICHOLAS BEETINGER after the decease of the said CHRISTIAN (to wit) 18 Jun 1759 obtained a warrant for 150 a. of land to be surveyed to him in trust for the heirs of CHRISTIAN LEFFELL decd adj CHRISTIAN HERR in Manheim Township, and the said PETER LEFFELL in

pursuance of a petition dated 14 Sep 1761 obtained an inquest to value the land and it was decreed that the said PETER should hold and enjoy the land paying the widow and other children their share of the valuation, and the said PETER LEFFELL on 12 Jun 1762 sold unto the said NICHOLAS BEETINGER the tr of land, and the said NICHOLAS BEETINGER on 15 Jan 1774 sold the tr of land unto the said MARTIN BASH ... . Wit: JOHN HECKENDORN, JOHN SHALLENBERGER. Ackn 10 Feb 1775 before WM LEAS justice. (F:pg 364)

27 Apr 1775. Deed, THOMAS MINSHALL of Hellam Township, York Co gent and MARY his wife for £3000 sold to JOHN HARE of same place farmer the residue of a tr of land not conveyed to DAVID MEHLINGER and also a 376 a. 14 perches tr of land adj the road from York to Wrights Ferry, the afsd tr, DAVID MEHLINGER, ABRAHAM FLURY & JAMES EWING esqr ... whereas the Proprietaries by their patent dated at Phila 12 Apr 1753 did grant unto the said THOMAS MINSHALL a 253 ½ a. tr of land in Hellam Township adj JOSHUA MINSHALL, ABRAHAM FLURY, HENRY STRICKLER, the Great Road to York, JOHN FLURIE, JOHN FISKE & ANDREAS WEYBRIGHT (Patent Book A vol. 19 pg 27) ... whereas the Proprietaries by their patent dated 23 Aug last did grant unto the said THOMAS MINSHALL a 253 a. 95 perches tr of land in Hellam Township adj the afsd tr, the road from York Town to Wrights Ferry, JAMES WRIGHT esqr & DAVID MEHLINGER (Patent Book AA vol. 14 pg 628), and the said THOMAS MINSHALL lately sold pt/o the first described tr of land unto DAVID MEHLINGER ... . Wit: [?], HENRY MILLER. Ackn 27 Apr 1775 before JOHN POPE justice. (F:pg 366)

27 Dec 1768. Deed. DANIEL BEITLER of Hellam Township, York Co yeoman and BARBARA his wife for £102 sold to CHRISTIAN STEINER of same place yeoman a 17 a. 74 perches tr of land in Hellam Township pt/o a 24 a. 83 perches tr of land ... whereas the Proprietaries by their patent dated at Phila 3 Jun 1761 did grant unto HENRY FURRY a 177 ½ a. tr of land in Hellam Township adj STEPHEN SHERK, JOHN FESTEELL, THOMAS MINSHALL, land late of JACOB FURREY & JOHN COMFORT (Patent Book AA vol. 1 pg 290), and the said HENRY FURREY being so seized in the tr of land died intestate, and FERONICA FURREY (widow and relict of said intestate) and the said CHRISTIAN STEINER adminrs of the estate of the said decd did exhibit their petition to the Orphans Court setting forth that the intestate died seized in the tr of land and the petitioners had rendered an account of their administration wherein it appeared that a balance of £4.3.9 only remained in their hands and there was due by said intestate £152 and prayed the Court to sell pt/o the land for the payment of the debts, and it was ordered by the Court that the said adminrs should make sale of 40 a. of the said tr of land to be sold at public vendue and the money arising for the payment of the intestate's debts, and the said adminrs did report to the Court on 24 May then last past they sold 24 a. only of the land

to the afsd DANIEL BEITLER for £157.14 he being the highest bidder which sum would be sufficient to satisfy the debts ... and the said adminrs confirmed unto the said DANIEL BEITLER the 24 a. 83 perches tr (pt/o a 177 ½ a. tr of land) adj THOMAS MINSHALL esqr, said CHRISTIAN STEINER & the road leading from York Town to Wrights Ferry ... . Wit: HENRY STRICKLER, JACOB BILLMEYER Junr. Ackn 27 Dec 1768 before THOMAS MINSHALL esqr justice. (F:pg 369)

17 May 1775. Deed. MICHAEL DANNER Senr of the Town of Hanover, York Co yeoman as trustee for the Menonist Congregation for £6 (by and with the consent of the members of the Menonist Congregation as testified by JOHN SCHENCK of Manheim Township, York Co minister and JACOB KAGY of Heidleberg Township, York Co minister and JOHN WELTY & JAMES MILLER of Manheim Township, York Co yeomen and elders) have agreed to release the equal and common privilege with the said Menonist Congregation of a 12 a. lot of land unto ADAM EICHELBERGER of Manheim Township innholder in trust for the use of the German Lutherans and German Reformed Calvinists and others of the neighbourhood for the purpose of erecting or joining with the said Menonist Congregation in erecting a schoolhouse and supporting a schoolmaster and if required a place for burial for the dead ... whereas the Proprietaries by their patent granted unto the said MICHAEL DANNER in trust for the only proper use of the Menonist Congregation a 12 a. tr of land called *Tanners Repository* in Manheim Township adj HENRY BOWMAN, MICHAEL NEWMAN, JOHN SCHENCK, ADAM EICHELBERGER (Patent Book AA vol. 12 pg 287) ... . Wit: RD MCALISTER, ARCHD MCCLEAN. Ackn 5 Jun 1775 before RD MCALISTER justice. (F:pg 372)

4 Jul 1774. Deed. DAVID BEATY Senr of Straban Township, York Co yeoman for £200 (£100 to be in hand by JNO BEATY of same co before the signing & delivering of these presents land and said BEATY is to pay £20 every year until the remainder be paid) sold to the said JNO BEATY a 300 a. tr of land whereon the said DAVID BEATY now dwells in Straban Township adj DAVID BEATY Junr, ALEXANDER MCCARTOR, JNO SCOT, GEORGE BLINHLENHOOF, THOMAS SLOAN & WILLIAM COOPER ... . Wit: JAMES BEATY, JAMES FLEMING. Ackn 19 May 1775 before ROBT MCPHERSON justice. (F:pg 374)

16 Mar 1775. Deed. HENRY LEPHART of Windsor Township, York Co miller and BARBARA his wife for £625 sold to JOHN HECKENDORN of York Township, York Co a 198 a. 151 perches tr of land in Windsor Township adj NICHOLAS COWFELT, LAWRENCE HERSHNER, CHRISTOPHER HELTZEL & CHRISTOPHER SHAFER, which was surveyed in pursuance of the application of said HENRY LEPHART No. 2419 for 200 a. dated 14 Jan

1767 ... . Wit: MARY LEAS, WM LEAS. Ackn 16 Mar 1775 before WM
LEAS justice. (F:pg 375)

17 Aug 1775. Deed of Mortgage. JOHN FEDER of Manchester Township,
York Co yeoman for better securing the payment of £138.17.10 and also 5
shillings sold to JOHN BEHR of the Town of York, York Co yeoman a 206 a. tr
of land in Manchester Township adj PETER SHAFER, JOHN BOYER &
GEORGE JACOB, whereon the said JOHN FEDER now dwells ... whereas the
said JOHN FEDER standeth bound unto the said JOHN BEHR for £277.15.8
conditioned for the payment of £138.17.10 on 1 Aug next ensuing ... provided
that if the said JOHN FEDER shall well and truly pay unto the said JOHN
BEHR £138.17.10 then this indenture to be void ... . Wit: JOHN MORRIS,
JACOB GARTNER. Ackn 17 Aug 1775 before WILLIAM LEAS esqr justice.
24 Feb 1776 JOHN BEHR discharged mortgage. Wit: SAML JOHNSTON
recorder. (F:pg 377)

22 May 1775. Deed. CHARLES LUKENS esqr high sheriff of York Co for
£270 sold to DAVID GRIER a 450 a. tr of land ... PHILIP BENTZ and AGNES
his wife in the Court of Common Pleas lately recovered against JACOB UPP
late of York Co yeoman decd a debt of £67.2.8 and £8.4.4 damages ...
SAMUEL EDIE esqr then high sheriff of York Co seized in execution a 450 a. tr
of land as the estate of the said JACOB UPP in the hands and custody of PETER
BENTZ adminr with the will annexed of the estate of said JACOB UPP adj
MARTIN FRY, TOBIAS FRY, JOHN BEITZEL, PHILIP GAUFF, PETER
PRAMBAUGH, LODOWICK SPEICE, ANTHONY WOLF & PHILIP BENTZ
in Dover Township ... CHARLES LUKENS esqr sheriff on 30 Jan 1775
exposed the land to sale at public vendue and the same sold to DAVID GRIER
of York Town for £270 he being the highest bidder ... . Wit: [?], [?]. Ackn in
open court 19 Jun 1775. SAMUEL JOHNSTON prothy. (F:pg 378)

12 Apr 1773. Quit Claim. JOHN KITZMILLER of Manheim Township, York
Co blacksmith and MARY his wife (the said JOHN KITZMILLER being one of
the sons and assignees of MARTIN KITZMILLER of same place) for the
premises and in discharge and fulfillment of an obligation and also 5 shillings
quit claim unto GEORGE KITZMILLER (another of the sons and assignees of
said MARTIN KITZMILLER) of same place miller all the privilege of the water
of Little Conewago Cr which runs through a tr of land and also liberty and right
of egress and regress to and from the dam ... whereas the Proprietaries by their
patent dated 11 Oct 1770 granted unto the said JOHN KITZMILLER a 188 ¼ a.
tr of land called *An-Miller* part in Manheim and part in Germany Townships adj
BARNARD BARDT, said MARTIN KITZMILLER & CONRAD
KEEFHAVER (Patent Book AA vol. 11 pg 424), and the mill pond, mill dam &
pt/o the mill race of the water corn and grist mill and shelling mill and hemp mill

of the said GEORGE KITZMILLER supplied with the stream of Little
Conewago Cr as also the original watercourse or channel of said stream layeth
within the afsd tr of land ... whereas the said JOHN KITZMILLER by an
obligation dated 9 Aug 1760 bound himself unto the said MARTIN
KITZMILLER that the said JOHN KITZMILLER after obtaining a patent of
confirmation for the afsd tr of land should convey all those necessary privileges
of the water of the stream afsd and other privileges in the obligation specified
and agreed upon unto said MARTIN KITZMILLER (the father) ... . Wit: [?],
ARCHD MCCLEAN. Ackn 12 Apr 1773 before RD MCALISTER justice.
(F:pg 380)

6 Oct 1766. Deed. THOMAS ARMOR of York, York Co surveyor for £40 sold
to ADAM HENIKE of York Township, York Co yeoman a 50 a. tr of land ...
whereas the Proprietaries by their warrant dated at Phila 13 Dec 1750 did grant
to CHARLES OHARA 50 a. of land adj DENNIS LOUGHERTY on a br of
Codorus Cr, and the said CHARLES OHARA on 1 Jan 1763 did convey the 50
a. tr of land unto ROBERT STEVENSON, and the said ROBERT STEVENSON
on 19 Aug 1765 did convey the 50 a. tr of land unto the afsd THOMAS
ARMOR ... . Wit: BARBARA WISE, GEORGE KUNTZ. Wit to receipt:
JOHN ADLUM. Ackn 6 Oct 1766 before JOHN ADLUM esqr justice. (F:pg
382)

9 Sep 1775. Deed. ADAM HEINICKE of York Township, York Co yeoman
and ELISABETH his wife for £20 sold to LUCAS ROUSE of York Town, York
Co minister of the Gospel a 20 a. 28 perches tr of land pt/o a 175 a. tr of land adj
CONRAD RICHEY ... whereas the Proprietaries by their patent dated at Phila
29 Oct 1771 did grant unto PHILIP BENTZ Junr a 175 a. tr of land called
Huntsmans Hall on Little Codorus in York Township adj CONRAD RICHY,
JOHN HORNISH & ADAM HEINICK's other land, and the said PHILIP
BENTZ and AGNES his wife on 13 Dec 1771 did sell the tr of land unto
MICHAEL HAHN, and the said MICHAEL HAHN and ELISABETH his wife
on 14 Dec 1771 sold the tr of land unto the said ADAM HEINICKE (Book G pg
1) ... . Wit: JOHN JONES, PAUL METZGER. Ackn 9 Sep 1775 before WM
LEAS justice. (F:pg 384)

22 Apr 1775. Deed. JOHN MCKINLEY of Chanceford Township, York Co
yeoman and MARGARET his wife for £786 sold to JACOB TREET and
NICHOLAS DEH both of Windsor Township, York Co yeomen three trs of land
in the whole 457 ½ a. ... whereas in pursuance of a warrant dated at Phila 21
May 1748 there was surveyed and laid out to ROBERT MORTON a 187 ½ a. tr
of land in Chanceford Township adj THOMAS MORGAN & ABRAHAM
BURKHOLDER, and the said ROBERT MORTON on 4 Mar 1761 did sell unto
the said JOHN MCKINLEY the afsd tr of land ... whereas there was a warrant

dated 21 May 1748 granted to EDWARD MCMAHAN for 50 a. of land to be surveyed in Chanceford Township, and the said EDWARD MCMAHAN on 21 Feb 1758 sold unto the said JOHN MCKINLEY the said warrant and all lands to be surveyed ... in pursuance of a warrant to the afsd JOHN MCKINLEY dated 20 Sep 1762 there was surveyed and laid out a 270 a. tr of land in Chanceford Township adj ROBERT MORTON, JOHN MCNULTY & JOSEPH WASON ... . Wit: BENJAMIN SADEN, ROULAND HUGHES, WILLIAM MCADAM. Wit to receipt: DAVID GRIER. Ackn 22 Apr 1755 before WILLIAM MCCASKEY justice. (F:pg 386)

6 Jul 1775. Deed. RICHARD MCCALISTER esqr of the Town of Hanover, Heidelberg Township, York Co for £3 sold to GEORGE SCHREYER of same place gunsmith a lot of ground in the Town of Hanover No. 73, in breadth 57'6" and in length 230' bounded by Frederick Street, Center Square & Lot Nos. 72, 71 & 74, pt/o a larger tr called *Digges' Choice* which the said RICHARD MCCALISTER holds in right of JOHN DIGGES decd ... paying unto the said RICHARD MCCALISTER on 1 May every year forever 8 shillings ... . Wit: HENRY SLAGLE, ARCHD MCCLEAN. Ackn --- 1775 before HENRY SLAGLE justice. (F:pg 389)

1 Aug 1775. Deed of Mortgage. JOHN MCLEAN of Manalan Township, York Co mason for better securing the payment of £46.13.4 and also 5 shillings sold to WILLIAM MCBRIDE of same place yeoman a messuage and 100 a. tr of land in Manalan Township adj CHARLES MCBRIDE, JOHN JOHNSTON, WILLIAM POLOCK & AMOS MAGINLEY ... whereas the said JOHN MCLEAN standeth bound unto the said WILLIAM MCBRIDE for £93.6.8 conditioned for the payment of £46.13.4 on 1 Feb 1777 ... provided that if the said JOHN MCLEAN shall well and truly pay unto the said WILLIAM MCBRIDE £46.13.4 then this indenture to be void ... . Wit: ROBT MCPHERSON, JENNEY MCPHERSON. Ackn 1 Aug 1775 before ROBERT MCPHERSON esqr justice. (F:pg 392)

15 Apr 1774. Deed. SAMUEL SCOTT of Hamilton Bann Township, York Co yeoman for £40 sold to my son JOHN SCOTT of same place two trs of land in Hamilton Bann Township (140 a.), one a 93 a. tr of land adj DAVID KENNEDY, THOMAS SHANNON & the tr hereafter described, being the same tr of land the said JOHN SCOTT now dwells on which was granted unto WILLIAM RANKIN by warrant dated 18 Oct 1754, and the said WILLIAM RANKIN sold unto me, the other tr of land was granted unto me by warrant dated 12 Oct 1773 adj DAVID KENNEDY & afsd tr of land ... . Wit: WILLIAM ORR, WILLIAM MCCLEAN Senr. Ackn 15 Apr 1774 before WM MCCLEAN justice. (F:pg 393)

1 Jun 1775. Deed. FREDRICK SCHWARTZ of Hopewell Township, York Co yeoman for £32.10 sold to JOHN GROVE of Lancaster Co yeoman a 70 a. tr of land whereon I now dwell in Hopewell Township adj GEORGE IRWIN, SAMUEL SMITH, WILLIAM GIFFEN & GARRET HENDRIX, which GEORGE COPELAND on 11 Aug 1772 conveyed unto me ... . Wit: JOHN MORRIS, [?]. Ackn 1 Jun 1775 before WM LEAS justice. (F:pg 394)

16 Sep 1775. Deed of Mortgage. JOHN EBY of Windsor Township, York Co yeoman for better securing the payment of £200 and also 5 shillings sold to NICHOLAS REISINGER of Manchester Township, York Co yeoman two trs of land, a 143 a. 24 perches tr of land in Windsor Township adj JACOB SHANE, MICHAEL BYER, CHRISTIAN LANDIS, CHRISTIAN WALTER & PETER REISINGER, whereon the said JOHN EBY now dwells, and an undivided ½ pt/o a 44 a. 7 perches tr of land called *Brothers Hill* in Windsor Township adj ADAM HAINDLE, JAMES HAMMOND, SAMUEL LANDIS & CHRISTIAN LANDIS ... whereas the said JOHN EBY standeth bound unto the said NICHOLAS REISINGER for £400 conditioned for the payment of £200 in payments before 1 Oct 1778 ... provided that if the said JOHN EBY shall well and truly pay unto the said NICHOLAS REISINGER £200 then this indenture to be void ... . Wit: JOHN MORRIS, GEORGE SCHLOSSER. Ackn 16 Sep 1775 before WILLIAM SCOTT esqr justice. 15 Dec 1778 NICHOLAS REISINGER discharged mortgage. Wit: ARCHD MCCLEAN recorder. (F:pg 395)

27 May 1775. Deed. PETER YOUNG of Mountpleasant Township, York Co yeoman and BARBARA his wife for £5 sold to GEORGE SPONSELLER of Germany Township, York Co yeoman two parcels of land pt/o a 80 a. tr of land, a 13 a. tr of land adj ANDREW SCHRIBER and a 13 ½ a. tr of land ... whereas the Proprietaries by their patent did grant unto the said PETER YOUNG a 80 a. tr of land in Germany Township called *Waterless Lot* adj ANDREW SCHRIBER, GEORGE SPONSELLER & PETER YOUNG (Patent Book AA vol. 13 pg 553) ... . Wit: JOHN GALENTIN, ARCHD MCCLEAN. Ackn 17 Jun 1775 before RD MCALISTER justice. (F:pg 397)

15 Oct 1774. Deed. GEORGE KEENTZ of York Town, York Co tavern keeper and FREDERICK ZAHRGER of Newberry Township, York Co blacksmith for £10 sold to JACOB SHULTZBERGER of Manchester Township, York Co farmer a 52 a. 70 perches tr of land pt/o a 105 a. 100 perches tr of land adj the heirs of JACOB GROVE & said JACOB SHULTZBERGER's other land ... whereas the Proprietaries by their patent dated at Phila 17 Jan 1774 did grant unto the afsd GEORGE KEENTZ and FREDERICK ZAHRGER a 105 a. 100 perches tr of land called *Fellowship* in Manchester Township adj JOHN or THOMAS CALHOON, the heirs of JACOB GROVE, PHILIP PENCE, JACOB

SHULTZBERGER, PETER BRENEMAN & JACOB SMITH (Patent Book AA vol. 14 pg 98) ... . Wit: [RHINHART LOTT?], WM LEAS. Ackn – Oct 1774 before MARTIN EICHELBERGER justice. (F:pg 399)

14 Sep 1775. Deed. WILLIAM WILLIS of Manchester Township, York Co mason for consideration of the yearly rent sold to STOPHEL SHLAGLE of York Town, York Co wheel wright full and free liberty, privilege and authority to erect a dam across the run that passes through the land of the said WILLIAM WILLIS a little above where the run crosseth Newberry Road ... paying yearly unto the said WILLIAM WILLIS on 1 Oct in every year £2.10 ... . Wit: JOHN JONES, WM KERSEY. Ackn 18 Sep 1775 before WM SCOTT justice. (F:pg 401)

9 May 1775. Deed. JOSEPH STEER of Warrington Township, York Co yeoman and GRACE his wife for £200 sold to JAMES DENISDON of same place mill right a 93 ½ a. tr of land in Warrington Township ... whereas the Proprietaries by their patent dated 13 Apr 1753 did grant unto the afsd JOSEPH STEER a 93 ½ a. tr of land in Warrington Township adj Beaver Cr (Patent Book A vol. 16 pg 370) ... . Wit: PETER CLEAVER, MICHAEL MILLER. Ackn 9 May 1775 before JOHN SMITH justice. (F:pg 402)

9 May 1775. Deed. JOSEPH STEER of Warrington Township, York Co yeoman and GRACE his wife for £325 sold to JAMES DENISDON of same place millwright a 169 ½ a. tr of land in Warrington Township ... whereas the Proprietaries by their patent dated 28 Oct 1773 did grant unto the afsd JOSEPH STEER a 169 ½ a. tr of land in Warrington Township (Patent Book AA vol. 14 pr 40) adj JOSEPH STEER's other land, JOSEPH SLOSS & JOSEPH ENGLAND ... . Wit: PETER CLEAVER, MICHAEL MILLER. Ackn 9 May 1775 before JOHN SMITH justice. (F:pg 404)

29 Apr 1775. Deed of Mortgage. GEORGE MILLER of Reading Township, York Co farmer for better securing the payment of £60 and also 5 shillings sold to ISAAC LEREW of Warrington Township, York Co cordwinder a 150 a. tr of land in Manahan Township adj SAMUEL NELSON, ROBERT ROSEBOROUGH, RICHARD PETERS esqr, WILLIAM NELSON & ALEXANDER WILSON, which the said GEORGE MILLER bought of EVAN MINSHALL this date ... whereas the afsd GEORGE MILLER stands bound unto the said ISAAC LEREW for £120 conditioned for the payment of £60 in payments before 15 May 1781 ... provided that if the said GEORGE MILLER shall well and truly pay unto the said ISAAC LEREW £60 then this indenture to be void ... . Wit: PETER SMITH, [?]. Ackn 29 Apr 1775 before JOHN SMITH justice. 14 Mar 1786 by virtue of a letter of atty from ISAAC LEREW,

GODFREY LENHART of York Town discharged mortgage. Wit: JACOB BARNITZ recorder. (F:pg 407)

19 Aug 1765. Deed. ROBERT STEVENSON of Warrington Township, York Co innholder for £13.7 sold to THOMAS ARMOR of York Town, York Co gent a 50 a. tr of land on a br of Codorus Cr near DENNIS LEFFERTY in York Township, which was granted unto CHARLES OHARA by warrant dated 13 Dec 1750 and by the said CHARLES OHARA conveyed to the said ROBERT STEVENSON on 1 Jan 1763 ... . Wit: GEO STEVENSON, JOHN BOYD. Ackn 2 Oct 1775 before WILLIAM RANKIN esqr justice. (F:pg 409)

24 Mar 1775. Deed. FREDERICK KUHN of Berwick Township, York Co innholder and CATHARINE his wife for £80 sold to FREDERICK YOUNCE of the Town of York, York Co blacksmith a 6 a. 110 perches lot of ground in York Township ... whereas on 28 Feb 1767 JOHN GITTINGER of North Hundred, Baltimore Co, MD yeoman and CATHARINE his wife sold to the said FREDERICK KUHN a 6 a. 110 perches lot of ground in York Township bounded by the line of York Town lands, land now of GEORGE MAUL, GODREY FRY & ADAM GERTNER (Book C pg 378) ... . Wit: JACOB THOMAS, HENRY KING. Ackn 24 Mar 1775 before DAVID MCCONAUGHY justice. (F:pg 410)

5 Apr 1775. Deed. JACOB LEFEVER of York Township, York Co yeoman and SUSANNA his wife for £60 sold to HENRY KING of the Town of York, York Co yeoman the s ½ of Lot No. 219 in the Town of York ... whereas the Proprietaries by a certificate dated 12 Sep 1749 did grant unto ANNA WOLF a lot of ground on the e side of Beaver Street in the Town of York, No. 219, in breadth 57'6" and in length 250', and by sundry conveyances the s ½ pt/o the lot is now vested in the afsd JACOB LEFEVER in breadth 28'9" and in length 250' ... . Wit: HERMAN MILLER, WILLIAM SCOTT. Ackn 5 Apr 1775 before WILLIAM SCOTT justice. (F:pg 412)

5 Apr 1775. Deed. JACOB LEFEVER of York Township, York Co yeoman for £20 sold to HENRY KING of the Town of York, York Co a lot of ground on the w side of George Street in the Town of York, No. 213, which was granted unto ANDREW KINKADE by GEORGE STEVENSON esqr one of the agents for the Proprietaries, and by the said ANDREW KINKADE conveyed unto JOHN BOYD on 16 Aug 1764, and by the said JOHN BOYD conveyed unto GOTLIEB ZEEGLE on 23 Aug 1764, and by the said GOTLIEB ZEEGLE conveyed unto MELCHOR FISHER on 25 Aug 1764, and by the said MELCHOR FISHER on 7 May 1774 conveyed to me ... . Wit: HERMAN MILLER, WILLIAM SCOTT. Ackn 5 Apr 1775 before WM SCOTT justice. (F:pg 414)

1 Mar 1775. Deed. NICHOLAS DEH (JOHN NICHOLAS DEH) of Windsor Township, York Co yeoman and ANNA MARGARET his wife for £312.10 sold to JACOB BEAVER of Hellam Township, York Co a 200 a. tr of land in Windsor Township adj WILLIAM WOMELEY & PETER TREET, which was surveyed and laid out unto JOHN BOYER in pursuance of a warrant dated 5 Apr 1754, and the said JOHN BOYER and MARGARET his wife on 14 Apr 1770 sold unto the said NICHOLAS DEH ... . Wit: SOLOMON WILLIAMS, [?]. Wit to receipt: WILLIAM BALEY. Ackn 10 Apr 1775 before WILLIAM BAILEY esqr justice. (F:pg 415)

5 Oct 1775. Deed of Mortgage. JOHN ALSPOAK of Winchester Town, Frederick Co, MD yeoman for better securing the payment of £93 and also 5 shillings sold to CONRAD SCHWARTZ of Lancaster Burrough, Lancaster Co, PA sadler two lots of ground in the Town of Petersburg, Germany Township, Nos. 82 & 83, adj JACOB EYLER, King Street leading from York Town to Frederick Town, MD & PETER LITTLE, in breadth 66' and in length 264', which PETER LITTLE and URSULA his wife on 8 Jun 1772 granted unto the said JOHN ALSPOAK ... whereas the said JOHN ALSPOAK standeth bound unto the said CONRAD SCHWARTZ for £186 conditioned for the payment of £93 on 5 Oct next ensuing ... provided that if the said JOHN ALSPOAK shall well and truly pay unto the said CONRAD SCHWARTZ £93 then this indenture to be void ... . Wit: JOHN SHULTZ, JOHN MORRIS. Ackn 5 Oct 1775 before WILLIAM BAILEY esqr justice. 1 Oct 1779 MICHAEL KELLAR of York Town in pursuance of a letter of atty from CONRAD SCHWARTZ discharged mortgage. Wit: ARCHD MCCLEAN recorder. (F:pg 417)

16 May 1775. Deed. RICHARD COX of Warrington Township, York Co and MARY his wife for £6 sold to NATHANIEL COX of same place a 100 a. tr of land (pt/o a 500 a. tr of land granted unto the said RICHARD COX by patent dated 24 Dec 1742) in Warrington and Huntington Townships adj other land of the said RICHARD COX & THOMAS NASH ... . Wit: WILLIAM COX Senr, WILLIAM COX Junr. Ackn 16 May 1775 before JOHN POPE esqr justice. (F:pg 419)

16 Oct 1775. Deed. JOHN THOMPSON of Mount Joy Township, York Co yeoman and SARAH his wife for £140 sold to WILLIAM WILSON of same place yeoman a 85 a. parcel of land in *Maske Manor*, Mount Joy Township adj other land of the said WILLIAM WILSON granted unto him by the said JOHN THOMPSON, WILLIAM GWIN, ROBERT MCKINNEY & WILLIAM THOMPSON, which WILLIAM THOMPSON brother of the said JOHN THOMPSON on 1 Sep 1774 did with other lands quit claim unto the said JOHN THOMPSON ... . Wit: ARCHD MCCLEAN, ROBT IRWIN. Ackn 16 Oct 1775 before RD MCALISTER justice. (F:pg 421)

15 Oct 1775. Deed. JOHN THOMPSON of Mountjoy Township, York Co yeoman and SARAH his wife for £300 sold to WILLIAM WILSON of same place yeoman a 170 a. parcel of land in Mountjoy Township adj land formerly of JOHN GIBSON, the *Manor of Mask*, land late of said JOHN THOMPSON, WILLIAM THOMPSON & land formerly of JOHN GIBSON, which WILLIAM THOMPSON brother of the said JOHN THOMPSON on 1 Sep 1774 did with other lands release unto the said JOHN THOMPSON ... . Wit: ARCHD MCCLEAN, ROBT IRWIN. Ackn 16 Oct 1775 before RD MCALISTER justice. (F:pg 423)

18 Oct 1775. Deed. ROBERT GREER (GRIER) of Chanceford Township, York Co yeoman and CATHARINE his wife for £220 sold to THOMAS SCOTT and ALLEN SCOTT both of same place yeomen a 171 ½ a. parcel of land in Chanceford Township which was surveyed and laid out to the said ROBERT GREER in pursuance of application No. 2385 for 200 a. dated 14 Jan 1767, adj WILLIAM ADAMS, other land of the said ROBERT GREER, JAMES FORSYTHE, JAMES MCENULTY & JAMES JOLLEY, and also a 200 a. tr of land in Chanceford Township adj the afsd tr of land, JAMES DUNCAN & STEPHEN MCKINLEY ... . Wit: JAMES ROBB, WM SCOTT. Ackn 18 Oct 1775 before WM SCOTT justice. (F:pg 425)

7 Jun 1775. Deed. MICHAEL SPARR of Dover Township, York Co farmer and BARBARA his wife for £230 sold to FREDERICK SPARR of same place farmer a 180 a. tr of land ... whereas the Proprietaries by their patent dated at Phila 9 Jun 1769 did grant unto NICHOLAS YONER a 194 a. tr of land in Dover Township called *Strabann* adj LEONARD FLOHR, land formerly of PATRICK CARRIGAN, PETER STREAR, GEORGE MITCHEL, MARTIN RYSINGER & PHILIP BECKER (Patent Book AA vol. 11 pg --), and the said NICHOLAS YONER on 24 Aug 1771 sold 180 a. pt/o the 194 a. tr of land adj MARTIN RYSINGER, PHILIP BECKER, LEONARD FLOHR, land formerly of PATRICK CARAGAN but now of JACOB YONER & GEORGE MITCHEL ... . Wit: [?], [JACOB YONER?]. Ackn 7 Jun 1775 before WM LEAS justice. (F:pg 428)

24 Aug 1771. Deed. NICHOLAS YONER of Dover Township, York Co cordwainer and ELIZABETH his wife for £230 sold to MICHAEL SPARR of same place farmer a 180 a. tr of land ... whereas the Proprietaries by their patent dated at Phila 9 Jun 1769 did grant unto the said NICHOLAS YONER a 194 a. tr of land in Dover Township called *Strabann* [*same as above*] ... . Wit: JOHN HECKENDORN, WM LEAS. Ackn 24 Aug 1771 before MICHAEL SWOOPE justice. (F:pg 430)

5 Sep 1775. Deed. CHARLES LUKENS esqr high sheriff of York Co for £150
sold to SAMUEL KELLAR a 100 a. tr of land ... whereas DANIEL
MESSERLY adminr de bonis non of PETER GOODLING decd late in a Court
of Common Pleas obtained a judgment against ANNA MARIA SHADRON
adminr with the will annexed of HENRY SHADRON decd who was adminr of
the said PETER GOODLING decd for £354 and 4 shillings 4 pence ½ penny
damages ... in pursuance of a writ the sheriff seized in execution as the estate of
the said HENRY SHADRON decd a message and a 100 a. tr of land in
Shrewsberry Township adj GEORGE KLINEFELTER, JACOB STONER &
others and on 24 Apr last past exposed the land to sale at public vendue and the
same sold to SAMUEL KELLAR for £151 he being the highest bidder ... . Wit:
JAS SMITH, R.N. CARNAN. Ackn 20 Sep 1775 in open court. SAMUEL
JOHNSTON prothy. (F:pg 433)

7 Jun 1775. Deed. ABRAHAM FLOWREY (FLOWERY) of Hellam
Township, York Co yeoman and SUSANNAH his wife for £150 sold to JOST
REEP of same place yeoman a 10 a. tr of land ... whereas the Proprietaries by
their patent dated 12 Apr 1753 granted unto THOMAS MINSHALL a 253 ½ a.
tr of land in the township afsd adj the dwelling plantation of the said THOMAS
MINSHALL (Patent Book A vol. 19 pg 27), and the said THOMAS
MINSHALL and MARY his wife on 30 Oct 1765 sold unto his brother
STEPHEN MINSHALL a 10 a. tr of land pt/o the 253 ½ a. tr of land adj JOHN
FISSEL, HENRY STRICKLER & JOHN FURREY, and the said STEPHEN
MINSHALL on 18 Dec 1766 sold unto PHILIP HOFF a ½ a. tr of land pt/o the
10 a. tr of land on the s side of the Great Road leading from York Town to
Wrights Ferry adj HENRY STRICKLER, JOHN FURREY & THOMAS
MINSHALL esqr, and DAVID MCCONAUGHY esqr late high sheriff of York
Co by virtue of sundry writs out of the Court of Common Pleas at the suit of
CASPER SINGER did take into execution the residue of the 10 a. tr of land as
the estate of the said STEPHEN MINSHALL to satisfy a debt of £53.14.4 and
64 shillings 5 pence damages, and also on 18 Jul 1768 exposed the land to sale
at publick vendue and the same sold to PHILIP HOFF for £56 he being the
highest bidder, and the said DAVID MCCONAUGHY on 10 Aug 1768
conveyed the tr of land unto the said PHILIP HOFF, and the said PHILIP HOFF
on 8 Aug 1772 sold unto DANIEL NEAF the 10 a. tr of land, and the said
DANIEL NEAF and ANN his wife on 26 Jul 1773 sold the 10 a. tr of land unto
the said ABRAHAM FLOWREY ... . Wit: JOHN MORRIS, [?]. Ackn 9 Jun
1775 before WM LEAS justice. (F:pg 435)

10 May 1775. Deed. GEORGE KOAH of Dover Township, York Co yeoman
and MARY MARGARET his wife for £93.12 sold to MICHAEL HOUSE of
Hidleberg Township, York Co yeoman Lot Nos. 38, 191, 192 & 193 in the
Town of Hanover ... whereas RICHARD MCCALLISTER by four indentures

(one of which was dated 29 Jan 1769 and the other three were dated 13 Mar
1769) conveyed unto the afsd GEORGE KOAH four lotts of ground in the Town
of Hanover in Hidleberg Township, to wit, Lot No. 38 on York Street in breadth
57'6" and in length 230' bounded by Lot No. 39, Lot No. 37, and also Lot. No.
191 on Pidgen Street in breadth 57'6" and in length 230' bounded by Lot No.
192 & Lot No. 190, and also Lot No. 192 on Pigeon Street in breadth 57'6" and
in length 230' bounded by Lott No. 193 & Lot. No. 191, and also Lot No. 193
on Pigeon Street in breadth 115' and in length bounded by Lot No. 190,
CHRISTOPHER BEAR & Lot No. 192, the said lots are pt/o a larger tr of land
called *Digges' Choice* which the said RICHARD MCCALLISTER holds in right
of JOHN DIGGES decd, Lot No. 38 subject to the yearly rent of 8 shillings to
the said RICHARD MCCALLISTER and Lot Nos. 191, 192 & 193 subject to
the yearly rent of 6 shillings ... . Wit: JOHN MORRIS, [?]. Ackn 10 May
1775 before WM BAILEY justice. (F:pg 439)

13 Apr 1754. Deed. ROBERT CANNON of Newberry Township, York Co
yeoman for £70 sold to TOBIAS HENDRIX of East Pennsborough Township,
Cumberland Co innkeeper a [*blank*] a. tr of land in Newberry Township adj
Yellow Breeches Cr, JOHN WELCH, REES MORGAN & THOMAS HUNTER
... . Wit: GEO STEVENSON, PHI SHEWBART, GEORGE MCMUN.
Proved 27 Oct 1775 by GEORGE STEVENSON esqr before SAML
JOHNSTON justice, the said ROBERT CANNON, and wits PHILIP SHUBART
& GEORGE MCMUN are since decd. (F:pg 442)

24 Apr 1775. Deed. PHILIP CRONE of Dover Township, York Co carpenter &
MARIA ELIZABETH his wife for £300 sold to JAMES BANE of Newberry
Township, York Co a 206 a. 115 perches tr of land in Newberry Township adj
GODLEIP FISHER, ROBERT WHINNERY, ELIAS EVANS, THOMAS
ARMOR, ELLIS ROGERS & MATTHIAS BOYER, which was surveyed and
laid out for the said PHILIP CRONE in pursuance of an application No. 5025 for
200 a. dated at Phila 1 Jun 1768 ... . Wit: WM MATTHEWS, MORDECAI
WILLIAMS. Ackn 24 Apr 1775 before WM RANKIN esqr justice. (F:pg 444)

19 Apr 1770. Deed. MATTHIAS MILAN (MALLAN) the elder of Reading
Township, York Co cooper for £200 sold to MATTHIAS MILAN the younger
of same place two trs of land, pt/o two [*later described*] trs of land, a 74 a. tr of
land adj JOHN LIGHTY, JOHN MILAN, MANUS BRUGH & PHILIP
HENEMAN, and a 28 ½ a. tr of land adj GEORGE ERNEST, JOHN MILAN &
JOHN LEASE ... whereas the Proprietaries by their patent dated at Phila 21 Nov
1747 (Patent Book A vol. 13 pg 297) did grant unto JOHN LEASE a 369 a. tr of
land in Reading Township then in Lancaster Co but now in York Co, and the
said JOHN LEASE together with HANNAH his wife on 1 Dec 1747 conveyed
unto the afsd MATTHIAS MILAN the elder two trs of land pt/o the afsd 369 a.

tr of land, a 170 a. tr of land adj land then of JOHN LEATHERMAN but now of
MANUS BRUGH, then vacant land but now of PHILIP HENEMAN, land then
of LAWRENCE HAINS but now of JOHN LIGHTY, land of JOHN ASPER &
the said JOHN LEASE, and a 40 a. tr of land adj the said JOHN LEASE & then
vacant land but now of GEORGE ERNEST ... . Wit: PETER SMITH, [?].
Ackn 19 Apr 1770 before JOHN SMITH justice. (F:pg 446)

19 Apr 1770. MATTHIAS MILAN (MALLAN) the elder of Reading
Township, York Co cooper for £200 sold to JOHN MILAN of same place
farmer two trs of land in Reading Township pt/o two [later described] trs, a 106
a. tr of land adj GEORGE ASPER, said JOHN LEASE, MANUS BRUGH,
MATTHIAS MILAN the younger & JOHN LIGHTY, and 18 a. a tr of land adj
GEORGE ERNEST, JOHN LEASE & MATTHIAS MILAN Junr ... whereas
the Proprietaries by their patent dated at Phila 21 Nov 1747 (Patent Book A vol.
13 pg 297) did grant unto JOHN LEASE a 369 a. tr of land [same as above] ...
and the said JOHN LEASE together with HANNAH his wife on 1 Dec 1747
conveyed unto the afsd MATTHIAS MILAN two trs of land pt/o the 369 a. tr of
land [same as above] ... . Wit: PETER SMITH, MARIA SMITH. Ackn 19
Apr 1770 before JOHN SMITH justice. (F:pg 449)

11 Sep 1775. Deed. MATHIAS BAKER of Germany Township, York Co
yeoman and THERESA his wife for £170 sold to PETER GOSHA of York Co
yeoman a tr of land in Germany Township, Lot No. 35 in the Town of
Petersburg bounded by Lot No. 36, a road leading from Cumberland Co to
Baltimore Town, Kings Street leading from York Town towards Frederick Town
& land late of PETER LITTLE, in breadth 66' and in length 264', being the
same lot of ground which PETER LITTLE with URSULA his wife on 8 Jun
1772 sold to the said MATHIAS BAKER ... . Wit: JOS BOUDE, BENJAMIN
SCHWEN. Ackn 11 Sep 1775 before RD MCALISTER justice. (F:pg 452)

20 May 1775. Deed of Mortgage. JONAS SCOGGIN of Mannallen Township,
York Co farmer for better securing the payment of £25 and also 5 shillings sold
to WILLIAM GRIFFETH of same place farmer 2/10 pt/o an undivided tr of land
in Huntington Township, by virtue of some conveyances and by virtue of a
survey made and also by a receipt under the hand of EDMUND PHYSIC dated
18 Oct 1753 for £10 paid by JOHN SCOGGIN father of the said JONAS
SCOGGIN, the said JOHN SCOGGIN became seized in a 156 ½ a. tr of land in
Huntington Township adj DAVID RICHEY, GEORGE ARMSTRONG &
JOHN MCGREW, and the said JOHN SCOGGIN died intestate and so seized
leaving to survive him two sons and seven daus (to wit) HANNAH who is decd
and left issue one son, CATHARINE, AMY & the afsd JONAS, ANN,
RACHEL, JOHN, MARY & ESTHER whereby 2/10 pt/o the whole tr
descended to the afsd JONAS SCOGGIN he being the eldest son, and the said

JONAS SCOGGIN on 14 Oct 1772 sold unto ROBERT PIERCE his 2/10 pt/o the land, and the said ROBERT PIERCE on 8 Jul 1774 conveyed back to the said JONAS SCOGGIN the 2/10 pt/o the land ... whereas the said JONAS SCOGGIN standeth bound unto the said WILLIAM GRIFFETH for £50 conditioned for the payment of £25 on 20 May 1779 ... provided that if the said JONAS SCOGGIN shall well and truly pay unto the said WILLIAM GRIFFETH £25 then this indenture to be void ... . Wit: DAVID POTTS, JOHN POPE. Ackn 20 May 1775 before JOHN POPE justice. (F:pg 454)

27 May 1775. Deed. ANDREW HERRAN (HERRON) of Cumberland Township, York Co, PA yeoman for £280 sold to ADAM BLACK of same place yeoman a 200 a. tr of land in Cumberland Township which was surveyed and laid out by MOSES MCCLEAN adj JOHN GOUDEY, JOHN LAREMORE, JOHN PORTERFIELD & SAMUEL HERRAN, which was sold to the said ANDREW HERRAN by his father ANDREW HERRAN on 28 Apr 1774 ... . Wit: ROBT MCPHERSON, JAS BLACK. Ackn 27 May 1775 before ROBT MCPHERSON justice. (F:pg 457)

18 Jun 1774. Articles of Agreement. JOHN COOPER doth agree that NICHOLAS COOPER shall have free and uninterrupted liberty of the water with the liberty of the race as it is now carreyed from my mill head of water when the mill is not grinding to water his meadow or other uses, and liberty to land with his fery boat & other vesals on my land anywhere on the Susquehanna River above Slate Point Rock ... the said JOHN COOPER shall have liberty at all times to build, raise and repair on the said NICHOLAS COOPER's side of the cr that turns said JOHN COOPER's mill & to damn as much land belong to the said NICHOLAS COOPER as shall be needful to keep sufficient water to the said mills and shall have liberty to carry any person over the river in his own vessel not for hire and to have spare water when the mill is not going ... . Wit: JOHN BOYD, WM ROWAN. Proved 10 Oct 1775 by JOHN BOYD & on 16 Oct 1775 by WM ROWAN before JOSIAH SCOTT justice. (F:pg 459)

1 Jun 1775. Deed. JAMES MCNARY the elder of Chanceford Township, York Co farmer for natural love and affection and 5 shillings sold to his son JAMES MCNARY the younger of Windsor Township, York Co farmer a 102 ½ a. tr of land pt/o a 167 a. tr of land adj GEORGE LIST, ANDREW PAXTON & JAMES MCGAFFOCK ... whereas the Proprietaries by their warrant dated at Phila 15 Mar 1743 did grant unto DAVID JONES a 167 a. tr of land (then in Lancaster Co) now in Chanceford & Windsor Townships, York Co adj CHARLES CARSON & LAWRENCE MCNAMARA, and JOHN JONES one of the sons and surviving heir at law of said DAVID JONES on 1 Aug 1766 conveyed unto the said JAMES MCNARY the elder the 167 a. tr of land ... .

Wit: THOMAS ARMOR, THOMAS ARMOR Junr. Ackn 3 Jun 1775 before
WM SCOTT justice. (F:pg 460)

17 May 1775. Deed. JACOB BLASSER of Manchester Township, York Co
yeoman and BARBARA his wife for £600 sold to DANIEL BEITLER of
Hellam Township, York Co yeoman a tr of land in Manchester Township adj
Big Codorus Cr, PHILIP KING & land of MARTIN CRONMILLER decd,
which the Proprietaries by their patent dated 9 Jul 1767 granted to ISRAEL
MORRIS (Patent Book AA vol. 8 pg 375), and by the said ISRAEL MORRIS
and PHEBE his wife on 24 Jul 1767 sold to the said JACOB BLASSER ... .
Wit: PAUL MEZGER, DAVID GRIER. Ackn 28 Oct 1775 before WILLIAM
SCOTT esqr justice. (F:pg 462)

11 May 1775. Deed. JAMES SMITH of York Co atty at law and ELEANOR
his wife for £120 sold to MARTIN SHUGART of York Co yeoman two lots of
ground in Botts Town on the s side of High Street adj JOHN JACOB BOTT &
others now in the tenure of JOHN JONES & CHRISTIAN NEWMAN ...
subject to the ground rents due to the heirs of HERMAN BOTT & their
assignees ... . Wit: MICHAEL GRAYBEL, WM SCOTT. Ackn 11 May 1775
before WM SCOTT justice. (F:pg 463)

11 May 1775. Deed. CHRISTOPHER RYNEMAN of Manheim Township,
York Co yeoman and URSULA his wife for £55, DOROTHY MILLER for £40
& ELISABETH MARGARET RYNEMAN for £40 (both also of same place)
spinsters (the said CHRISTOPHER RYNEMAN, DOROTHY MILLER &
ELISABETH MARGARET RYNEMAN being children of CHRISTOPHER
RYNEMAN the elder late of Manheim Township yeoman decd by ANNA
CATHARINA his wife) sold to WILHELM RYNEMAN of Manheim
Township, York Co yeoman (also one of the sons of the said CHRISTOPHER
RYNEMAN the elder decd by the said ANNA CATHARINA) a 63 a. 87
perches tr of land ... whereas the Proprietaries by their patent dated at Phila 17
Oct 1767 did grant unto the said CHRISTOPHER RYNEMAN (the father) a 63
a. 87 perches tr of land in Manheim Township called *Heidleberg* adj the
temporary line, HENRY FIET & JACOB COGHANOUR (Patent Book AA vol.
10 pg 139), and the said CHRISTOPHER RYNEMAN (the father) became
seized in the said tr of land together with divers other lands adj thereto and in
MD, and being so seized died intestate about the middle of Jun now last past
leaving ANNA CATHARINA his relict and widow and issue by her the afsd
CHRISTOPHER RYNEMAN, DOROTHY who intermarried with HENRY
MILLER who was a lunatic and who went away about 2 years past and hath not
been since heard of, and ELISABETH MARGARET yet feme sole and also the
said WILHELM RYNEMAN, and the said WILHELM RYNEMAN hath purch
from the other heirs their right and title in the land ... . Wit: ARCHD

MCCLEAN, THOS LATTA. Ackn 12 May 1775 before THOS LATTA justice. (F:pg 464)

11 May 1775. Quit Claim. ANNA CATHARINA RYNEMAN widow and relict of CHRISTOPHER RYNEMAN late of Manheim Township, York Co yeoman decd for £10 quit claim unto WILHELM RYNEMAN one of the sons of the afsd CHRISTOPHER BYNEMAN by the said ANNA CATHARINA all manner of dower which the said ANNA CATHARINA RYNEMAN hath in a 63 a. 87 perches tr of land ... . Wit: ARCHD MCCLEAN, THOS LATTA. Ackn 12 May 1775 before THOS LATTA justice. (F:pg 468)

6 Nov 1775. Deed. FREDERICK SOWER of Frederick Co, MD weaver and JULIANA his wife for £100 sold to GEORGE SCHROYER of the Town of Hanover, Heidleberg Township, York Co gunsmith a lot of ground in the Town of Hanover, No. 78, in breadth 57'6" and in length 230', bounded by Frederick Street & Lot No. 77, which RICHARD MCCALISTER and MARY his wife on 30 Nov 1763 did grant to the afsd FREDERICK SOWER (Book A vol. 2 pg 20) ... . Wit: ARCHD MCCLEAN, ARCHD MCCALISTER. Ackn 6 Nov 1775 before RD MCCALISTER justice. (F:pg 468)

1 Jun 1775. Deed. WILLIAM GETTYS of Mountpleasant Township, York Co storekeeper and MARY his wife for £170 sold to JOHN MARTIN of the Town of Petersburgh, Germany Township, York Co taylor Lot No. 18 in the Town of Petersburgh under subject of the yearly ground rent of 7 shillings unto PETER LITTLE ... whereas by an indenture of release dated 18 Jan 1769 PETER LITTLE of Germany Township and URZULA his wife released unto ISAAC DROGGET of the Town of Hanover tobacconist a lot of ground in the Town of Petersburgh, No. 18, adj Kings Street (being the road leading from York Town to Frederick Town, MD), the new road leading through the said town from Black's Gap to Baltimore, JOSEPH FLOUT & Lot No. 19, in breadth 66' and in depth 264', and the said ISAAC DROGGET and ELISABETH his wife on 5 Oct 1772 sold the lot of ground unto JOHN MEYERS, and the said JOHN MEYERS (by the name & addition of JOHN MEYER of the Town of Petersburgh, York Co storekeeper) and MARY his wife on 27 Feb 1773 sold the lot of ground unto the said WILLIAM GETTYS ... the said ISAAC DROGGET by indenture of mortgage dated 13 Apr 1771 granted the said lot of ground unto CASPER REINECKER of the Town of Hanover innholder for securing the payment of a debt due by the said ISAAC DROGGET unto the said CASPER REINICKER (Book D pg 411), and of which incumbrance of mortgage neither the said JOHN MEYERS nor the said WILLIAM GETTYS had any knowledge of at the time of the passing the afsd grants unto them, for removing the incumbrance and remedying the inconvenience that would arise therefrom and in order that the title unto said lot of ground should pass clear unto the said WILLIAM GETTYS,

the said CASPER REINECKER upon payment of said mortgage money unto him by the said ISAAC DROGGET did by his deed poll dated 26 Apr 1774 forever quit claim unto the said WILLIAM GETTYS all the afsd lot of ground (Book E pg 496) ... . Wit: ARCHD MCCLEAN, RD MCCALISTER. Ackn 29 Jun 1775 before RD MCALISTER justice. (F:pg 470)

27 Jun 1775. Deed. JOHN MARTIN of Mountpleasant Township, York Co (formerly of the Town of Petersburgh, Germany Township, York Co) taylor for £132.10 sold to WILLIAM BRONNER of the Town of Petersburgh afsd taylor Lot No. 18 in the Town of Petersburgh subject to the yearly ground rent of 7 shillings to PETER LITTLE [same as above] ... . Wit: ARCHD MCCLEAN, JAMES MARTIN. Ackn 29 Jun 1775 before RD MCALISTER justice. (F:pg 473)

10 Mar 1775. Deed. THOMAS ARMOR of York Town, York Co surveyor for £40 sold to DANIEL GLASS of Warrington Township, York Co a 80 a. 108 perches tr of land adj THOMAS ATHERTON, JOHN MCMULLEN & others in Warrington Township, surveyed in pursuance of JOSEPH WALLACE's application No. 5524 and order of survey dated 19 Jun 1769 who on 1 Sep 1769 conveyed the same unto me (Book E pg 316) and also JOHN CRAFFORD on 24 Jan last conveyed unto me all his right to the said land ... . Wit: [?], LENHARD KAIGE. Ackn 15 May 1775 before WM SCOTT justice. (F:pg 475)

14 Oct 1775. Bond. CHARLES LUKENS of York Town, JAMES RANKIN of York Township and JAMES DILL of Manahan Township all of York Co are firmly bound unto GEORGE the third for £2000 ... the condition of this obligation is such that if the said CHARLES LUKENS on 2 Oct instant was elected sheriff for York Co and if he shall well and truly pay to the several suitors the several sums of money belonging which shall come to his hands and shall do from time to time during his continuance in the office of sheriff well and faithfully execute the said office and perform every duty and truly in him reposed then this obligation to be void ... . Wit: CORNELIUS SHERIFF, ROBT STEVENSON. Ackn 3 Nov 1675 before SAML JOHNSTON esqr justice. (F:pg 476)

10 Oct 1775 at Phila. Commission. CHARLES LUKENS appointed sheriff of York Co by JOHN PENN. (F:pg 477)

24 Jan 1775. Deed. JOHN CRAWFORD of Warrington Township, York Co farmer for £3 sold to THOMAS ARMOR of York Town, York Co surveyer a tr of land adj WILLIAM GRIFFITH, JOHN MCMILLAN, ADAM WILEY, THOMAS ATHERTON & my land in Warrington Township which was

surveyed by CHARLES LUKENS surveyor on 15 Dec last in pursuance of an application No. 5524 dated 19 Jun 1769 granted unto JOSEPH WALLACE ... . Wit: FRANCIS WORLEY, THOS ARMOR Junr. Ackn 24 Jan 1775 before WILLIAM SCOTT esqr justice. (F:pg 478)

10 Nov 1775. Deed of Mortgage. JACOB BURKHARD of Manheim Township, York Co yeoman and SALOME his wife for better securing the payment of £300 and also 5 shillings sold to MICHAEL GUNDACKER of Lancaster Borough, Lancaster Co yeoman two trs of land, a 213 a. tr of land in Manheim Township adj CHRISTIAN HERSHEY & CHARLES YOUNG, and a 140 ½ a. tr of land adj THOMAS WILSON, JACOB BOLLINGER, ANDREW HERSHEY & MARK TURNEY ... whereas the said JACOB BURKHARD standeth bound unto the said MICHAEL GUNDACKER for £600 conditioned for the payment of £300 on 10 Nov 1776 ... provided that if the said JACOB BURKHARD shall well and truly pay unto the said MICHAEL GUNDACKER £300 then this indenture to be void ... . Wit: [?], EBERHART MICHAEL. Ackn 15 Nov 1775 before WILLIAM BALEY (BAILEY) esqr justice. 4 Jul 1789 MARGARET GUNDACKER and PETER MILLER surviving executors of the will of MICHAEL GUNDACKER discharged mortgage. Wit: J. BARNITZ recorder. (F:pg 479)

15 May 1775. Deed. JOHN WRIGHT of Hellam Township, York Co gent for £25 sold to JACOB PROBST of York Town, York Co yeoman Lot No. 36 in the Town of York ... whereas the Proprietaries by their patent dated at Phila 21 Oct 1765 did grant unto ELEANOR WRIGHT and JAMES WRIGHT executors of the will of JOHN WRIGHT decd (the father of the afsd JOHN WRIGHT) a lott of ground on the w side of Duke Street in the Town of York, No. 36, in breadth 57 ½' and in length 250', bounded by Lot. No. 35 (Patent Book A vol. 18 pg 413), and by the death of ROBERT WRIGHT (who died intestate and without issue) one of the sons and heirs at law of the said JOHN WRIGHT the elder decd, and releases from JAMES EWING & PATIENCE his wife, JOHN HOUSTON & SUSANNA his wife dau of said JOHN WRIGHT the elder decd the said lott of ground became vested in the said JOHN WRIGHT the younger ... . Wit: FREDERICK YOUCE, HENRY MILLER. Ackn 15 May 1775 before WILLIAM SCOTT justice. (F:pg 480)

17 Nov 1775. Deed of Mortgage. LEONARD KIRKINHEISER of Manheim Township, York Co yeoman for better securing the payment of £100 and also 5 shillings sold to WYRICK BENS of the Town of York, York Co yeoman a 100 a. tr of land in Manheim Township adj JACOB LENGERFELTER, ULRICK HOOVER & the heirs of ENGLE JONES, which the Proprietaries by their patent dated at Phila 8 Dec 1773 did grant unto the said LEONARD KIRKINHEISER ... whereas the said LEONARD KIRKINHEISER standeth

bound unto the said WYRICK BENS for £200 conditioned for the payment of £100 on 1 May 1777 ... provided that if the said LEONARD KIRKINHEISER shall well and truly pay unto the said WYRICK BENS £100 then this indenture to be void ... . Wit: JOHN MORRIS, JOHN HAUSLER. Ackn 18 Nov 1775 before WILLIAM LEAS esqr justice. 9 Nov 1776 WYRICK BENS discharged mortgage. Wit: SAML JOHNSTON recorder. (F:pg 482)

16 Sep 1775. Deed. CHRISTIAN ROTH of Paradise Township, York Co yeoman and JULIANA his wife for £150 sold to PETER RATZ of same place yeoman a 150 a. parcel of land in Paradise Township adj JOHN [JASSEPH or IASSEPH?], PAUL FEGELY & CASPER SNEIDER, which was granted unto the said CHRISTIAN ROTH by warrant dated at Phila 24 Feb last past ... . Wit: GEO LEWIS LESLER, GEORGE GUTYAHR. Ackn 20 Nov 1775 before WM LEAS justice. (F:pg 484)

7 Aug 1775. Deed of Mortgage. CONRAD LEHER of the Town of York, York Co taylor for better securing the payment of £25 and also 5 shillings sold to PHILIP ENTLER of same place yeoman a messuage and lott of ground on the e side of Water Street in the Town of York, No. 175, bounded by Lot No. 174, in breadth 57'6" and in length 230', whereon the said CONRAD LEHER now dwells ... whereas the said CONRAD LEHER standeth bound unto the said PHILIP ENTLER for £50 conditioned for the payment of £25 in payments before 1 Oct 1777 ... provided that if the said CONRAD LEHER shall well and truly pay unto the said PHILIP ENTLER £25 then this indenture to be void ... . Wit: JOHN MORRIS, MICHAEL [blank]. Ackn 7 Aug 1775 before WILLIAM LEAS esqr justice. (F:pg 486)

2 Oct 1775. Deed. THOMAS ARMOR of York Town, York Co yeoman and SARAH his wife for £53 sold to CHRISTIAN HARE of Lancaster Co, PA yeoman a 138 a. tr of land ... whereas the Proprietaries by their patent dated 29 Mar 1760 did grant unto DANIEL SLEGLE a 138 a. tr of land in Mount Pleasant Township adj ANDREW HARRIER, ANDREW HERRIER's heirs, THOMAS MCCARTY, PAUL TIMIN & LUDWIG SCHRIVER (Patent Book A vol. 20 pg 506), and the said DANIEL SLEGLE and BARBARA his wife sold unto the said THOMAS ARMOR the tr of land on 2 Feb 1761 (Book A pg 483) ... . Wit: FREDERICK HOUSMAN, ROBT BIGHAM Junr. Ackn 4 Nov 1775 before WILLIAM RANKIN esqr justice. (F:pg 488)

30 Nov 1775. Deed. JACOB SHANK of York Town, York Co shoemaker adminr of the estate of JACOB WOLF formerly of York Town cooper decd who died intestate for £100 sold to JOHN KUNKLE of same place cooper and stiller Lot No. 167 in the Town of York ... whereas by consent of the Proprietaries there was surveyed and laid out unto HENRY MESSERSMITH a lott of ground

in the Town of York, No. 167, as by a certificate under the hand of THOMAS
COOKSON esqr then one of the agents for the Proprietaries dated 15 Jun 1748,
and the said HENRY MESSERSMITH afterwards died intestate seized of the
lott of ground leaving a widow ELIZABETH, and SAMUEL his eldest son,
ANNA MARIA w/o JACOB RUDISILLY, CHRISTIANA w/o BALTZER
SPANGLER & MATTHIAS his younger son, and the said ELIZABETH
MESSERSMITH widow and relict of said decd on 21 Apr 1763 did sell the lott
of ground unto NICHOLAS OTT, and the said NICHOLAS OTT on same date
sold the lot of ground to PETER LEONHART, and the said PETER
LEONHART on 30 Apr 1763 sold the lott of ground to NICHOLAS SHAFFER,
and the said NICHOLAS SHAFFER on 20 Jul 1765 sold the lott of ground to
JACOB WOLFF (WOLF), and SAMUEL MESSERSMITH eldest son of the
said HENRY MESSERSMITH and ELISABETH his wife, the said JACOB
RUDISILLY and ANNA MARIA his wife, BALTZER SPANGLER and
CHRISTIANA his wife and MATTHIAS MESSERSMITH on 22 Jul 1765 did
quit claim unto the afsd JACOB WOLFF all their right in the lott of ground, and
the said JACOB WOLFF in his lifetime by Articles of Agreement dated 4 Nov
1774 for £100 paid by JOHN KUNKLE of the Town of York did agree with the
said JOHN KUNKLE that he the said JACOB WOLFF would convey unto the
said JOHN KUNKLE the afsd lot of ground on 5 Nov next ensuing, and whereas
the said JACOB WOLFF lately died intestate without having executed any
conveyance for the lot of ground to the said JOHN KUNKLE and administration
of the estate was granted to the said JACOB SHANK .... Wit: DAVID
GRIER, CORNELIUS SHERIFF. Ackn 2 Dec 1775 before SAMUEL
JOHNSTON justice. (F:pg 490)

4 Nov 1774. Articles of Agreement. Between JACOB WOLF of Frederick Co,
MD copper and stiller and JOHN KUNKLE of the Town of York, York Co
copper and stiller [same as mentioned above] .... Wit: JOHN MORRIS,
MICHAEL GEISELMAN. Proved 24 Nov 1775 by JOHN MORRIS &
MICHAEL GEISELMAN before SAML JOHNSTON justice. (F:pg 493)

9 Oct 1775. Deed. GOTTLIEB ZIEGEL of the Town of York, York Co
innkeeper and BARBARA his wife for £4 sold to PHILIP DEITSCH of same
place schoolmaster a house and lot of ground in York Town on the w side of
George Street, No. 283, in breadth 57 ½' and in 250' bounded by Lot No. 284 &
Lot No. 282, which JOHN BURKBECK on 10 Feb 1770 conveyed unto the said
GOTTLIEB ZIEGEL .... Wit: MATTHIAS DEBTOR, GEO LEWIS
LESLER. Ackn 9 Oct 1775 before WM SCOTT justice. (F:pg 494)

25 Aug 1775. Deed of Mortgage. JACOB STOBER of Paradise Township,
York Co yeoman for better securing the payment of £300 and also 5 shillings
sold to GEORGE MICHAEL STOBER of same place yeoman a 260 ½ a. tr of

land in Paradise Township adj FREDERICK STOBER, RUDOLPH
KLINEPETER, JACOB HARMAN & CASPER SPANGLER, which the said
GEORGE MICHAEL STOBER granted to the said JACOB STOBER on 22
May last past ... whereas the said JACOB STOBER standeth bound unto the
said GEORGE MICHAEL STOBER for £600 conditioned for the payment of
£300 in payments, £100 payable in yearly payments of £5 from 22 May 1778,
and £200 in payments of £25 yearly from the day of the death of the said
GEORGE MICHAEL STOBER ... provided that if the said JACOB STOBER
pay unto the said GEORGE MICHAEL STOBER £300 then this indenture to be
void ... . Wit: GEORGE CRAFT, JOHN MORRIS. Ackn 4 Dec 1775 before
WILLIAM LEAS esqr justice. (F:pg 496)

24 Jul 1775. Deed. THOMAS SCOTT of Chanceford Township, York Co
yeoman and JENNET his wife for £105 sold to ROBERT LONG of Dremore
Township, Lancaster Co taylor a 150 a. tr of land adj JOHN FINLEY, JAMES
JOLLEY, ROBERT GRIER, JOHN MCCLORG, JAMES ELDER &
ALEXANDER MCCULLOUGH ... whereas ROBERT SUMMERS settled and
improved on a tr of land in Chanceford Township adj JOHN FINLEY, JAMES
JOLLEY, JOHN EDMUNDSON, WILLIAM WILSON & others and obtained a
warrant dated 9 Mar 1753 for 75 a. of land and being seized thereof died having
first made his will and ordered his executors to sell the said tr of land and did
appoint JOSEPH WASON & JOSEPH BOGLE executors, and the said JOSEPH
WASON & JOSEPH BOGLE on 2 Mar 1768 did sell unto JAMES GUY the
afsd tr of land, and the said JAMES GUY and ISABELLA his wife on 7 Apr
1768 by an assignment endorsed on the back of the conveyance did make over
all their right to the conveyance unto the afsd JOSEPH WASON, and the said
JAMES GUY by another conveyance on 8 Apr same year did sell unto the afsd
JOSEPH WASON the afsd tr of land, and the said JOSEPH WASON on 17 Sep
1768 for £103 sold the tr of land unto the afsd THOMAS SCOTT ... . Wit: JOS
READ, WM MCCASKEY. Ackn 24 Jul 1775 before WM MCCASKEY
justice. (F:pg 498)

1 May 1775. Deed. ISAAC MORRIS of Warrington Township, York Co
blacksmith for £450 sold to DEWALD HESS of same place a 179 a. 43 perches
tr of land ... whereas HENRY FLICK obtained two warrants to include his
improvement for 180 a. of land in Warrington Township dated in Phila 27 Apr
1772 and 25 May same year, and the said HENRY FLICK on 16 May 1773 sold
unto DANIEL CROUSE a 179 a. 43 perches tr of land in Warrington Township
adj ANTHONY EURY, JOSHUA DAVIES, DETER UPACK & GEORGE
HIKES, and the said DANIEL CROUSE on same date sold unto ISAAC
MORRIS the tr of land ... . Wit: WILLIAM ROSS, JACOB WILLIAMS.
Ackn 9 May 1775 before JOHN SMITH justice. (F:pg 500)

2 Jul 1774. Deed. MICHAEL BARD of York Township, York Co innkeeper and DOROTHEA his wife for £940 sold to JOHN HERBAUCH of same place a 200 a. tr of land in York Township ... whereas the Proprietaries by a licence under the hand of SAMUEL BLUNSTON esqr (then agent for said Proprietaries) dated at Lancaster 9 Dec 1734 granted unto ULRICH WISSLER (by the name of WOOLRICK WEESLER) 250 a. on land on Little Codorus Cr about a mi above THOMAS PENN to be taken on both sides of said cr for the conveniency of building a mill, and the said ULRICH WISSLER assigned on 12 Nov 1745 to ½ pt/o the afsd licence to his son in law JOHN BOWER, and the said ULRICH WISSLER and JOHN BOWER on 28 Mar 1749 sold the licence and land unto CONRAD HOLTZBAUM, and the said CONRAD HOLTZBAUM and CATHARINA his wife on 18 Sep 1763 sold unto GEORGE STEVENSON esqr a 200 a. tr of land pt/o the 250 a. of land adj MELCHOR HENNEBERGER, HERMAN MILLER, said CONRAD HOLTZBAUM (Book B pg 492) ... whereas SAMUEL EDIE esqr high sheriff of York Co in pursuance of sundry writs issued out of the Court of Common Pleas at the suit of JAMES BENEZET merchant, did take in execution the afsd 200 a. tr of land as the estate of GEORGE STEVENSON to satisfy a debt of £1772 and £9.14.6 damages, and on 7 Sep last past exposed the same to sale by publick vendue and sold unto the said MICHAEL BARD for £940 he being the highest bidder, and the said SAMUEL EDIE in pursuance of the sale on 21 Jun last past conveyed the 200 a. unto the said MICHAEL BARD together with the grist mill, shelling mill & saw mill ... . Wit: GODFREY LONBERGER, HENRY MILLER. Ackn 2 Jul 1774 before WM BAILEY justice. (F:pg 502)

21 Jun 1774. Deed. SAMUEL EDIE esqr high sheriff of York Co for £940 sold to MICHAEL BARD a 200 a. tr of land with a grist mill, shelling mill & saw mill ... whereas JAMES BENEZET lately in the Court of Common Pleas recovered against GEORGE STEVENSON late of York Co a debt of £1772 and £9.14.6 damages ... and the sheriff seized in execution a 200 a. tr of land with a grist mill, shelling mill & saw mill [*same as above*] ... and sold at publick vendue to MICHAEL BARD for £940 he being the highest bidder ... . Wit: THOMAS HARTLEY, HENRY MILLER. Ackn 7 Oct 1774 in open court. EDWARD SHIPPEN prothy. (F:pg 505)

31 Oct 1775. Deed of Mortgage. SARAH BUTLER and THOMAS BUTLER of Heidleberg Township, York Co for better securing the payment of £52 and also 5 shillings sold to CASPER REINECKER of York Co innholder four pieces of ground in Heidleberg Township, known on the plan of lotts laid out by PATRICK MCSHERRY as No. 17, No 13, No. 16 and No. 14 ... whereas the said SARAH and THOMAS BUTLER stand bound unto the said CASPER REINECKER for £104 conditioned for the payment of £52 on or before 13 Nov next ensuing ... provided that if the said SARAH BUTLER and THOMAS

BUTLER shall well and truly pay unto the said CASPER REINECKER £52 then this indenture to be void ... . Wit: JOS BOUDE, ARCHD MCCALISTER. Ackn 31 Oct 1775 before RICHARD MCCALISTER esqr justice. 10 Mar 1777 CASPER RENECKER discharged mortgage. Wit: SAML JOHNSTON recorder. (F:pg 507)

5 Dec 1763. Deed. JACOB EYLER of Manheim Township, York Co carpenter one of the sons of CONRAD EYLER late of Lancaster Co decd for 5 shillings sold to VALENTINE EYLER of same place my share of a tr of land originally granted unto the afsd CONROD EYLER by warrant dated at Phila 3 Oct 1738 on a br of Codorus Cr on the w side of Susquehannah River then pt/o Lancaster Co now in Manheim Township, York Co, whereon the afsd VALENTINE now dwells ... . Wit: THOS ARMOR, RICHARD MCCALISTER. Ackn 13 Jan 1768 before HENRY SLAGLE justice. (F:pg 508)

8 Dec 1763. Deed. FREDRICK CROYDER of Fredricks Co, VA and BARBARA his wife one of the daus of CONRAD EYLER late of Lancaster Co, PA decd for 10 shillings sold to VALENTINE EYLER of Manheim Township, York Co their share in a tr of land [same as above] ... . Wit: W. BROOKE, JACOB KLEH, JOHN MORRIS. Proved 18 Jan 1776 by JACOB KLEH before HENRY SLAGLE justice. (F:pg 509)

2 Jan 1764. Deed. LAWRENTZ SCHNEP at the Atkin River in NC & ELIZABETH his wife one of the daus of CONROD EYLER late of Lancaster Co, PA for 10 shillings sold their share in a tr of land unto VALENTINE EYLER of Manheim Township, York Co [same as above] ... . Wit: JOHN LEW BEARD, MICHAEL KARLE, CHRISTINA BENTZ. Proved 16 Sep 1765 by MICHAEL CARL (KARLE) before HENRY SLAGLE justice. (F:pg 510)

6 Dec 1763. Deed. JACOB VERTREAZ of Frederick Co, VA and CATHRINE his wife one of the daus of CONROD EYLER late of Lancaster Co, PA decd for £10 shillings sold to VALENTINE EYLER of Manheim Township, York Co their share in a tr of land [same as above] ... . Wit: HENRICH BEIDINGER, HENRY COKUS, JACOB KLEH. Proved 18 Jan 1776 by JACOB KLEH before HENRY SLAGLE justice. (F:pg 511)

27 May 1772. Quit Claim. FREDERICK GALWIX of Manheim Township, York Co yeoman and MARY his wife one of the daus of CONRAD EYLER late of York Co yeoman decd for £7 quit claim unto VALENTINE EYLER of York Co yeoman one of the sons of the said CONRAD EYLER decd our right to the estate real or personal of the said CONRAD EYLER decd especially in a 233 a.

tr of land in Manheim Township ... . Wit: ROBT WHITE, JOS BOUDE. Ackn – May 1772 before RD MCALISTER justice. (F:pg 512)

7 Feb 1776. Deed of Mortgage. DAVID EVENS of Dover Township, York Co farmer for better securing the payment of £109.18.6 and also 5 shillings sold to DAVID GRIER, MICHAEL HAHN & ADAM DIHL all of York Co a 100 a. tr of land whereon the said DAVID EVENS now dwells in Dover Township adj HENRY YESLER, WILLIAM BALEY esqr, PHILIP GAUFF, PETER BRUMBAUGH, LUDWIG SPEES & ANTHONY WOOLF ... whereas the said DAVID EVENS standeth bound unto the said DAVID GRIER, MICHAEL HAHN & ADAM DIHL for £219.17 conditioned for the payment of £109.18.6 before 7 Feb 1778 ... provided that if the said DAVID EVENS shall well and truly pay unto the said DAVID GRIER, MICHAEL HAHN & ADAM DIHL £109.18.6 then this indenture to be void ... . Wit: PHILIP WOLFF, CONRAD WOULFF. Ackn 7 Feb 1776 before WILLIAM BAILEY esqr justice. 5 Dec 1782 ADAM DIEHL discharged mortgage. Wit: ARCHD MCCLEAN recorder. (F:pg 512)

25 Aug 1775. Deed. JOHN COX of Newberry Township, York Co farmer for £150 sold to JOHN BEHR of Strasburg Township, Lancaster Co farmer a 77 a. tr of land pt/o a 140 a. tr of land adj JACOB BEHR & JACOB SHITTER ... whereas in pursuance of a warrant granted un DANIEL MCLOUGHERY dated 31 Oct 1745 there was surveyed and laid out a 140 a. tr of land in Newberry Township adj Big Conewago Cr, FREDERICK STONE, WILLIAM UPDEGRAFF & JACOB SHITTER, and the said DANIEL MCLOUGHERY died intestate leaving his sons JOHN, DANIEL, JEREMIAH & PATRICK, also daus SARAH w/o AMBROSE UPDEGRAFF & CATHRINE w/o JONAS ODENBAUGH, who by sundry mesne conveyances did make over all their right to said tr of land unto WILLIAM UPDEGRAFF, and the said WILLIAM UPDEGRAFF and SARAH his wife on 4 Sep 1770 sold unto the said JOHN COX the tr of land ... . Wit: THOS ARMOR, VALENTINE ROTHROCK. Ackn 2 Nov 1775 before WM RANKIN esqr justice. (F:pg 514)

14 Dec 1775. Deed. CHRISTIAN WALTER of Windsor Township, York Co yeoman and BARBARA his wife for £225 sold to JOHN MYER of same place blacksmith a 80 a. 131 perches tr of land in Windsor Township which in pursuance of a warrant dated 20 Feb 1767 was surveyed and laid out unto the said CHRISTIAN WALTER adj WENDALL REISINGER, JACOB STAGNER, ADAM HAINDAL & CHRISTIAN LANDUS, which was originally improved and possessed by NICHOLAS REISINGER, and the said NICHOLAS REISINGER on 1 Aug 1759 sold the tr of land unto PETER REISINGER, and the said PETER REISINGER on 20 Aug 1759 sold the tr of

land unto the said CHRISTIAN WALTER ... . Wit: JOHN MORRIS, JACOB
STAGNER. Ackn 14 Dec 1775 before WM LEAS justice. (F:pg 515)

12 Feb 1776. Articles of Agreement. JACOB DILINGER Senr for £80 sold
unto JACOB DILINGER Junr (both of Windsor Township, York Co) yeoman
his now dwelling plantation and 260 a. tr of land in Windsor Township adj FEIT
BENER, WILLIAM MICHAEL, ANDREW GILBERT & others, also all his
horses, cows, sheep and swine and all his tools and gears, excepting and
reserving for the said JACOB DILINGER the elder and MARIA BARBARA his
wife the old dwelling house and room in the stable for one cow which is to be
kept for their use during their natural life, and the said JACOB DILINGER Junr
doth agree to deliver unto the said JACOB DILINGER Senr and MARIA
BARBARA his wife yearly during their natural lives in the fall season two
hogsheads of good cider, 60 lbs. weight of good beef, 60 lbs. weight of good
pork, 20 lbs. of hackled hemp or flax, 4 lbs. of wood, 15 bushels of good wheat
and 10 of rye, 11 gallons of apple liquor and 3 lbs. PA money and the £80
purchase money to be paid, to wit, £20 in 2 years after decease of said JACOB
DILINGER the elder to be paid to FREDERICK DILINGER, £20 to JOSEPH
DILINGER in one year next after the said first payment, the said FREDERICK
and JOSEPH being sons of the said JACOB DILINGER the elder, £20 more in 4
years next after the decease of said JACOB DILINGER Senr to be paid to
JOSEPH TRITT & MARGARET TRITT grandchildren of said JACOB
DILINGER Senr & £20 more in 5 years after the decease of said JACOB
DILINGER Senr to PHILIP GOHN son in law to said DILINGER the elder,
which several sums is in full the £80, and the said JACOB DILINGER Senr doth
order that in one month after his decease that the said JACOB DILINGER Junr
shall pay unto JOHN NICHOLAS HOWERT who is a grandson of said JACOB
DILINGER Senr 5 shillings in right of his mother who is intermarried with
MICHAEL HOWERT, and the said JACOB DILLINGER Senr and JACOB
DILINGER Junr do agree with each other that if JOHN DILINGER one of the
sons of the said JACOB DILINGER Senr doth return home from the Army and
gives security for his performing ½ pt/o the conditions afsd then he shall have ½
pt/o the land and effects in this article named and described, and for the true
performance of the covenants and agreements herein mentioned the parties bind
themselves to each other in the sum of £200 ... . Wit: PAUL SLAGLER,
WILLIAM SCOTT, HENRY KING, ADAM GARTNER. Ackn 12 Feb 1776
before WM SCOTT justice. (F:pg 517)

13 Feb 1776. Deed of Mortgage. CONRAD MEIXEL of Dover Township,
York Co yeoman for better securing the payment of £148 and also 5 shillings
sold to PHILIP JACOB JULIUS & ADAM MILLER each of York Co yeomen a
100 a. tr of land in Newberry Township adj JACOB DOUDLE, ANDREAS
MELLHORN & others, which JACOB MILLER eldest son and heir at law of

JACOB MILLER late of York Co decd this date sold unto the said CONRAD
MEIXEL ... whereas the said CONRAD MEIXEL standeth bound unto the said
PHILIP JACOB JULIUS & ADAM MILLER for £296 conditioned for the
payment of £148 in payments before 2 Nov 1783 ... provided that if the said
CONRAD MEIXEL shall well and truly pay unto the said PHILIP JACOB
JULIUS & ADAM MILLER £148 then this indenture to be void ... . Wit: GEO
EICHELBERGER, JOHN MORRIS. Ackn 13 Feb 1776 before WILLIAM
BAILEY esqr justice. (F:pg 518)

13 Feb 1776. Deed. JACOB MILLER of Newberry Townships, York Co
yeoman for £148 sold to CONRAD MEIXEL of Dover Township, York Co
yeoman a 100 a. tr of land in Newberry Township [*same as above*] ... whereas
the said JACOB MILLER the elder lately died intestate possessed of the tr of
land leaving a widow ELISABETH and the said JACOB MILLER his eldest son
and heir at law and MICHAEL MILLER, GEORGE MILLER, HENRY
MILLER, PETER MILLER, MATHIAS MILLER, ADAM MILLER & EVE
MILLER his children to survive him, and upon the petition of the said JACOB
MILLER the eldest son of the decd it was ordered by the Orphans Court that
partition of said tr of land should be made ... on 5 Sep last CHARLES LUKENS
esqr then sheriff of York Co returned that the tr of land would not admit of
partition without spoiling the whole and the same was valued at £80, and it was
ordered by the Court that the said JACOB MILLER the eldest son should pay
unto the said ELIZABETH MILLER the widow yearly during her natural life
£1.9.11 3 farthings in full for her right of dower, and the said JACOB MILLER
also to pay the other children each £5.11 1 penny, and in one year after the death
of the said widow the further sum of £2.5.6 ½ penny to each of them in full of
their share of said valuation, and it was also ordered by the Court that upon the
said JACOB MILLER making the several payments afsd and giving good
security for the same that he should hold the said tr of land ... . Wit: GEO
EICHELBERGER, JOHN MORRIS. Ackn 13 Feb 1776 before WILLIAM
BAILEY justice. (F:pg 520)

13 Feb 1776. Quit Claim. ELIZABETH MILLER the widow of JACOB
MILLER late of Newberry Township, York Co yeoman for £25 quit claim unto
CONRAD MEIXEL all my estate right to the [*above mentioned*] tr of land
formerly belonging to my late husband JACOB MILLER decd or my part by
reason of my dower ... . Wit: GEO EICHELBERGER, JOHN MORRIS. Ackn
13 Feb 1776 before WILLIAM BAILEY justice. (F:pg 522)

15 Feb 1776. Deed of Mortgage. PHILIP SMELTZER of Windsor Township,
York Co yeoman for better securing the payment of a debt and also 5 shillings
sold to ANTHONY AMENT of same place yeoman a messuage and 250 a. tr of
land with a grist mill thereon in Windsor Township adj ANDREW KUHN,

JAMES HINES & land late of GEORGE WACHTEL, being the same lately belonging to JOHN AMENT and conveyed by SAMUEL EDIE esqr late high sheriff in pursuance of sundry writs unto the said ANTHONY AMENT on 15 Apr 1773, and the said ANTHONY AMENT did convey the messuage and tr of land unto the said PHILIP SMELTZER on 19 Apr 1773 ... whereas the said PHILIP SMELTZER stands bound unto the said ANTHONY AMENT in several sums of money conditioned for the payment of the several sums of money in payments before 15 Apr 1780 ... provided that if the said PHILIP SMELTZER shall well and truly pay unto the said ANTHONY AMENT the afsd debt then this indenture to be void ... . Wit: ANDREAS BILLMEYER, WILLIAM SCOTT. Ackn 15 Feb 1776 before WM SCOTT justice. 3 May 1783 ANTHONY AMENT discharged mortgage. Wit: ARCHD MCCLEAN recorder. (F:pg 522)

16 Nov 1775. Quit Claim. WALTER LITTLE of Chanceford Township, York Co cooper and HANNAH his wife (one of the daus of JAMES DICKSON decd) in consideration of THOMAS JOHNSTON who married ANN (the other dau of the said JAMES DICKSON) having quit claimed unto the said WALTER LITTLE all his estate right to ½ pt/o a 209 a. 150 perches tr of land and also 5 shillings quit claim unto THOMAS JOHNSTON of same place yeoman a 105 a. tr of land pt/o a 209 a. 150 perches tr of land in Chanceford Township adj WILLIAM MORRISON & WILLIAM CULLY ... whereas in pursuance of two warrants, one for 100 a. dated 19 Jul 1749 and the other for 80 a. dated 1 Apr 1751 there was surveyed and laid out unto WILLIAM DIXON and JAMES DIXON a 209 a. 151 perches tr of land in Chanceford Township adj ROBERT LEMON, JOHN DOUGHERTY, WILLIAM CULLY, WILLIAM MORRISON Junr & WILLIAM MORRISON the elder, and the said WILLIAM DIXON died before any division of the tr of land was made having first made his will and therein bequeaths his pt/o the land unto his son JOHN DIXON who sold the same unto the afsd JAMES DIXON but never conveyed in the lifetime of the said JAMES, and the said JAMES DIXON being so seized of the tr of land made his will dated 12 Feb 1768 and did give the afsd tr of land unto two of his daus, to wit, "I bequeath unto my daus HANNAH & ANN DIXON the plantation JOHN DICKSON formerly live on only allowing my sister ELIZABETH the privilege of her house while she lives", and the afsd JOHN DICKSON on 1 Apr 1768 did sell all his estate right in the afsd tr of land unto the afsd HANNAH & ANN DICKSON (Book C vol. 3 pg 445) ... . Wit: ALEXR MCCASKEY, WM MCCASKEY. Ackn 16 Nov 1775 before WM MCCASKEY justice. (F:pg 524)

16 Sep 1775. Deed. JOHN BLOUSE of York Township, York Co cordwinder and ANN MARY his wife for £30 sold to WILLIAM SCOTT esqr of York Town, York Co a 100 a. tr of land in York Township adj HENRY

MESSERSMITH, MICHAEL WIDNER, HENRY BERNINGER & others ... .
Wit: THOS CROSS, ANDREAS BILLMEYER. Ackn 16 Sep 1775 before
WILLIAM BAILEY justice. (F:pg 526)

12 Apr 1755. Deed. ANTHONY COABLE (KOBLE) of Codorus Township,
York Co yeoman for £140 sold to JACOB SHAR of Manum Township, York
Co a warrant made over to me by ADDAM REED formerly of Codorus
Township with all my right and property of said warrant ... . Wit: JAMES
ROBISON, MICHAEL DANNER. Proved 20 Feb 1776 by JAMES ROBISON
before WM SCOTT justice. (F:pg 527)

18 Dec 1775. Deed of Mortgage. ADAM SHERMAN of Germany Township,
York Co yeoman and CATHARINE his wife for better securing the payment of
£146.14 and also 5 shillings sold to CONRAD KEEFHABER of Manheim
Township, York Co yeoman a 248 a. 154 perches tr of land in Germany
Township adj ABRAHAM SELL, JOHN SHAWMAN, GEORGE
STEVENSON & JOHN ZEHR, which was granted by the Proprietaries unto the
said ADAM SHERMAN by patent dated at Phila 23 Jun 1770 (Patent Book AA
vol. 11 pg 355) ... whereas the said ADAM SHERMAN stands bound unto the
said CONRAD KEEFHABER for £293.8 conditioned for the payment of
£146.14 on 18 Dec next ensuing ... provided that if the said ADAM SHERMAN
shall well and truly pay unto the said CONRAD KEEFHABER £146.14 then
this indenture to be void ... . Wit: NICHOLAS KEEFHABER, DOROTHY
SLAGLE, HENRY SLAGLE. Ackn 17 Feb 1776 before HENRY SLAGLE
esqr justice. 27 Nov 1802 the heirs of CONRAD KEEFHABER discharged
mortgage. Wit: J. BARNITZ recorder. (F:pg 528)

7 Dec 1775. Deed. MICHAEL HAHN and DAVID GRIER both of York Co
for £50 sold to PHILIP GAUFF of Dover Township, York Co farmer a 50 ¼ a. tr
of land pt/o a 450 a. tr of land adj WILLIAM BAILEY esqr, other land of the
said PHILIP GAUFF & DAVID EVANS, and the said MICHAEL HAHN &
DAVID GRIER against the heirs of JACOB UPP decd and will warrant and
forever defend by these presents ... whereas CHARLES LUKENS esqr high
sheriff of York Co on 22 May 1775 for £270 paid by DAVID GRIER did sell
unto the said DAVID GRIER a 450 a. tr of land in Dover Township adj
MARTIN FRY, TOBIAS FRY, JOHN BEITZEL, PHILIP GAUFF, PETER
BRAMBAUGH, LODOWICK SPEICE, ANTHONY WOLF & PHILIP BENTZ
... . Wit: ROBT MCPHERSON, DANIEL SPANGLER. Ackn 7 Dec 1775
before SAML EDIE justice. (F:pg 530)

13 Jan 1776. Deed of Mortgage. VALENTINE CRANTZ of Manchester
Township, York Co yeoman for better securing the payment of £50 and also 5
shillings sold to ROBERT STRETTELL JONES of the City of Phila esqr a

messuage and 233 ½ a. tr of land in Manchester Township adj MARTIN
EICHELBERGER, JOHN STEWART, JACOB SCHMEISSER, the road
leading to York, JOSEPH GRAYBILL, MICHAEL EBERT & PHILIP
ROTHROCK, which is pt/o a larger tr of land which SAMUEL EDIE esqr high
sheriff of York Co on 1 Jun 1774 sold unto the said VALENTINE CRANTZ,
and the said VALENTINE CRANTZ on 13 Jan 1775 mortgaged (Book F pg
156) the said messuage and tr of land unto the said ROBERT STRETTELL
JONES to secure payment of £250 which said principal yet remains unpaid ...
whereas the said VALENTINE CRANTZ together with FREDERICK MEHL of
German Town, Phila Co skindresser stand jointly and severally bound unto the
said ROBERT STRETTELL JONES for £100 conditioned for the payment of
£50 on 13 Jan next ensuing ... provided that the said VALENTINE CRANTZ
shall well and truly pay unto the said ROBERT STRETTELL JONES £50 then
this indenture to be void ... . Wit: PETER MILLER, ABRM SHOEMAKER.
Ackn 13 Jan 1776 before BENJAMIN CHEW justice. (F:pg 531)

19 Sep 1775. Deed. LAWRENCE POLOY of the Town of York, York Co
yeoman and BARBARA his wife for £52 sold to ADAM SCHNEIDER of same
place labourer a lot of ground on the e side of George Street in the Town of
York, No. 274, in breadth 57'6" and in length 230', bounded by Princess Street
& Lot No. 275, which originally was taken up and improved by GOTTFRIED
ZELLHARD ... . Wit: JOHN MORRIS, DANIEL HOFF. Ackn 20 Sep 1775
before WM SCOTT esqr justice. (F:pg 533)

2 Jan 1776. Deed. HENRY STAUFFER of York Township, York Co miller
and BARBARA his wife for £32.5 sold to JOSEPH WELSHHANCE and
JACOB WELSHHANCE both of York Town, York Co gunsmiths a 1 a. 30
perches tr of land pt/o a 163 ¼ a. tr of land in York Township adj HENRY
STAUFFER's grist mill ... whereas the Proprietaries by their patent dated at
Phila 22 Apr 1774 did grant unto JOSEPH DONALDSON a 163 ¼ a. tr of land
in York Township adj HENRY SPANGLER, DAVID JAMESON esqr,
MICHAEL HENGST, FRANTZ JACOB MILLER, JOSEPH SHANK,
BALTZER SPANGLER & MICHAEL FISSEL (Patent Book AA vol. 14 pg
276), and the said JOSEPH DONALDSON and FRANCES his wife for £1300
sold to the said HENRY STAUFFER on 26 Oct 1774 the said 163 ¼ a. of land
... . Wit: NICHOLAS BERNHART (BERNARD), JACOB LETTER. Ackn 2
Jan 1776 before WM SCOTT justice. (F:pg 534)

8 Mar 1773. Deed. FREDERICK RUHL of York Town, York Co cordwainer
and CATHARINE his wife for £38 sold to JACOB WELSHHANCE of same
place gunsmith a 3 a. 64 perches tr of land ... whereas the Proprietaries by their
patent dated at Phila 16 May 1760 did grant unto JAMES SMITH a 101 a. tr of
land in York Township (Patent Book AA vol. 1 pg 6), and the said JAMES

SMITH and ELEANOR his wife on 3 Oct 1766 conveyed the tr of land unto JOHN HAY (Book C vol. 3 pg 192), and the said JOHN HAY and JULIANA his wife on 13 Jun 1768 conveyed unto JACOB UPDEGRAFF a 12 a. 85 perches tr of land pt/o the afsd tr adj York Town land, JOHN HAY, the Great Road leading from York Town to Wrights Ferry, GODFREY FREY & FREDERICK KUHN, and the said JACOB UPDEGRAFF and BARBARA his wife on 24 Dec 1770 conveyed unto the said FREDERICK RUHL a 3 a. 64 perches tr of land pt/o the afsd tr adj the Great Road, GODFREY FREY, FREDERICK KUHN & land of the said JACOB UPDEGRAFF (of which this is part) … . Wit: ADAM GARTNER, JACOB BILLMEYER Junr. Ackn 8 Mar 1773 before JOHN ADLUM justice. (F:pg 537)

17 Feb 1776. Deed of Mortgage. CHARLES LUKENS of the Town of York, York Co esqr and MARGARET his wife for better securing the payment of £150 and also 5 shillings sold to JOSEPH PASCHAL of the City of Phila merchant, only acting executor of the will of ISAAC PASCHALL late of said city merchant decd, a messuage and lot of ground on the n side of High Street in the Town of York, in breadth 32 ½' and in length 230' bounded by GEORGE CHRISTIAN SINN & JACOB EICHINGEN (it being the w ½ of Lot No. 104 which JOHN LUKENS of the City of Phila esqr and SARAH his wife on 25 Sep 1771 did grant unto the said CHARLES LUKENS) … whereas the said CHARLES LUKENS standeth bound unto the said JOSEPH PASCHAL for £300 conditioned for the payment of £150 on 17 Feb next ensuing (it being the monies of the estate late of said ISAAC PASCHALL decd) … provided that if the said CHARLES LUKENS shall well and truly pay unto the said JOSEPH PASCHAL £150 then this indenture to be void … . Wit for CHARLES LUKENS: PETER MILLER, ABRAHAM SHOEMAKER. Wit for MARGARET LUKENS: CORNS SHERIFF, SAML JOHNSTON. Ackn 18 Mar 1776 before SAML JOHNSTON justice. 27 Nov 1778 By virtue of a letter of atty from JOSEPH PASCHALL, GEO EICHELBERGER discharged mortgage. Wit: ARCHD MCCLEAN recorder. (F:pg 539)

16 Mar 1776. Deed of Mortgage. JOSEPH CHAMBERS of Manchester Township, York Co yeoman for better securing the payment of £500 and also 5 shillings sold to JOSEPH FOX of the City of Phila esqr a 325 a. tr of land on the w side of Sasquahannah River in Manchester Township adj Conewaga Cr, THEOBALD SHULTES, JOHN BROWN & JAMES LOGAN esqr, which PHILIP MORNINGSTAR and EVA his wife on 21 Jun 1766 granted unto the said JOSEPH CHAMBERS … whereas the said JOSEPH CHAMBERS stands bound unto the said JOSEPH FOX for £1000 conditioned for the payment of £500 on 16 Mar 1777 … provided that if the said JOSEPH CHAMBERS shall well and truly pay unto the said JOSEPH FOX £500 then this indenture to be void … . Wit: CALEB PARR, SILAS WATTS. Ackn 16 Mar 1776 before

THOMAS WILLING justice. 26 Jul 1779 by virtue of a letter of atty from
JOSEPH FOX, JAMES ROLL discharged mortgage. Wit: ARCHD
MCCLEAN recorder. (F:pg 541)

27 Mar 1776. Deed of Mortgage. GEORGE MARSH of Newberry Township,
York Co turner for securing the payment of £110 and also 5 shillings sold to
JOHN JARRET of Whiter Marsh Township, Phila Co farmer a 200 a. tr of land
in Newberry Township adj Yellow Breeches Cr, THOMAS CANNON,
GEORGE ASHBRIGE, WILLIAM JONES, Widow VANE, THOMAS (alias
SAMUEL) WHITESIDES, JOHN CALHOUN, PETER TITTLE & JAMES
SHARP, which by patent dated 14 Apr 1773 (Patent Book AA vol. 13 pg 454)
was granted unto JOSEPH WHITESIDE who on 19 Apr 1773 granted the tr of
land unto the afsd GEORGE MARSH ... whereas the said GEORGE MARSH
standeth bound unto the said JOHN JARRET for £220 conditioned for the
payment of £110 on 22 Apr 1778 ... provided that if the said GEORGE MARSH
shall well and truly pay unto the said JOHN JARRET £110 then this indenture to
be void ... . Wit: CORNS SHERIFF, SAML JOHNSTON. Ackn 27 Mar 1776
before SAML JOHNSTON justice. 11 Nov 1801 DAVID MARSH atty for
DOROTHY BAIKING adminr of the estate of JOHN JARRETT decd
discharged mortgage. Wit: J. BARNITZ recorder. (F:pg 542)

19 Apr 1773. Deed. JOSEPH WHITESIDE of Newberry Township, York Co
farmer for £405 sold to GEORGE MARSH now of German Township, Phila Co
turner a 200 a. tr of land in Newberry Township [same as above] ... . Wit:
JOHN EDMUNDSON, ELLIS LEWIS. Ackn 24 May 1773 before WILLIAM
RANKIN esqr justice. (F:pg 544)

INDEX

216

Spotsylvania County, Virginia Deed Books, 1722–1734

Spotsylvania County, Virginia Deed Books, 1734–1751

York County, Virginia Deeds, Orders, Wills, Etc., 1698–1700

York County, Virginia Deeds, Orders, Wills, Etc., 1700–1702

York County, Virginia Deeds, Orders, Wills, Etc., 1705–1706

York County, Virginia Deeds, Orders, Wills, Etc., 1714–1716

York County, Virginia Deeds, Orders, Wills, Etc., 1716–1718

York County, Virginia Deeds, Orders, Wills, Etc., 1718–1720

York County, Virginia Deeds, Orders, Wills, Etc., 1728–1732

York County, Virginia Land Records: 1694–1713

York County, Virginia Land Records: 1713–1729

York County, Virginia Land Records: 1729–1763

York County, Virginia Land Records: 1763–1777

York County, Virginia Wills, Inventories and Court Orders, 1702–1704

York County, Virginia Wills, Inventories and Court Orders, 1732–1737

York County, Virginia Wills, Inventories and Court Orders, 1737–1740

York County, Virginia Wills, Inventories and Court Orders, 1740–1743

York County, Virginia Wills, Inventories and Court Orders, 1745–1759

www.ingramcontent.com/pod-product-compliance
Lightning Source LLC
Chambersburg PA
CBHW070413270326
41926CB00014B/2800